From ORPHANED BOY to PROPHET OF GOD

THE STORY OF JOSEPH F. SMITH

From ORPHANED BOY *to* PROPHET OF GOD

THE STORY OF JOSEPH F. SMITH

BLAINE M. YORGASON

The Living Scriptures®

Ogden, Utah

Published by The Living Scriptures®
Ogden, Utah

This book is a work of both fiction and non-fiction. Chapter beginning
narrative (printed in colored ink), which contains references to actual
historical characters, places, and incidents, is the product of the author's
creativity or is represented fictitiously. The majority of this book's content
(printed in black ink) is historical non-fiction based on the author's
research, containing end notes (chapter 21) and bibliography (chapter 22).
The views expressed herein are the responsibility of the author and do
not necessarily represent the position of Living Scriptures, Inc.

First Printing, 2001
Printed in the United States of America
10 9 8 7 6 5 4 3 2 1

ISBN 1-56473-175-8

For Kathy—
With Eternal Love!

$\mathcal{F}$OREWORD

When Jared F. Brown, President of Living Scriptures, first contacted me about writing *From Orphaned Boy to Prophet of God: The Story of Joseph F. Smith*, I was troubled as well as excited. He explained that he wanted this to be the first in a multi-volume series that would be called *Stories of the Modern Prophets*. This excited me, for I have held these men and their accomplishments in awe and reverence for nearly as long as I have memory. I was especially enjoying the Church of Jesus Christ of Latter-day Saints Priesthood and Relief Society's study of the life and teachings of President Joseph F. Smith. To think of delving into President Smith's and other prophets' lives, sufficient to come up with a series of 400-page manuscripts, was thrilling.

    The difficult part of Mr. Brown's plan—the part which troubled me—was his description of the approach he was seeking. First, he wanted each manuscript to be written in an interesting story format that is *not* fictional and did not use fictional characters to carry the theme. Second, he wanted this series of books to be historical but not ponderous—the stories not of prophets, but of how the Lord turned boys and men into them. Third, he felt like each book should be advantageous to scholars without being burdened by footnotes or other types of documentation. Fourth, he wanted numerous photographs without turning them into photo albums. And finally, he wanted each of these volumes to be so unique that they would stand alone, independent of all other biographies and books about these great men.

As might be imagined, meeting these expectations proved more than challenging. After immersing myself in literature pertaining to Joseph F. Smith I finally began writing. Over the next sixty days I created a dozen or more versions of chapter one—none of which felt satisfactory....

Then in the middle of one night I awakened with the impression—an idea—to begin each chapter with an historical vignette—a short, delicate literary sketch of some significant event in the life of President Smith. These would be independent segments, stories filled with the emotion like that which Joseph F. must have experienced, that would be entertaining to young and old alike—bringing to life events that in any other format can seem like dry, historical details.

At the end of each vignette the historian in me would take over, and I would build a chronological account of the historical facts surrounding that story from President Smith's life. This part of each chapter would be fully documented with sources consulted and/or quoted, though I would use end notes rather than footnotes so the pages would flow more easily.

The photographs, I felt, should be left up to Laurie Bonnell Stephens and the creative staff at Living Scriptures, who are already producing *The Modern Prophets*™ video documentaries on each of these great men.

With renewed excitement I started over, and sample chapters confirmed that this innovative way of telling the facts of Joseph F. Smith's life was the very approach Jared Brown had been seeking all along.

Though difficult, it turns out that this is some of the most enjoyable writing I have ever done. Not only am I privileged to develop a more intimate understanding of our modern prophets and how the Lord has prepared them for His work, but I have the opportunity to take significant moments from their lives and dramatize them in a way that shows their very human side. This satisfies both my training as a historian and my life-long love of stories. I don't believe this format has ever been used, at least in this manner, and I am pleased to be a part of it.

Blaine M. Yorgason
February 2001

THE DREAM OF MANHOOD

It was long after dark when Elder Joseph F. Smith collapsed onto the thin woven mat that served as his bed. Not only did he feel hungry, sticky, and grimy—conditions that seemed constant in the Sandwich, or Hawaiian, Islands—but never in his life had he felt more discouraged. Here he was, an elder in The Church of Jesus Christ of Latter-day Saints, called by God's prophet, Brigham Young, to serve a mission to these native people. But he was also just fifteen years old and a poverty-stricken orphan, serving without purse or scrip. Wherever he went he was met with scorn, either because of his age or the rags he was forced to wear.

"I am Elder Smith," he had declared only hours before to a group of both white and native men he and his companion had encountered along their way. "This is my companion, Elder Pake, and we have come to you with a message from the Lord."

"From the Lord?" a dark-bearded white man had sneered. "Listen to that, boys! This young whippersnapper says he's been sent from the Lord! Must be mighty lean pickings where he comes from!"

The natives in the group had chuckled, but none of them had spoken.

"Or the barrel'd bin dredged bung-empty afore they came up with him," another of the white men snickered.

"Why, lad, you don't even shave! Since when does the Lord call ragamuffin little boys to the ministry?"

"Why, uh—" Joseph F. had stammered, feeling his face turn bright red with shame for his age and appearance. "I... I..."

"You head on back and find your mammy, boy, and stop wasting the time of real men!"

Abruptly Joseph F. had felt the bile of anger boiling up within him—the fierce temper that had become such a burdensome part of his life. In an instant he was furious, not so much because he was being ridiculed as because these fools were rudely ignoring the important work to which he had been called!

Well, he could teach them a lesson or two about such things— yes, and proper manners, too! He was big for his age, strong as the proverbial ox, and he knew exactly what his fists could do. After all, he had been ill treated, abused, and trod on by these nefarious gentiles and ethnics just long enough. As far as he was concerned, it was no longer a virtue, if they would not treat him as he merited, if they would not obey his testimony, and his counsels, but persist in their wickedness, hard-heartedness and indifference, their lyings, deceitfulness, and hard-hearted cruelty as regards the servants of the Lord, then perhaps it was time for him, Joseph F. Smith, to apply a little of the "laying on of hands!" Yes, siree—

"Both Enoch and Samuel were boys when they were called of God to be prophets," Elder Pake had abruptly interjected in very good English, stopping Joseph F.'s intended mayhem in its tracks.

What was the matter with him? he had then found himself asking. How could he have come so close to beating up on these men, or at least trying to, when he had been sent to them with a message of peace? Of love? When was he ever going to finally gain control of himself—of his wicked temper—

Joseph F. Smith at
nineteen years of age

CA. 1858

King Collection

"And... and so was Joseph Smith a boy when he was called of God," he had added lamely, his squeaking, trembling voice, sounding childish even to himself. "The true gospel of... of Jesus Christ has been restored through Joseph Smith's ministry, and we have come this day to declare it to you!"

"Then come back when your voice has changed," one of the men had laughed as he turned away, the others following suit.

"And in the meantime, take this two bits and find yourself a decent shirt," the group's obvious leader had hooted as he followed the others, flipping the young missionary a quarter as he turned. "The one you're wearing is the wrong kind of holy for a preacher-man!"

Even now, hours later, Joseph F. felt his ears burning and tears of shame welling up in his eyes at the memory of the men's lighthearted mockery. He was more thankful than he could say that Elder Pake had helped him to refrain from losing his temper. Yet still, how could one serve the Lord under such conditions? How could he keep going when he was so destitute of funds as to be nearly naked and was always on the ragged edge of starvation? Would it never get any better? Would he never be able to simply go forth in power to do the work to which he had been called?

Staring up into the darkness of the native hut, the young missionary found himself thinking of the last time he had seen his father. Five years old, he had been standing by the road in front of his large frame home in Nauvoo, Illinois, when Hyrum Smith and several others, including his Uncle Joseph, the Prophet, had ridden up on horseback.

"Son," Hyrum had said, "we have been ordered to go to Carthage to meet with the governor." Then, leaning down from his saddle, he had picked Joseph F. up and drew him close. "I must leave you now," he said as he lifted the boy's cap and tousled his hair. "Be a brave boy and help your dear mother all you can."

After kissing and hugging Joseph F. warmly, his father had then placed him back down in the road. With a last smile Hyrum kicked his horse into motion, and little Joseph F. had not moved until the party of riders had gone from his sight.

Now a long and difficult ten years had passed by, and Joseph F. understood two things with absolute certainty. First, his brave father had given his very life for the cause of truth. He and Joseph had been murdered in the Carthage Jail, and their testimonies, sealed with their blood, would stand forever as a witness for the Lord.

Second, in Hyrum's last plea to his son had been the implicit declaration that he, Joseph F., could do no less than his father! If he was to gain the everlasting approval of Hyrum Smith the martyr, as well as the same glorious reward in Christ, he, Joseph F., must dedicate himself to performing the same good works. Somehow he must live in the same glorious manner as his father had lived and died. Instead of being ruled by anger, he must be kind, gentle, tenderhearted, full of wisdom and knowledge, ever willing and able to bear witness of the gospel of Christ as restored through his uncle. In short, as the youthful Christ had once declared, he, too, must be about his father's business and be about it successfully!

Only, he asked himself as he stared helplessly up into the darkness, how would that be possible? How could he manage to do a man's work in the ministry, when he was only a foolish, mostly naked, angry, wilful boy —

The youngest son of martyred Church Patriarch and Assistant Church President Hyrum Smith and his wife Mary Fielding Smith, Joseph F. Smith had an abiding faith in the truthfulness of the work to which he had been called. Still, there were times when a person — even a person with a firm testimony — got discouraged.

"I was very much oppressed..." he explained years later,

"almost naked and entirely friendless, except the friendship of a poor, benighted, degraded people. I felt as if I was so debased in my condition of poverty, lack of intelligence and knowledge, just a boy, that I hardly dared look a white man in the face."[1]

His present missionary experience, Joseph F. knew, had started with the death of his sweet mother on September 21, 1852. He had been thirteen at the time, suddenly an orphan, yet still living with his younger sister, stepbrother, stepsisters, and sweet old "Aunty" Hannah Grinnels in his mother's cabin on Mill Creek. He kept busy day and night, doing chores around the home and working away as herd boy, wood cutter, field hand and general roustabout during harvest. When all the work was done each season, Joseph F. and his sisters, including Martha Ann, attended school, doing their best to pick up a little education. It had been in school where his ferocious temper had finally landed him in trouble—trouble which turned out to be an important step toward his being called as a missionary to the islands.

The teacher at their school liked to impose discipline with a leather strap, something few but him appreciated. Joseph F., rapidly growing from a boy into a man, found himself dealing not only with a developing sense of justice but with rather uncommon physical prowess as well. A clash had been inevitable.

One day, due to some minor infraction, the male teacher had undertaken to apply his leather-strap discipline on Martha Ann.

"Don't whip her with that!" Joseph had ordered loudly from the back of the room.

Instantly the teacher turned and started for Joseph F., leather strap at the ready, intent on giving Martha Ann's upstart brother her punishment. What the teacher had not taken into sufficient consideration was the fifteen-year-old's burgeoning physical strength. Instead of Joseph F. being whipped, the fifteen-year-old boy had "licked [the teacher] good and plenty."[2]

The embarrassing incident had not only ended the teacher's career as an educator but also Joseph F.'s formal education. More significantly, it had reached the ears of his stepfather (Heber C. Kimball), President Brigham Young, and the other Brethren of the Church, who did not look kindly on boys with weaknesses such as uncontrolled tempers. At the next general conference, to his great surprise and consternation, Joseph F.'s name had been read over the pulpit as one of twenty-one missionaries called to serve in the Pacific Isles. The calling was Heber C. Kimball's and Brigham Young's way of caring for the motherless and fatherless son of greatness, while at the same time instilling a little much-needed discipline and self-control into his heart.

Once in his field of missionary labor, Joseph F. found the work of the ministry both hard and discouraging. On one occasion he recorded in his journal: "I have ate enough dirt and filth, put up with anough inconveniances slept sufficiently in their filth, muck & mire, lice and everything else. I have been ill treated, abused, and trod on by these nefarious ethnicks just long anough. I believe it is no longar a virtue, if they will not treat me as I merit, if they will not obey my testimony, and my counsels, but persist in their wickedness, hard heartedness and indifference, their lyings, deceitfulness, & hard hearted cruelty as regards the servents of the Lord, I will not stay with them, but leave them to their fait... This evening we had a pint of poi each & with it I ate 6 chile pepers and retired, more to alleviate the gnawing of a hungry gut than to seak repose and rest."3

Perhaps on a night such as that, the poi and peppers, or whatever he had been given to eat, had alleviated nothing. Perhaps Elder Smith's stomach was still growling with hunger; perhaps anger at his parents' unjust deaths was still boiling within him, and perhaps he had absolutely no idea what to do about his destitute circumstances or his unbridled emotions. Certainly he felt "'very much oppressed'… in a 'condition of poverty, lack of intelligence and knowledge.' "4 Under those conditions he offered up a silent, fervent plea for divine help; lay down upon his hard, thin mat; and slept.

Early the next morning he awakened with a start, aware that he had just experienced a most vivid and powerful dream. Nearly sixty-five years later, on April 7, 1918, while speaking in General Conference in the Tabernacle in Salt Lake City, President Joseph F. Smith spoke movingly of that divinely appointed dream. In his address he called it a literal thing, a reality:

I dreamed that I was on a journey, and I was impressed that I ought to hurry—hurry with all my might, for fear I might be too late. I rushed on my way as fast as I possibly could, and I was only conscious of having just a little bundle, a handkerchief with a small bundle wrapped in it. I did not realize just what it was, when I was hurrying as fast as I could; but finally I came to a wonderful mansion, if it could be called a mansion. It seemed too large, too great to have been made by hand, but I thought I knew that was my destination. As I passed towards it, as fast as I could, I saw a notice, "Bath." I turned aside quickly and went into the bath and washed myself clean. I opened up this little bundle that I had, and there was a pair of white, clean garments, a thing I had not seen for a long time, because the people I was with did not think very much of making things exceedingly clean. But my garments were clean, and I put them on. Then I rushed to what appeared to be a great opening, or door. I knocked and the door opened, and the man who stood there was the Prophet Joseph Smith. He looked at me a little reprovingly, and the first word he said: "Joseph, you are late." Yet I took confidence and said:

"Yes, but I am clean—I am clean!"

He clasped my hand and drew me in, then closed the great door. I felt his hand just as tangible as I ever felt the hand of man. I knew him, and when I entered I saw my father, and Brigham, and Heber, and Willard, and other good men that I had known, standing in a row. I looked as if it were across this valley, and it seemed to be filled with a vast multitude of people, but on the stage were all the people that I had known. My mother was there, and she sat with a child in her lap; and I could name over as many as I remember of their names, who sat there, who seemed to be among the chosen, the exalted.

The Prophet said to me, "Joseph," then pointing to my mother, he said: "Bring me that child."

I went to my mother and picked up the child and thought it was a fine baby boy. I carried it to the Prophet, and as I handed it to him I purposely thrust my hands up against his breast. I felt the warmth; I was alone on a mat, away up in the mountains of Hawaii; no one was with me. But in this vision I pressed my hand up against the Prophet, and I saw a smile cross his countenance. I handed him the child and stepped back. President Young stepped around two steps, my father one step, and they formed a triangle. Then Joseph blessed that baby, and when he finished blessing it they stepped back in line; that is, Brigham and father stepped back in line. Joseph handed me the baby, wanted me to come and take the baby again; and this time I was determined to test whether this was a dream or a reality. I wanted to know what it meant. So I purposely thrust myself up against the Prophet. I felt the warmth of his stomach. He smiled at me, as if he comprehended my purpose. He delivered the child to me and I returned it to my mother, laid it on her lap.

When I awoke that morning I was a man, although only a boy. There was not anything in the world that I feared. I could meet any man or woman or child and look them in the face, feeling in my soul that I was a man every whit. That vision, that manifestation and witness that I enjoyed at that time has made me what I am, if I am anything that is good, or clean, or upright before the Lord, if there is anything good in me. That has helped me out in every trial and through every difficulty.

Now, I suppose that is only a dream? To me it is a reality. There could never be anything more real to me. I felt the hand of Joseph Smith, I felt the warmth of his stomach, when I put my hand against him. I saw the smile upon his face. I did my duty as he required me to do it, and when I woke up I felt as if I had been lifted out of a slum, out of despair, out of the wretched condition that I was in; and naked as I was, or as nearly as I was, I was not afraid of any white man nor of anyone else, and I have not been very much afraid of anybody else since that time. I know that that was a reality, to show me my duty, to teach me something, and to impress upon me something that I cannot forget. I hope it never can be banished from my mind.5

Shortly after he had been given the dream, in a letter to his father's cousin, Elder George A. Smith, young Joseph F. wrote the following, showing clearly the change in his thinking that had occurred: "I know that the work in which I am engaged is the work of the living and true God, and I am ready to bear my testimony of the same, at any time, or at any place, or in whatsoever circumstances I may be placed; and hope and pray that I may ever prove faithful

Illustration by Robert T. Barrett

in serving the Lord, my God. I am happy to say that I am ready to go through thick and thin for this cause in which I am engaged; and truly hope and pray that I may prove faithful to the end...

"I had rather die on this mission, than to disgrace myself or my calling. These are the sentiments of my heart. My prayer is that we may hold out faithful to the end, and eventually be crowned in the kingdom of God, with those that have gone before us."[6]

In order to better understand the miraculous transition from angry, willful, ineffective boy to powerful, tenderhearted, peace-loving prophet, seer, revelator, and President of The Church of Jesus Christ of Latter-day Saints, it becomes necessary to examine Joseph F.'s parentage and earliest beginnings—and to trace the difficult but necessary path of learning, living, and preparation which the Lord asked him to follow.

2

HYRUM SMITH— BELOVED BROTHER

"O, my dear brother, Hyrum, I can't tell you how badly I feel! That your sweet Jerusha is gone, taken from you and your little ones in your hour of need, pains my soul more than I can say."

Bleakly Hyrum Smith looked up into his younger brother's face. His wife, Jerusha Barden Smith, had passed away October 13, 1837, while he had been on a mission to strengthen the Church in Far West, Missouri. It had been well into November before he had received word of her passing and made his way back to Kirtland, and for all that time his five small children had been mostly under the care of his eldest daughter, Lovina, who was barely eleven.

Joseph had been away, too, in Terre Haute, Indiana, before going on to Far West, where he had joined Hyrum for the journey home. Had he been in Kirtland he would have seen to the care of Hyrum's family. And indeed, many had stepped in and done what they could, particularly had his parents, Joseph Sr. and Lucy, and dear friend "Aunty" Hannah Woodstock Grinnels. But oh, if only he, Hyrum, might have been there at Jerusha's side!

Though a heavy snow was falling outside, it was not yet terribly cold, and as Hyrum reached out and built up the fire he and Joseph were sharing, he felt thankful. It took constant work just keeping the wood chopped and the two fires going in the home, and Hyrum wondered that his parents and children had been up to the task. Of course "Old George" Mills, a retired soldier and another of Hyrum's and Jerusha's boarders, had been a fine hand with the axe at the woodpile. But occasionally Old George's thinking grew erratic, Hyrum knew, and so he could not always be counted upon—

"Mother declares that Jerusha was a woman whom everybody loved that was acquainted with her," Joseph stated quietly, "for she was every way worthy. I wholeheartedly agree. Our family has been so warmly attached to her that, had she been our own sister, we could not be more afflicted by her death."

"Yes," Hyrum breathed as he rubbed at his eyes, "she was dearly loved. And I must tell you that Aunty Grinnels, who has taken lodging with us for some time, has been wonderful with tiny baby Sarah. She has devoted herself to Sarah's care, and she is anxious to continue to do so."

Standing, Hyrum paced back and forth across the room. "Lovina tells me her final words were, 'Tell your father when he comes that the Lord has taken your mother home and left you for him to take care of.'" Sighing deeply, the tall, thin man returned to his chair. "What am I to do, Joseph? How am I to care for them? Baby Sarah is hardly a month old! Even with Aunty Grinnels' aid, how will I be able to feed her, nourish her, nurture her? Little Jerusha isn't much older, and sweet Hyrum is hardly older than either of his sisters. Of a truth, they are all still babies. How can I care for such little ones?"

Joseph Smith smiled tenderly, desiring with all his heart to help ease his elder brother's burden. From the day of his birth, Joseph had been loved and admired by his elder brother Hyrum. Described by their mother as remarkable for his tenderness and sympathy, Hyrum's heart had never hardened in the least toward

Joseph; if anything, his affection had grown more ardent as the boys matured. Hyrum was not only solicitous of his brother's well-being, but he had held as precious his own God-given witness of Joseph's divine calling as prophet, seer, and revelator. He knew as well that Joseph had translated the Book of Mormon from ancient golden plates delivered to him by an angel, and Hyrum continued to give frequent testimony that Joseph had restored to earth Christ's only true and living Church.

Throughout Joseph's ministry, trials, and tribulations, his faithful, loving brother had humbly stood to share in all the hardships, persecutions, and tribulations that accompanied the opening of the heavens and the restoration of divine truth. Though six years his senior, Hyrum had never been jealous of his younger brother's rights and calling or displayed the least spirit of jealousy or envy because the Lord had called his brother instead of him to usher in the Restoration. Never had there been a time when Hyrum would not have laid down his own life in defense of his beloved younger brother.

"John is now six," Joseph finally stated, "and he will prove to be a big help. And of course, Lovina has already proven her mettle..."

"Yes, Joseph," Hyrum interrupted, his voice reflecting his exhaustion and discouragement, "they will help, for both of them are sober children, mature beyond their years. But children, especially small ones, need their mother—Oh, why did the Lord see fit to take Jerusha now? I don't understand!"

"His ways are not our ways," Joseph replied quietly after he had thrust another log into the fire. "Nevertheless, if you would like, I will inquire of the Lord what it is that He would have you do."

"Would you, Joseph? Please? My own mind seems so distraught right now, that I don't know if I could hear even if He should speak with a voice of thunder!"

CHAPTER TWO

"Then I will do it," Joseph stated confidently as he rose to his feet and shrugged into his greatcoat. Then, abruptly, he smiled again. "In fact, dear brother, even as we speak, I am receiving a rather interesting impression. Are you familiar with the young Englishwoman, Mary Fielding?"

Born February 9, 1800, at Tunbridge, Vermont, Hyrum was the third child and second son of Lucy Mack Smith and Joseph Smith, Sr. While an older sister had not survived birth and had been buried unnamed, Hyrum's older brother, Alvin, had been born two years before, on February 11, 1798, also in Tunbridge.

Much alike in both temperament and personality, Hyrum and Alvin were noble young men, possessed of the purest of thoughts and intentions. In a poetic manner Joseph later described Alvin, who died at age twenty-five, as being without guile. "He lived without spot from the time he was a child. From the time of his birth he never knew mirth. He was candid and sober and never would play; and minded his father and mother in toiling all day. He was one of the soberest of men, and when he died the angel of the Lord visited him in his last moments."1 It is apparent, as Hyrum's life is examined through the perspective of history, that he was much like his older brother.

Little is known of the details of Hyrum's youth, except that it was spent assisting his parents as they went from one failed financial venture, and home, to another. Though Joseph Sr. and Lucy Smith had every reason to expect stability and prosperity when they began married life, they had no idea that the Lord already had his hand in their affairs or that "in the accomplishment of His work, the plans of men frequently fail."2 So it was to be with the Smith family fortunes.

As one crop or financial endeavor after another proved a failure, either from the ravages of the elements or the actions of

Lucy Mack Smith,
grandmother of Joseph F. Smith

CA. early 1850's

Church Archives, The Church of Jesus Christ of Latter-day Saints

dishonest men, the family grew ever closer, ever more reliant upon each other. On long winter evenings, as the cold New England winds whipped deep snow about the eaves of their various rented cabins and homes, the Smiths no doubt gathered close about the fire to read from the Holy Writ and then to share the lessons of life they were garnering.

At age twelve, Hyrum was enrolled in an academy at nearby Hanover (now Dartmouth University). At home Mother Smith gave birth to her ninth child, baby Catherine, and the future looked bright with promise. Within a year, however, in 1813, an epidemic of typhoid fever[3] broke out in the Connecticut River Valley, and Hyrum was forced to leave school and return home when several in his family grew ill. Sophronia's illness was the most serious, and for ninety days she lay deathly ill. Mother Smith's prayers for her daughter were answered, and at last Sophronia recovered.

Almost instantly, it seemed, another crisis developed. While recovering from a mild case of the disease, young Joseph, age seven, was stricken with a severe pain in his shoulder. The terrible swelling which developed over the next several days was relieved by lancing and the release of a full quart of purulent material from beneath his arm. About two weeks later, during breakfast, a pain shot "like lightning"[4] from his shoulder down into the bone of his leg, and for the next few weeks Joseph suffered almost more than he could bear. When Mother Smith grew ill from the strain and effort of caring for him, it was thirteen-year-old Hyrum who stepped forward to relieve her.

As she later recorded, "Hyrum, who was rather remarkable for his tenderness and sympathy, now desired that he might take my place. As he was a good, trusty boy, we let him do so, and, in order to make the task as easy for him as possible, we laid Joseph upon a low bed and Hyrum sat beside him, almost day and night for some considerable length of time, holding the affected part of [Joseph's] leg in his hands and pressing it between them, so that his afflicted brother might be enabled to endure the pain which was so excruciating that he was scarcely able to bear it."5 The operation that finally relieved Joseph's pain and saved his leg is a well known story in Church history.

Interestingly, not only Joseph, but all in the family, and perhaps Hyrum most of all, were affected positively by this experience with typhoid. Hyrum's compassionate nature and his great concern for young Joseph and the others in his family matured him beyond his years. But Joseph's suffering especially elicited Hyrum's tenderest regards and cemented the brothers' love and devotion to each other. "Hyrum's feelings found expression in his self-appointed but unassuming guardianship of his brother, which ended only when he fell mortally wounded by an assassin's bullet in Carthage Jail"6 more than thirty tumultuous years later.

More failed crops and other adversities led to yet another move, to Norwich, Vermont, where on March 25, 1816, baby brother Don Carlos was added to the family. When three years of crops failed there, each for a different reason, the family was forced to move again. This was a most difficult move, for Joseph Sr. was forced to go on ahead, leaving the responsibility for moving the large family with his wife and eldest sons. It was a trying time, yet 1818 found them together again, clearing land for a new home and farm near the village of Palmyra, in western New York state. Now the Lord had them where they needed to be.

Though they'd had only two cents cash money when they had arrived, once again the Smiths' hopes were high for a bright and stable future. Until 1820, everything they touched or did prospered. Hyrum and Alvin, by then twenty and twenty-two years old respectively, were thin but strapping young men of uncommon strength. Alvin stood about six feet two inches tall, and Hyrum was a little shorter. Both Hyrum and Alvin, and occasionally even Joseph, were in constant demand as hired workers on their neighbors' farms, and their combined incomes blessed the family immensely.

Although the Smiths' newfound prosperity would prove a prelude to an impending storm, the two and one-half years of economic stability were long enough for them to put down strong roots and enable them to survive the events that were about to unfold.

The spring air of 1820 was filled with the sounds of religious debate. Western New York was in the grip of a wave of revivalism, a mighty effort by local Presbyterian, Baptist, and Methodist leaders to save the "unchurched" from going to hell.7 The Smiths had heard of the revivals, but not until Hyrum came in one evening with the news did they learn that a camp meeting was to be held near their farm. This galvanized some of the family. Were they in need of religion? Certainly none of them had been saved. Of course they read and believed in the Holy Writ and were not by nature sinful. They were industrious, honest, sober, clean people who most certainly believed in God and his Holy Son. Still, some felt the need to investigate, to discover if perhaps they had missed something that would bring them their salvation.

All the family began attending, some at one time of the day and some at another, and the messages they heard from the various ministers and preachers, while filled with fervor and partiality toward one or another interpretation of scripture, were neverthe-less congenial. Soon over four hundred people had "confessed" and been "saved,"8 and many of them had also been baptized into one or another of the churches.

By the second week of May, however, the atmosphere at these camp meetings had become tense with shouting and ill will. The confusion, uncertainty, and anger manifested between the religious sects not only contributed to the breaking up of the revival itself, but it also spread to the Smith family. Hyrum, who had joined the Presbyterians through baptism, wondered why his minister was so jealous of the leaders of the other religions. And though his mother, sister Sophronia, and brother Samuel Harrison had also been baptized, the remainder of the family "exhibited far too little concern for their souls. Even Joseph, who had favored the Methodists, [had] hesitated to declare himself."9 However, Joseph had become very engrossed in his study of the New Testament and was particularly intrigued by a scriptural passage in the Book of James, which a Methodist minister had brought to his attention:

> If any of you lack wisdom, let him ask of God, that giveth to all men liberally, and upbraideth not; and it shall be given him. But let him ask in faith, nothing wavering. For he that wavereth is like a wave of the sea driven with the wind and tossed. (James 1:5–6)

Though Hyrum had no idea what was happening in a nearby copse one particular spring day, that night after work and chores the atmosphere in the Smith home must have been electric. As he, Alvin, Sophronia, little William, and the others took their favorite places, there must have been hushed whispers concerning what they were about to hear. But instead of it being Mother or Father Smith who led the discussion, this night the flickering light from both the fire and the coal oil lamp fell on young Joseph.

In one brief hour the Smiths had become "something more than a family engaged in agricultural and business pursuits. The very air seemed charged with apprehension. A revelation from God had been given. The ancient concept of God [had been] reestablished. Visions had not been done away with. Prayers could be literally answered, and the biblical pronouncement of the reality and power of the evil one was reaffirmed. All the sects and

Illustration by Robert T. Barrett

Joseph Smith's First Vision

creeds presently upon the earth were mere machinations of mens' minds. They bore no official sanction from Jesus Christ, the author of salvation.

"The implications of the revelation were overwhelming. From the status of common frontiersmen, the Smiths were now thrust by a strange chain of events and a curious public into a new and strange role. A younger member of the family had unwittingly triggered the powers of heaven and unleashed a blast of knowledge and power strong enough ultimately to change the world."[10]

For serious-minded Hyrum, the whole affair must have been both startling and exhilarating. "So overwhelmed was he by his brother's story that his mind at first failed to grasp the full import of such an experience. But as the days passed, the true significance of it was borne in upon his understanding. He remembered how seriously Joseph had listened to the revivalists and how his meditations exceeded even his study of the Bible. Joseph's refusal to join any of the various sects had given offense to some, one person in particular; for someone had tried to kill him. But the bullet had missed him and lodged in the neck of a cow. Hyrum wondered what new perils would come to Joseph with the announcement of his story."[11]

And perils most certainly did come. Scoffing, scorning, mocking, persecutions, theft, robbery, and even further attempts at murder plagued young Joseph continually. And to a greater or lesser extent, every other member of the Smith household suffered the same. Many neighbors and friends withdrew their society and became outright enemies, while religious leaders of all denominations became bitter persecutors. Yet through it all the family stood by Joseph, for each of them knew that Joseph had told the truth, and that "to deny such an experience would be to offend God; for [Joseph] knew that he had had a vision, and he dared not deny it."[12]

On September 22, 1823, Joseph called another family council.

There he announced to his expectant parents and siblings the visit, three times during the night before, of a glorious angel. As Hyrum gave rapt attention, he learned that this messenger, who gave his name as Moroni, had come to reveal the existence and location of an ancient book, "written upon gold plates, giving an account of the former inhabitants of [the American] continent, and the sources from whence they sprang. He also said that the fullness of the everlasting Gospel was contained in it, as delivered by the Savior to the ancient inhabitants."13

Again there was no doubt in the minds of the family members that Joseph was telling the truth. Not only had he always been truthful, but even as he spoke the Lord was bearing witness to them, through the power of the Holy Ghost, of the truthfulness of Joseph's experiences. And it was good that He bore such witness, for difficulties and persecution continued to assail every member of the family.

On November 19, 1823, after he had completed a good portion of a new frame home for the Smiths, Alvin, the eldest son, passed away suddenly. Before dying, he admonished Joseph to be a good boy so that he might obtain the Record from Moroni." 'Be faithful in receiving instruction,' " he added, " 'and in keeping every commandment that is given you.' "14

Lucy tells us that "Alvin manifested, if such could be the case, greater zeal and anxiety in regard to the Record that had been shown to Joseph, than any of the rest of the family."15 But with Alvin gone, Hyrum was suddenly the eldest, and from then on he manifested the same intense zeal toward Joseph's divinely appointed work as had Alvin.

Three years later, on November 2, 1826, Hyrum married Jerusha Barden of Palmyra, a young woman noted for her singular beauty and fine character. Rather than being allowed to establish a home, however, almost immediately he became embroiled in an attempt by others to steal the family's farm and new home from his parents. It took until the end of January, 1827, for him to settle the matter, and in the meantime, Joseph had married Emma Hale, of Harmony, Pennsylvania.

Hyrum and Jerusha finally settled down, taking their place in the community, involving themselves in the local Presbyterian church, and for Hyrum accepting positions of civic responsibility. His hope was to remain in the area for the balance of his life, carving a niche for himself and his family in western New York.

On September 16, 1827, Jerusha gave birth to Lovina, their first child. About a week later, as she and Hyrum were visiting with her three sisters who were admiring the new baby, Don Carlos ran into the room in a state of great excitement. Seeing him, Hyrum bolted into the bedroom, hurriedly emptied the contents of a small wooden chest onto the floor, and raced with it out the door and toward the Smith home, heedless of the shocked expressions on the faces of the women. Don Carlos's look had told him that Joseph had finally obtained the plates. Hyrum had promised Joseph the chest as a place to secure and hide them, and he had forgotten to deliver it.16

For the next two years, as persecution continued to rage and the translation of the plates moved sporadically forward, Hyrum and Jerusha helped Joseph and Emma when they could. They prayed for them always, and gave much time in assisting the larger Smith family in their work on the farm.

In the spring of 1829, after Samuel had been baptized by Joseph in Pennsylvania and then returned to the family in New York, Hyrum determined to learn what course the Lord would have him pursue. Going to where Joseph was living in Harmony, Hyrum asked if he would make such an inquiry of the Lord. In response, the Lord declared:

Portrait of Hyrum Smith   ᴄᴀ. *early 1840's*

Behold thou art Hyrum, my son; seek the kingdom of God,
and all things shall be added according to that which is just.
Build upon my rock, which is my gospel; Deny not the spirit of revelation, nor the spirit of prophecy, for wo unto him
that denieth these things; Therefore, treasure up in your
heart until the time which is in my wisdom that you shall
go forth... Behold, I am Jesus Christ, the Son of God. I am
the life and the light of the world. I am the same who came
unto mine own and mine own received me not; But verily,
verily, I say unto you, that as many as receive me, to them
will I give power to become the sons of God, even to them
that believe on my name.[17]

The Lord also advised Hyrum to seek not for riches but for wisdom,
telling him that the mysteries of God should be unfolded unto him
and that he should be made rich, inasmuch as he that has eternal
life is rich. He was also warned to declare only repentance unto this
generation—though not until after he had sought to obtain God's
word. Then his tongue would be loosed, and he would receive the
power of God unto the convincing of men. Moreover, he was to
study the word of God, both the word that had gone abroad and
the words which were being translated, until he had obtained all
which God would grant unto the children of men in this generation.[18]

 Shortly thereafter Joseph and Emma moved back to New
York, staying with the Whitmers in Fayette while Joseph forged
ahead with translating the remainder of the Record. In June, 1829,
Joseph baptized Hyrum in Seneca Lake, while Jerusha was preparing
at home to give birth to their second daughter. Mary was born
June 27, 1829, and early in July, to add to his joy, Hyrum received
word that witnesses were needed who could testify to the world
that they had both seen and held in their hands the gold plates on

which the record had been engraved.

Three had already been shown the plates by the Angel Moroni, Hyrum learned, and had heard the voice of God bearing witness to them. But he, along with his father and brother Samuel Harrison had been chosen as three of eight additional witnesses, and they were also to see and hold in their hands the ancient record.

This occurred in a secluded place near the Smith farm, with Hyrum and each of the other seven men literally handling the plates and turning the thin gold pages one after another as they felt the fine, careful engravings of the ancient scribes. It was a crowning moment not only for Joseph, who now had witnesses to attest to his truthfulness, but for Hyrum. Now he was like Joseph. Now he also knew, nothing doubting! He had both seen and felt the ancient golden record, and his life and testimony could never be the same!

Though trials, sorrows, persecutions, and difficulties would follow him and his family from New York to Kirtland—including his sweet Jerusha's untimely death and Joseph's inspired impression that Mary Fielding should take her place—Hyrum Smith would never waver. He could not, for he knew that his younger brother was in very deed a prophet of God, and that made all the difference!

MARY FIELDING— DAUGHTER OF GOD

"You want me to marry you?" Mary Fielding, thirty-six years old and never married, stared at Hyrum Smith in surprise.

"Not me, Sister Mary," the thirty-seven-year-old widower explained hastily. "It is the Lord who desires it. He gave a revelation regarding the two of us to my brother Joseph. As I said, it is the Lord's will that you marry me."

Mary was absolutely dumbfounded. She had emigrated from Canada to Kirtland not many months before, in part to learn more of the Lord's true gospel from the mouth of Joseph Smith, whom she knew to be a living prophet of God. Only, this was hardly what she'd had in mind—

"But... Brother Smith, I don't even know you! How can I possibly marry you?"

Hyrum smiled patiently. "You can get to know me, I suppose. You see, Sister Mary, my wife, Jerusha, passed away while I was on a mission to Far West. She said to one of our children when on her deathbed, 'Tell your father when he comes that the Lord has taken your mother home and left you for him to take care of.' She then died with a full assurance of her part in the First Resurrection."

"How... many children do you have, Brother Smith?"

"We had six, though our second, little Mary, has already departed for those heavenly climes where her mother now abides."

"And the ages of the five remaining?" Mary Fielding questioned, feeling unaccountably drawn to this tall, soft-spoken man.

"Lovina has just turned ten; John has just turned five; Hyrum is three; Jerusha is one and an half; and baby Sarah was born only a few days before my dear Jerusha passed away. They are now motherless, Sister Mary, and my brother Joseph, feeling anxious for their welfare, inquired of the Lord what I was to do. It was made known to him that I was to marry as quickly as possible and that if you will have me, I am to marry you. Of course, all is voluntary in this Church—"

"Brother Smith," Mary responded, holding up her hand to stop him, "I joined this Church because the Lord has revealed to me that it is true and that your brother, Joseph Smith, is a prophet of God—the Lord's mouthpiece on the earth at this time. If I am to believe his revelations regarding the gospel of Jesus Christ, how can I then doubt his revelation regarding you and me? Now, if you will kindly introduce me to your children, I will begin mothering them immediately. Our marriage may follow as soon thereafter as satisfactory arrangements can be made."

The mother to be of Joseph F. Smith, Mary Fielding was born July 21, 1801, in Honidon, Bedfordshire, England, a quaint country estate owned by her father's uncle. Mary was the eldest daughter of John and Rachel Ibbotsen Fielding, who were known as Nonconformists—people who had left the Church of the English Crown and affiliated themselves with various sects, such as the Methodists and Calvinists. Though in doing so they had given up certain rights and privileges granted by the Crown, Nonconformists were men and women of independent spirit, free thinkers, and lovers of freedom. By and large, it was

Mary Fielding

N.D.

Nonconformists such as the Fieldings who would be drawn to the message of the Mormon missionaries during the decades to come.

A tenant farmer on the estate, John Fielding provided for his children, Mary included, opportunity to participate in all manner of work and play that acquainted them with farming and animal husbandry. Little did he know that certain of his children were being prepared for a day far in the future when they would have to accommodate their lives to an agricultural environment in both plain and desert and to depend wholly upon the soil in both places for a living.

Rachel Fielding's gifts to her children were multiple. "She managed her affairs well and exercised economy. She was good to the poor and relieved their wants beyond her means. She took a large share of the care of the family upon herself. This left her husband more at liberty for his religious and pulpit engagements...

Her conduct toward her children was kind and tenderly affectionate, though seldom manifested by a caress, or ill-judged commendations. She showed her love by her precepts, and her firmness in opposing gratification of every desire which she knew to be harmful to their best interests. She was a prayerful woman and took part in leading prayer in the Rectory at Colmworth. While her husband was easy going, she was business-like and capable. She was a mother-doctor and inoculated the babies of the village; people looked up to her."[1]

Mary, who grew to be much like her mother, also had great insight into financial situations and was frugal, resourceful, and self-reliant. By her twenties she was earning her own way through life, practicing thrift and managing her own funds. She had developed a mind of her own and at all times showed initiative and self-control.

Cultured and refined, she cultivated etiquette and was well

trained in the more genteel arts of homemaking. She knew something of art and was acquainted with a variety of good books, authors, and verses, though her Bible was her refuge and Psalms her favorite comfort. Her letters reveal clear thinking and an adroit use of words, and she is reputed to have been a gifted singer.

In 1834, Mary, then thirty-three years old, emigrated to Canada. There she joined her younger brother, Joseph Fielding, and her younger sister, Mercy Rachel Fielding, who had both preceded her to the New World and were living outside Toronto and working a rented farm. Both had emigrated in order to secure better positions for themselves. Mary "was also a pioneer in every sense of the word, resolute, unflinching, tough-minded in the face of opposition, and tempered like fine steel. She was nurtured not to the soft life, but to the hard way, tinged with the aesthetic."2

Of her it was said, "To sweetness of disposition, she added strength of mind and power of instant decision. But over all the strength and firmness of her soul she drew the veil of modest womanhood so closely that only her very own realized how great was her gift, how supreme were her powers."3

Highly spiritual, Mary's devoutness to God and Christ increased under the direction of John Taylor, a Methodist minister some years Mary's junior, who with his wife had also come to Canada from England. John Taylor was an intense young man who preached regularly to his small flock concerning the virtues of the Lord's ancient and only true gospel. This message had resonated in the ears of the three Fielding siblings, and they had become faithful followers.

Early in 1836 Parley P. Pratt, a former minister and now a missionary for a new American religion, stopped at the Taylor home in Toronto. He had gone to that city because of a remarkable prophecy pronounced upon his head a few weeks before by Elder Heber C. Kimball, who had stopped at Elder Pratt's home in

Kirtland, Ohio. Elder Kimball, who enjoyed the gift of prophecy to a remarkable degree, promised Parley's wife that she would be healed of consumption, an affliction she had endured for six years, and would bear a son—this after ten childless years of marriage. Laying his hands next on the head of Parley P. Pratt, he declared:

> Thou shalt go to Upper Canada, even to the city of Toronto, the capital, and there thou shalt find a people prepared for the fullness of the Gospel, and they shall receive thee, and thou shalt organize the Church among them, and it shall spread thence into the regions round about, and many shall be brought to the knowledge of the truth and shall be filled with joy; and from the things growing out of this mission, shall the fullness of the Gospel spread into England, and cause a great work to be done in that land.4

Events transpired just as Elder Kimball prophesied. Elder Pratt's wife got well and bore a son, Parley P. Pratt, Jr. Elder Pratt went on a mission to Toronto, and the first home to which he was led by the Spirit was that of Methodist minister John Taylor and his wife, Leonora. Once the Taylors had heard the message of Elder Pratt, they were anxious to assist him in sharing it with their little flock. On a warm spring day shortly thereafter, Elder Pratt and Brother Taylor approached the Fielding home, about nine miles outside of Toronto.

At Elder Pratt's first appearance, while Joseph Fielding visited with the American stranger, his two sisters fled to a neighbor's home, for they had heard nothing good about "Mormonism."5 But quickly allaying their fears through reason and logic, Elder Pratt was soon able to set aside their prejudices. Of his dialogue and further experiences with Joseph Fielding, Elder Pratt has written:

"Ah," said I, "why do they oppose Mormonism?"

"I don't know," said he, "but the name has such a contemptible sound; and, another thing, we do not want a new revelation, or a new religion contrary to the Bible." "Oh," said I, "if that is all we shall soon remove your prejudices. Come, call home your sisters, and let's have some supper. Did you say the appointment was not given out?" "I said, sir, that it was not given out in the meeting house, nor by the minister; but the farmer by whom you sent it agreed to have it at his house." "Come then, send for your sisters, we will take supper with you, and all go over to meeting together. If you and your sisters agree to this, I will agree to preach the old Bible gospel, and leave out all new revelations which are opposed to it."

The honest man consented. The young ladies came home, got us a good supper, and all went to meeting. The house was crowded; I preached, and the people wished to hear more. The meeting house was opened for further meetings, and in a few days we baptized brother Joseph Fielding and his two amiable and intelligent sisters, for such they proved to be in an eminent degree. We also baptized many others in that neighborhood, and organized a branch of the Church, for the people there drank in truth as water, and loved it as they loved life.6

The baptism of the Fieldings was performed in a small stream called Black Creek, in May, 1836. Reverend John Taylor and his wife Leonora were also baptized that day. Years later John Taylor would become the third president of the Church.

Responding to the spirit of Gathering, the Fielding siblings soon moved southward to Kirtland, Ohio, to join with the main body of the Church. There "Mary noticed that everybody worked for a living. There was no privileged clergy. Certain simple forms of recreation were not considered sinful. Events, such as socials, dramatic productions, or a cotillion dance, were opened with prayer. The Mormon Word of Wisdom proscribed tea, coffee, tobacco and strong drink. There were no rich, and every effort was made to make the poor comfortable. Nearly everyone went to church, and anyone could be expected to be called upon to pray or preach.

"The striking Temple in their midst was awe-inspiring to Mary. The tempo of her religious and social life quickened to a marked degree requiring certain adjustments in her habits, mode of living, and thinking."[7]

In Kirtland, "Mary was beautiful to look upon. When she and her equally handsome sister, Mercy, came to Kirtland in 1837, trim, straight, dark-haired and dark-eyed, with delicately blooming cheeks and finely molded, graceful figures, clad in dainty silks of modern grace, they were the observed of all observers. Their refined and stately ways made them a shining mark in Kirtland society. Wherever they went they were spoken of as those 'Lovely English girls.' "[8]

Before long, Mercy Rachel was married to Elder Robert B. Thompson, described as "one of the Literati of the Church,"[9] and the two of them were called to serve a mission in Canada. Near the same time, on June 4, 1837, the Prophet Joseph approached Heber C. Kimball while he was seated in the front stand above the sacrament table on the Melchizedek side of the Kirtland Temple and whispered, " 'Brother Heber, the Spirit of the Lord has whispered to me: "Let my servant Heber go to England and proclaim my Gospel, and open the door of salvation to that nation." ' "[10]

Quickly this privately whispered revelation was put into action. Elder Kimball, Dr. Willard Richards, and Orson Hyde prepared for immediate departure to England, and Joseph

Fielding, a native of Great Britain who knew England well and had open-minded family living in many parts of that land, was appointed to accompany them. All this, of course, was in further fulfillment of Heber C. Kimball's own prophecy, pronounced upon the head of Parley P. Pratt over a year before.

Prior to their departure, the three apostles and Elder Fielding sat in council with the Prophet Joseph Smith. He told them that when they arrived in England they should, to "adhere closely to the first principles of the Gospel, and remain silent concerning the gathering, the Vision, and the Book of Doctrine and Covenants, until such time as... it should be clearly made manifest by the Spirit to do otherwise."[11] After being set apart by blessing, the missionaries were ready to depart—to what would turn out to be unprecedented success in their labors.

> But the name of Fielding, after those of the apostles, was principal in accomplishing these results. The sisters Mary and Mercy, with Joseph, half converted by their letters, the congregation of their reverend brother in Preston, before the advent there of the apostles. In their brother James' chapel, the first apostolic sermon in foreign lands was preached by Heber C. Kimball, and it was one of the Fielding sisters... who gave the Elders the first money for the "gospel's sake" donated to the church abroad.[12]

Upon their departures from Kirtland (Mercy and her husband took the same ship out into Lake Erie on their way to Canada as did her brother Joseph and the balance of those departing for England), Mary slipped Elder Kimball five dollars to assist him in his labors. The money—a substantial sum at the time—proved to be a godsend, for Elder Kimball had not a dollar to his name, and Mary's gift paid his and Elder Orson Hyde's passage through to

Buffalo. In years to come, Elder Kimball did not forget this timely
gift and rendered equally timely service to Mary.

Still single, Mary returned alone to Kirtland, no doubt wondering what would be in store for her in the coming days. She took
a job as a teacher and a little later took boarding with a family
named Dort.

In the latter part of 1837, with Joseph Smith and Brigham
Young also in Canada on a mission, certain dissenters united in an
attempt to overthrow the Church, claiming to be the "'old
standard'"13 and renaming themselves the Church of Christ.
Brigham Young, one of the loyal apostles, had earlier incurred their
wrath by declaring openly that he knew Joseph Smith was a
prophet and had not transgressed and fallen as the apostates had
declared. But now both he and the Prophet were out of the
country, and the apostates intended to keep it that way.

Mary, very conscious of what was happening, wrote a letter to
her missionary sister Mercy Rachel, stating in part:

> I do thank my Heavenly Father for the comfort and peace
> of mind I now enjoy in the midst of all the confusion and
> perplexity and raging of the devil against the work of God
> in this place, for although there is a great number of
> faithful, precious souls, yea, the salt of the earth, yet it may
> truly be called a place where Satan has his seat; he is fre-
> quently stirring up some of the people to strife and con-
> tention and dissatisfaction with things they do not under-
> stand...
>
> [Only a few days past, Brother Joseph Smith and
> Brigham Young] had got to within four miles of home...
> when they were surrounded with a mob and taken back to
> Painsville and secured, as was supposed, in a tavern where
> they intended to hold a mock trial, but to the disappoint-

ment of the wretches, the housekeeper was a member of the Church, who assisted our beloved brethren in making their escape...

No doubt the hand of the Lord was in it, or it could not have been effected...

Notwithstanding all that he had to endure, [Brother Joseph] appeared in the House of the Lord throughout the Sabbath, in excellent spirit, spoke in a very powerful manner, and blessed the congregation in the name of the Lord...

I fear for Kirtland. Oh, that we as a people may be faithful, for this is our only hope, and all we have to depend upon.14

It was under such difficult and trying circumstances, apparently only days after Mary Fielding had penned this letter, that Hyrum Smith approached her with his unusual proposal of marriage. His proposal was accepted, and a short time later, on December 24, 1837, Mary Fielding became the wife of Hyrum Smith, then Second Counselor in the Presidency of The Church of Jesus Christ of Latter-day Saints.

BORN IN TRYING TIMES

"Oh, my darling Hyrum, I can hardly bear to think of leaving our temple behind!"

Seated on the wagon bench beside his new wife while they waited for the remaining wagons to catch up, Hyrum Smith nodded silently. It was mid-March of 1838, a warm spring day in Kirtland, and all things seemed propitious for travel. Yet his heart was also heavy, for not only was he leaving the gleaming white temple in the hands of his and Joseph's enemies, which seemed terribly difficult, but he was also leaving his parents, younger brothers, and their families, assuming that they would be able to follow a few days later.

Yet they must leave, and Hyrum knew it! Their lives were in danger at the hands of former neighbors and friends, for Satan was raging in the hearts of wicked men wherever the gospel standard was being raised.

Thinking of Satan and his power over the hearts of those who chose to live in unrighteousness, he recalled the frightening experience of Brother Heber C. Kimball and the others who were now laboring in far-off England. Shortly after they had established a toehold in Preston, Elder Kimball had written, and on the morning of the day when their first baptisms were to be performed in the River Ribble, he had been seized by an invisible power while blessing Elder Isaac Russell and had fallen senseless to the floor. Ministered to by Elders Orson Hyde and Isaac Russell, he had sat on the bed in great agony and pain while the three of them distinctly saw the evil spirits who had attacked. Elder Willard Richards had come into the room at that time and beheld the same scenes.

These tidings had sobered Hyrum thoroughly, yet when Joseph heard it he had declared that the report had given him great joy, for he knew then that the work of God had taken root in that land. It was this that caused the devil to make a struggle to kill Brother Kimball.

Yes, Hyrum thought ruefully, and every other servant of God that Satan could get his hands on, as well as their families and dear ones—himself, Mary, and the nine others who were making up his present caravan included! Joseph, Sidney, and their families had been forced to flee in January; he, Mary, and their entourage were departing now; his aged parents and others would follow shortly; and lastly the faithful members of the Seventy would lead the remaining righteous Saints as they abandoned Kirtland, leaving that fair city to the devices of the wicked.

There was a terrible spirit of apostasy in the Church as the great ones fell! Oh, how he prayed that the spirit of mobocracy that had destroyed so many of the Saints and their dreams in Jackson County had by now died away from Missouri completely. How he prayed that the Saints would be left to find peace in the new counties of Daviess and Caldwell—counties that had been created especially for the members of the Church. He prayed, too, most fervently, that the spirit of apostasy now so rife in Kirtland would not follow to their new home.

Yet deep within Hyrum Smith there existed a fear that Missouri would not prove as peaceful as all were hoping—

"It was about this season, Mary, back in '33, when I removed the first shovelful of dirt for the foundation." Hyrum's eyes had never left the temple of which he was now speaking. "Reynolds Cahoon and I dug almost every foot of that trench with our own hands, and my cousin, George A. Smith, hauled the first load of limestone from the quarry. Oh, Mary, what great and terrible sacrifices the Saints have made to build that noble edifice up to the glory of the Lord!"

"It would have filled my heart with joy had I only been here to take part."

"Yes," Hyrum smiled, "I don't doubt you, sweet Mary." For a moment Hyrum was silent. "You are right, though. I am also troubled when I think of giving it over into the hands of wicked apostates!"

Mary nodded. "I suppose all the Saints feel that way. But such men and women can never take away from us those things for which the temple was built! All of us have our sweet memories of it, most have had our testimonies of God's reality strengthened through the glorious manifestations of his Holy Spirit therein, and no one can ever take away from Joseph the keys of authority over this earth and its peoples that Jehovah and his eternal servants bestowed upon him and Oliver there."

"You are right, my dear." Tenderly Hyrum reached his arm around his new wife and drew her close. "And we will yet build another temple, even more glorious than this, for the Lord has revealed to Joseph that our ceremonies here were not complete and that God has even greater power he deigns to bestow upon the heads of faithful Latter-day Saints. You and I will live to see it, Mary, for the Lord has promised it! Perhaps it will even be in Far West!"

"Whether or not that turns out to be so, it will certainly be in

Far West that I will give birth to my first child."

Stunned, Hyrum pulled back. "You... you're... expecting?"

"I believe I am," Mary smiled sweetly. "Perhaps it will even be the second son I have been praying for the Lord to give you, a younger brother for John. Now, Old George, Aunty Grinnels, my sister Mercy and her husband Robert, and all your dear children have come up and are waiting behind us, dear. Hadn't we better be starting?"

And with a whoop of pure joy, Hyrum snapped the reins and complied.

Joseph F., Mary's first child, was born near the end of 1838, perhaps the harshest and most difficult year that members of The Church of Jesus Christ of Latter-day Saints ever passed through. Mob violence was sinking to unprecedented levels of cruelty and depravity, and "like the Patriarch Jacob of old, [Joseph F.] could say as his days grew near their close: 'few and evil have the days of the years of my life been,' yet could he add, 'but with it all, the Lord, my Redeemer, has blessed me with an abundance of His choicest blessings.' "[1]

As the new wife of Hyrum Smith, Mary found herself caught in the hate-driven maelstrom's very center. Immediately, her concerns and fears for the safety and well-being of her husband, as well as his prophet-brother Joseph, rose to new heights. Her maternal instincts were to love, protect, and preserve, and with each new act of violence, or rumor of the same, the tensions in Mary's life increased.

At the same time, she also assumed the great responsibility of being mother to Hyrum's five children, which "she accepted and performed with unwavering fidelity up to the day of her death, and much of the time under the most trying circumstances and difficulties that could possibly be imagined, in the midst of mobs, drivings, robbings and even the murder of her loving husband. When she became the wife of Hyrum Smith, strife, bitterness and hate, were rife in Kirtland, and gaining momentum through the aid of false brethren."[2]

Early in January Joseph Smith and Sidney Rigdon were driven from Kirtland by an enraged mob composed primarily of former Latter-day Saints who had become disaffected. In late March Hyrum and Mary led a second caravan out of Kirtland. At the Ohio and Erie Canal, Hyrum sent on by water all his household furniture and a number of farming implements. This lightened his loads considerably, a blessing since the weather had been wet and the roads more like a bog than a highway.

Despite the lightened loads, however, rainy weather continued for much of the 870-mile journey, and all suffered. Such conditions were particularly distressing to the women whose long skirts and petticoats dragged in the water and mud. It was difficult to dry things, and so their wet clothing had to dry on their bodies as they trudged along.[3]

The caravan arrived in Far West in May—about the same time Joseph and others were beginning initial surveys of additional new community sites north of Far West for the gathering Saints. One such newly platted city was called Adam-ondi-Ahman, which according to John Corrill meant " 'the valley of God in which Adam blessed his children.' "[4] Another became known as Haun's Mill.

Immediately upon their arrival in Far West, Hyrum and Mary set up housekeeping for their large and extended family—first in tents and then, when it was completed, in a small frame home. How Mary must have enjoyed that home—her first as a wife and soon-to-be mother! In it she came into her own as the managing force of the household, and all domestic activities now revolved around her. Hyrum was a public figure and was away from home considerably, but Mary adapted herself to this and quickly earned her husband's praise and complete trust.

The meaning of the trip to Far West and its importance in Mary Smith's future is quite clear. It made her familiar with long-distance travel by wagon-train. She had learned what to expect from day to day and the need to go prepared for any eventuality. She was now an experienced veteran of the long trail—no longer the novitiate. She had learned the right way to dress for such a journey; the diet to sustain health and good morale; the preservation and preparation of food in all kinds of weather; cleanliness and its importance to a sense of well-being; the care of a baby and how to travel with children; comfort stops; tents and how to handle them; animals and their care [on the trail]; and how to meet unexpected difficulties as they arose. However, the trip had been taxing, and [due to her pregnancy] she had good reason not to feel well, but she came through it safely and thoroughly seasoned to the rigors of the long trail. She could undertake such a journey on her own if ever it should become necessary. To know of this great experience in Mary's life is to gain a new insight into her background and an appreciation of the extensive groundwork laid for her later achievements. Under the guiding hand of her husband, she had received a rigid training which established in her the confidence to cope with bigger difficulties that lay ahead.5

At the time, it was hoped that the Smiths, with the rest of the Saints, could find peace and rest and freedom from mob violence and hate. Unfortunately, and in obvious confirmation of Hyrum's fears as he had left Kirtland, the spirit of apostasy could not be so easily escaped. Beginning in Kirtland once the temple was completed in 1836, it had spread like wildfire, according to Eliza R. Snow, as the Saints began seeking the things of the world rather than the things of God.6 By the springtime of 1838 this apostasy had stretched its tentacles across a thousand miles of America and was bidding fair to destroy the Church in Missouri.

In March 1838 the High Council in Far West had excommunicated W. W. Phelps and John Whitmer, the latter of whom, with Hyrum, had been one of the eight witnesses to the Book of Mormon. In April Oliver Cowdery and David Whitmer, two of the three special witnesses of the Book of Mormon, and Lyman Johnson, an apostle, had been excommunicated. In May the same judgment was rendered against William E. McLellin, another of the apostles.

In June Sidney Rigdon gave what has become known as the "Salt Sermon," an oration intimating that dissenting members ought to be " 'trodden under foot of men' " in a literal way. This address scandalized the Church and did much to prejudice the minds of nonmembers wherever it was published throughout the state.7

On July 4TH the cornerstones for a temple at Far West were laid. Sidney Rigdon was once again the orator of the day, and his theme, as characterized by Joseph Smith, was the Mormon Declaration of Independence.

Unfortunately, when Sidney Rigdon's two fiery addresses were published, they did much to inflame the minds of non-Mormons throughout Missouri. Meanwhile wagon trains of Saints continued to roll into Far West and other new communities, keeping Hyrum, Joseph, and Sidney busy directing them to where they might settle and sitting in council meetings conducting the affairs of the people.

Increased activity of the Saints aroused mob action against them. While the business of organizing an orderly government went on, the mob element was busy inciting the old settlers against the Mormons. Already plans were laid to prevent the Saints from voting at the polls at Gallatin, Daviess County, Missouri. On the day the voting took place a skirmish occurred with the Mormons obtaining the upper hand. The Missourians feared the loss of their suffrage. The following day rumors spread that several casualties among the brethren had occurred and that Missourians had been prevented from voting, and that the majority of the citizens of Daviess County were determined to drive the Saints from the county. Immediately, Hyrum left... with the Prophet and Sidney Rigdon for Gallitan to investigate affairs... To their great relief and joy they learned that none of the brethren had been killed, although several had been severely wounded.8

While Hyrum, Joseph and others sought desperately for a way to calm peoples' minds and restore peace, a mob threatened the Saints in De Witt, Carroll County. Late in August, Governor Lilburn W. Boggs ordered out a part of the state militia to quell the civil disturbances in Caldwell, Daviess, and Carroll counties.

"The mounting force of evil like a tidal wave was about to sweep over [the Saints]. In Hyrum's family, now located in a comfortable house at Far West there was a feeling of tension and uneasiness... Mary Fielding Smith, Hyrum's wife, was soon to become a mother, and the worry and concern endured by Hyrum for his wife and family was almost overwhelming."9

By the first part of September mobbers began gathering at Millport, Daviess County, though by the end of the month the militia under Generals Atchison, Doniphan, and Parks had forced

Governor Lilburn W. Boggs

N.D.

Church Archives, The Church of Jesus Christ of Latter-day Saints

most of them into Carroll County, where they viciously attacked De Witt. On October 4TH Hyrum and Joseph arrived in De Witt to assist the Saints, but by the 11TH, weakened by starvation and an almost constant bombardment which had taken several lives, the Saints were forced to abandon their property and flee to Far West.

On October 25 a battle was fought between about seventy-five brethren and a mob led by the Reverend Samuel Bogart on Crooked River, in Ray County. Two days later Governor Boggs issued his infamous extermination order, which gave the Saints the choice between banishment from Missouri and death.

Three days later, a mob under the leadership of Colonel William O. Jennings attacked the little settlement of Saints at Haun's Mill, killing seventeen men and boys, including small children, and wounding a great number more. That same afternoon a mob-militia under command of General Samuel D. Lucas, about two thousand strong, arrived near Far West, and the Mormon citizens, Hyrum and Mary Smith and their family included, prepared to defend themselves.

For a day the mob/militia gathered, joined by many who had once been the Saints' leaders but had now become apostate. As the mob awaited another six thousand reinforcements, many of them amused themselves by sniping at the Saints. Meanwhile, the news of the murders at Haun's Mill had left the Saints shuddering and fully aware of the danger they were in, and Church leaders met in solemn council. All knew that the extermination order had been given; none doubted that it could just as easily be carried out.

"Mary Smith saw the anxiety on her husband's face; yet he tried not to alarm her. The hour called for great stamina and mighty faith. They strengthened each other, and both were fortified with a calm courage. Together, they steeled themselves and put their trust in the Almighty."10

On the 31ST of October, Joseph Smith, Sidney Rigdon, Parley

P. Pratt, and others were betrayed to the mob/militia by Colonel George N. Hinckle, leader of the Saints' defensive forces. The next day, Hyrum Smith and Amasa M. Lyman were also betrayed by Hinckle and taken as prisoners into the mobbers' camp. "Mary witnessed the scene [of the arrest] and reeled under the impact of the awful moment. Fear seized the other members of the household, the color draining from their faces... Hyrum remonstrated with Hinkle [*sic*] and protested that he could not go, that his family was sick, and that he also was sick. Hinkle said that he didn't care, that Hyrum would have to go. The prisoner's cloak and hat were brought. The guard surrounded him and marched him toward the army camp... forced along at the point of bayonets to the prisoner compound. There, to his great joy, he found Joseph and the other prisoners safe and well. Hyrum lay on the ground that night in November weather with only his mantle for a covering."[11]

Parley P. Pratt, who witnessed Hyrum's arrest, stated, "As I returned from my house towards the troops in the square, I halted with the guard at the door of Hyrum Smith, and heard the sobs and groans of his wife, at his parting words. She was then near confinement; and needed more than ever the comfort and consolation of a husband's presence."[12]

An illegal tribunal, which the militia leaders called a court-martial, was held during that night, and the prisoners, none of whom had been allowed to appear in his own defense, were sentenced to be shot the following morning. The order of execution read as follows:

Brigadier-General Doniphan:
Sir:—You will take Joseph Smith and the other prisoners into the public square of Far West, and shoot them at 9 o'clock to-morrow morning.

Samuel D. Lucas,
Major-General Commanding 13

The reply of General Doniphan, which no doubt saved Hyrum,
Joseph, and the others from their awful fate, has become legendary.

It is cold-blooded murder. I will not obey your order. My
brigade shall march for Liberty tomorrow morning, at 8
o'clock; and if you execute these men, I will hold you
responsible before an earthly tribunal, so help me God.
A. W. Doniphan,
Brigadier-General 14

On November 2, Joseph, Hyrum, and the other prisoners were
taken back into Far West under strong guard and permitted to see
their terrified families, though they were denied the privilege of
conversing with them or even uttering a fond farewell.

The foul-mouthed sergeant ordered Mary Smith to get
[her husband] some clothes within two minutes...
The sight of him standing in manacles... rumpled,
unshaven, and pale from his ordeal definitely was enough
to unnerve completely a wife whose first child was about
due... The scene was rare drama, silent drama, filled with
torture and pain for both of them expressed in the
anguished gaze of two people whose hearts were breaking
for each other...
The unfeeling guard, with hideous oaths and threats,
commanded Mary to take her last farewell of her husband for
his die was cast and his doom sealed, and she need never think
that she would see him alive again. In the critical condition of
her health, this heartrending scene and what followed came

near ending her life. However, her reserve of vigor and inner strength sustained her in the terrible ordeal.15

Hyrum later recorded, " 'I was obliged to submit to their tyranni- cal orders, however painful it was, with my wife and children cling- ing to my arms and to the skirts of my garments, and was not permitted to utter to them a word of consolation, and in a moment was hurried away from them at the point of a bayonet.' "16

Under command of General Lucas and Robert Wilson, the prisoners were then taken to Independence, suffering constant abuse and threats of being hanged from the next available tree as they traveled. Arriving in Independence on the 4TH of November, they were shackled and put on public display. That same day General Clark arrived at Far West, where he took most of the remaining brethren prisoners. The next morning he assembled the people and delivered an insulting speech, in which he advised the Saints to scatter abroad and never again organize themselves with bishops, presidents, and so forth. Concerning Hyrum, Joseph, and the rest of those who had been taken to Independence, he reiterated that their fate was fixed, their die cast, and their doom sealed, and as had the guard at Mary's door, he quite boldly stated that they would never be seen by their friends or families again.

Mary, only days away from delivering her firstborn child, could hardly contain her grief and anguish. "In the critical condition of her health, this heartrending scene and what followed came near ending her life...

She struggled with all her might to compose her grief and obtain relief from the pain in her bosom. [Yet] it seemed that her heart would break... However, her reserve of vigor and inner strength sustained her in the terrible ordeal...

[as she] plead with her God to protect Hyrum and return him to her."17

On Friday, November 9, Hyrum, Joseph, Parley P. Pratt, and the four other prisoners in Independence were taken to Richmond, Ray County, where they were put in chains, all linked together so that none of them could move independently of the others, and otherwise much abused by their guards. According to Elder Pratt, these men were some of the most "noisy, foulmouthed, vulgar, disgraceful rabble that ever defiled the earth."18 Hyrum, before a court of law in Nauvoo in 1843, described the guards' behavior.

> They tantalized us and boasted of their great achievements at Haun's Mill and at other places, telling us how many houses they had burned, and how many sheep, cattle, and hogs they had driven off belonging to the "Mormons," and how many rapes they had committed, and what squealing and kicking there was among the [women], saying that they had lashed one woman upon one of the damned "Mormon" meeting benches, tying her hands and her feet fast, and sixteen of them abused her as much as they had a mind to, and then left her bound and exposed in that distressed condition. These fiends of the lower regions boasted of these acts of barbarity, and tantalized our feelings with them.19

On Tuesday, November 13, a mock trial of the prisoners began at Richmond, which was to last sixteen long and exhausting days and end with Hyrum and some of the others being imprisoned in Liberty Jail. That same gloomy November Tuesday, Mary Fielding Smith went into labor in mob-ravaged Far West, delivering her first-born son and Hyrum's seventh child—tiny Joseph F. Smith.

5

A Jail Called Liberty

"Is this where you want me, Don Carlos?"

"That's it, Mary. These mattresses and pillows are the best I could do, so squirm around a bit and do your best to get comfortable."

"Thank you," Mary smiled weakly in the frigid, early morning air. "Oh, these warm bricks feel so good! Mercy Rachel, I can take the babies now."

"All right, Mary, here's little Joseph F., all snug as a bug in a rug."

"Is he awake, do you think?" Mary fussed with three-month-old Joseph F.'s blankets, making certain he was fully covered.

"I shouldn't think so. He ate just half an hour ago and seemed very contented when I bundled him up. Are you ready for Mary Ann?"

"Hand her to me. I'm sure I can take her."

Mercy Rachel handed her own eight-month-old baby daughter in through the puckerhole at the rear of the wagon, after which she allowed Don Carlos to help her up and inside.

"All right, sisters," Don Carlos said as he closed up the rear hole in the wagon's canvas cover, "we'll pick up Emma and young

Joseph III, and then we'll be on our way!"

It was biting cold, yet all through the day Don Carlos kept the wagon moving southward along the rutted, frozen road, the steam from the horses' nostrils and shaggy winter coats giving mute evidence of the season. Somehow they managed a winter camp under some leafless trees that night, with no one doing much talking as the women endeavored to care for the babies and keep them warm. By daylight they were on the road again, pushing the tired teams ever onward, until in the bitter cold of early evening Don Carlos brought the animals to a halt before the jail in Liberty, Missouri.

Numb with cold and moving stiffly, the youngest Smith brother then descended from the wagon, approached the guard at the door, and requested permission for his party to see the prisoners, Hyrum and Joseph Smith.

"All right, sisters," he said a little later as he lowered the wagon gate and gently helped the three women to the ground, "these heartless fellows are fearing a jailbreak, but when I explained Mary's condition and the nerve it took for all of you to come, this one at the door, his heart fairly melted. 'Bravery ought to be rewarded,' he declared." Don Carlos grinned. "Of course it didn't hurt when I explained that we also had with us two tiny infants, one of whom had never met his father. 'I've a son of my own!' the guard told me, 'and if I hadn't ever bin allowed to see him, by d---, I'd move heaven and earth to do so! Bid the women enter, and welcome!'"

Don Carlos' expression grew instantly sober. "Remember, though, the guards inside will be an altogether different kettle of fish. This one at the door warned me against them and instructed me to inform you that their trigger fingers are itchy, and they're too cold and miserable to care much about who they shoot—man, woman or child."

Silently nodding their understanding, the women shuffled toward the door. The big iron key turned in the grating lock, and all but Don Carlos, who first went to put up the teams, entered into the lamp-lit upper room of the jail.

"Where... are they?" Mary asked as she looked around the small, nearly empty room. "Where are our husbands?"

"Not up here," the guard sneered as he covered them with his rifle. "This is too good for the likes of them! Yes'm, they're down in the pit below that trap door, and if you want to see 'em, you'll have to join 'em there!"

Mary, her entire body tingling with emotion, crept down the stairs behind Emma and her son, flickering candles lighting the way. At the bottom she turned and received her baby from Mercy Rachel's extended arms. Mercy and her daughter then descended, and the door in the floor closed over all of them.

The damp foulness of the dungeon was intense. As Mary peered at the gaunt, bearded faces, long straggly hair, and burning eyes of the prisoners, she felt a horror sweep over and through her. They were being treated like animals—no, like criminals of the deepest dye! Yet to them, as their faces brightened, she realized that she and the others must appear like rays of living light.

Gritting her teeth she held her frail and trembling figure still, tiny Joseph F. clutched tightly in her arms. She must stand. Hyrum must see her standing! He must not see her in her weakness—

"M... Mary, is it you?" a voice whispered hoarsely. "Is it... truly you?"

Then Hyrum was shuffling toward her, his arms outstretched, his tall, thin frame bent over so his head would not slam against the low ceiling. Deep and heartfelt happiness suddenly enveloped Mary—both of them—and for a long moment they simply touched each other's hands. It had been such a long time since they had seen each other, such a desperately long time, filled with so many

heartaches and abuses, yet now that they were together, they hardly even knew what to say.

"How are you, Hyrum?" she asked, unable to think of anything better.

"Just fine, Mary," he lied easily. "And you?"

"I am quite all right now," she responded, unbidden tears finally starting from her eyes as she realized she was telling the truth. "I... Oh, Hyrum, I am sorry for these foolish tears! This is your son, Joseph Fielding. I have named him after our two brothers, you see."

Tenderly taking the infant into his arms, Hyrum examined the alert child's face and then carefully nuzzled him with his whiskered lips.

"He's a dandy," he declared as he swiped at his own eyes, trying to rid them of the tears of joy he was feeling. "You have done well, Mary; very well indeed! We shall call him Joseph F., to distinguish between him and all the other Josephs who seem to be running around the country these days."

Turning then, he held his new son up for all to see. "Brethren," he declared with choking voice, "come and see this fine new son that the Lord has sent to Mary and me. His name is Joseph Fielding, but as anyone can plainly see, he is the spitting image of his papa!"

"His proud papa," the Prophet chuckled as he became the first to take the infant from Hyrum's hands. "Neither can I blame you, dear brother, for he is a handsome child, and he does seem to have that fine Smith nose we are all noted for!"

The brethren all laughed, and then one after another they held Mary's and also Mercy Rachel's babies, feeling the wonder of new life even in the depths and despair of their pitiful dungeon.

For the rest of that night Mary, Hyrum, and tiny Joseph F. sat close and visited; Joseph, Emma, and young Joseph did the same;

and Mercy Rachel and Don Carlos stayed as far back as possible, near the ever-watchful guard, surveying the heartrending scene. Deep and heartfelt happiness permeated them all; a touch of a hand, a tender embrace, a spoken word, even a smile were as manna to their starving souls.

The visit was the tonic that Mary seemed to have needed. The sun had risen again in her life, pushing back the dark cloud of gloom that had settled over her the day Hyrum had been marched away at the point of a bayonet. Knowing that he was yet alive, seeing him, touching him, hearing with her own ears his tender affections—these were all that Mary needed.

Perhaps she also received a blessing of health under the hands of these servants of the Most High God; perhaps little Joseph F. received the same, along with his name. She would never tell. What was obvious, from that night onward, was that light had come back into her eyes, and she was prepared to continue onward with the difficult work that the Lord had called her to do.

Following Joseph F.'s birth on November 13, 1838, Mary's health took a serious turn for the worse. "With her soul racked with fear for the safety of her companion, and her body racked with pain due to [her] constant suffering under the cloud of oppression and persecution,"1 she found herself unable even to nurse her newborn child. But her sister Mercy Rachel, already nursing her own baby Mary Ann and despite her terrible fears concerning her own missing husband who had fled in the direction of Illinois some two weeks before, simply added the nursing of tiny Joseph F. to her agenda. At the same time, she took charge of the rest of the Smith household in behalf of her sister.

Day after dreary day, Mary lingered in her afflicted state, her situation seriously aggravated by a terrible cold and fever. Meanwhile all in the home and community, including baby Joseph F., suffered from cold and the lack of food, for the mobs had used up the woodpiles, trampled the corn and grain fields, butchered or stolen the livestock, emptied and burned the corncribs, and set fire to the stacks of feed put up for the animals.

Speaking of one such occasion long afterward, Joseph F. reminisced:

> After my father's imprisonment by the mob, my mother was taken ill, and continued so for several months... While in this condition of health, and her husband in jail, a company of men led by a Methodist preacher named [Samuel] Bogart [who also led the mob at Crooked River where Apostle David W. Patten was slain] entered her house, searched it, broke open a trunk, and carried away papers and valuables belonging to my father. I, being an infant, and lying on the bed, another bed being on the floor, was entirely overlooked by the family (my mother being very sick, the care of me devolved upon my Aunt Mercy and others of the family) during the fright and excitement. So when the mob entered the room where I was, the bed on the floor was thrown on to the other completely smothering me up, and here I was permitted to remain until after the excitement subsided.2

"When thought of and discovered," Joseph F. concluded, "my existence was supposed to have come to an end; but subsequent events have proved their suppositions erroneous, however well founded! No thanks, however, to the Rev. Mr. Bogart and his friends."

Eight decades later, Elder Melvin J. Ballard declared that when Joseph F. was found, "the boy was so black that life was almost extinguished, but the hand of the Lord was over him: from that moment the Spirit of the Lord attended him in the midst of trials, in the midst of vicissitudes, and has preserved his life marvelously to complete that which the Lord had in store for him to do."3

No doubt aggravated by the lack of proper nourishment, the days of Mary's illness extended into weeks, then months. "Mary lay pale and weak; she was unable to wait on herself. She fought to stay away from the 'brink' and remain alive. Christmas was cheerless for the family. The weather was cold as well as the house, which was impossible to heat throughout. [Yet through it all, Mary] was sustained by the words: 'Yea, though I walk through the valley of the shadow of death I will fear no evil: for thou art with me; thy rod and thy staff they comfort me.' (Psalms 23:4.)"4 There is no question that the terrible happenings in Far West nearly cost Mary, and her baby, their lives.

Meanwhile, Hyrum, Joseph, and four other prisoners had been hauled from Richmond to Liberty in a large wagon. There the six men were fitted by a blacksmith with shackles and chains, securing them to each other with only two to three feet of chain between. Thus linked together they were forced into the cold, damp darkness of the jail's basement, where for months they were held in close confinement. For coverings they had only their clothing; for pillows, chunks of firewood; and Hyrum's bed was the square side of a hewn white-oak log. The small, open windows let in little light but more than sufficient cold; there was no heat other than that provided by their own bodies; their toilet facilities consisted of an old bucket that all were forced to share; the ceilings were so low that Hyrum and most of the others could never stand fully upright; and their food was anything but adequate and decent.

"Thus," Joseph said, "in a land of liberty, in the town of Liberty, Clay county, Missouri, my fellow prisoners and I in chains, and

Liberty Jail

CA. 1858

Church Archives, The Church of Jesus Christ of Latter-day Saints

dungeons, saw the close of 1838."5

Early in 1839, after a visit from Don Carlos Smith during which Hyrum expressed his loneliness for Mary and his sorrow over never having seen his two-month-old son, Don Carlos brought word to Mary that her husband was anxious to see her. Emma and her son Joseph III were also invited to see the Prophet Joseph. Immediately plans began to be made in both households.

Anticipating the visit with her husband, and sensing what his joy would be like when he was able to finally see and hold his new son, lifted Mary's spirits and gave her renewed energy. Yet her precarious health would add to the risky nature of the journey: forty miles through snowdrifts and over rough and frozen roads; mobbers still roaming the countryside looking for Mormons; no inns where they could find warmth or food; and always the frigid air assailing her weakened lungs.

Then, too, there were the two babies, hers and Mercy Rachel's, for certainly her sister and baby daughter would have to accompany them in order for Mercy Rachel to continue nursing little Joseph F. Could the two babies stand the journey? It would take a minimum of two days and a night in each direction, all in the bitterest winter temperatures. Were the tiny babies' constitutions up to it? Mary didn't know, but Mercy Rachel thought the risk was worth it, Emma agreed, and so the date of their departure was set for around the 1st of February, 1839.

The hazardous journey, and perhaps even more hazardous visit, portrayed fictionally at the beginning of this chapter, took place as scheduled. The line that night between the forces of good and evil was drawn thin and tight. A single wrong word, a gesture misinterpreted, and a finger would have tightened on a trigger and mayhem may have erupted. " 'The night was spent in fearful forebodings,'" Mercy Rachel later declared, "'owing to a false rumor having gone out that the prisoners contemplated making an attempt to escape which greatly enraged the jailer [*sic*] and guards."6

This was the setting in which little Joseph F. finally met his father and Mary was briefly reunited with Hyrum. "It was a unique event in the annals of the period. True, Emma Smith and the wives of some of the other brethren had visited their husbands the previous December, and Emma again now. But none did so under such hazardous circumstances as did Mary. Yet, heroically, she made the supreme effort to see her husband once more even if it should cost her her life."7

As far as Hyrum and the rest of the prisoners were concerned, despite the brief visit from their loved ones, there still seemed to be no good reason for any of them to hope for survival. Between his mother's frail condition and his father's desperately dangerous circumstances, the future did not look bright for little Joseph F. Few friends were able to stand by them, and no one was allowed to champion their cause. If the state or nation had sympathy for them no one knew it. The enemy had succeeded in ripping the family apart, and the tiny baby boy would be affected by the trauma of what began there in Far West for the remainder of his life.

Years later, while serving as president of the European Mission, Joseph F. wrote:

The day was cold, bleak and dreary, a fit and proper anniversary of the dark and trying day of my birth; When my father [Hyrum] and his brother [Joseph] were confined in a dungeon for the gospel's sake and the saints were being driven from their homes in Missouri by a merciless mob. The bright sunshine of my soul has never thoroughly dispelled the darkening shadows cast upon it by the lowering gloom of that eventful period.8

For Hyrum and the other prisoners, "the coming trial with the 'court' being what it was held little hope for acquittal on legal grounds. Reports reaching them of the scattered and poverty-ridden Saints being driven [from the state] by [the] ruthless mob, together with their anxiety over the safety and welfare of their families, was almost more than they could endure."9

Back in Far West, Mary continued in poor health while Mercy Rachel continued to nurse little Joseph F. Meanwhile, all the Saints had been dealing with the overwhelming prospect of getting everyone out of the state before spring, when Governor Boggs's extermination order was due to go into effect.

On the sixth of February, only days after the wives of Hyrum and Joseph had arrived back in Far West from their visit to Liberty, Stephen Markham started for Illinois with Emma and her children, as well as Jonathan Holmes and his wife. Approximately a week later, Mary, tiny Joseph F., and the rest of Hyrum's children—with their extended family of Mercy Rachel and daughter, Aunty Grinnels, Jane Wilson (a young woman afflicted with nervous fits whom Hyrum and Mary had recently "adopted"), and Old George Mills—started on their own two-hundred-mile, frigid winter journey.

According to Mercy Rachel:

Shortly after our return (from Liberty jail) to Far West we had to leave our cold unfurnished house and start in lumber wagons for Illinois, my sister (Mary) again being placed on a bed in an afflicted state. This was about the middle of February, the weather extremely cold. I still had the care of both babies (Joseph and Mary Jane). We arrived at Quincy about the end of the month. My husband (Robert Thompson) had engaged a room for our accommodation but my sister was obligated to be with me on account of the baby.

The whole of Brother Hyrum's family of ten remained with us until April.10

As the suffering of both prisoners and fleeing Saints continued through March and toward April, 1839, it would have been natural for questions to arise in their minds. What was the purpose of this ordeal? Was it necessary for the Lord to exact such an extreme test of their faith? Had the Lord somehow abandoned them? Had so many of them lived beneath themselves, both spiritually and temporally, that the Lord had left them to their just desserts? And finally, had the Prophet Joseph himself, been abandoned?

On March 15 and again on March 20, 1839, the Prophet Joseph and those imprisoned with him wrote two remarkable letters, answering many of the "why" questions and making known the mind and will of the Lord regarding his servants in their distressing conditions. To Hyrum, the sentiments seemed as messages both to and from his own heart, and by them he set the course for the remainder of his life. His youngest son, Joseph F., would do the same.

In the first letter, to a Mrs. Norman Bull, who had tried to visit the brethren in Liberty but had been denied admittance, Joseph declared:

No tongue can tell what inexpressible joy it gives a man, after having been enclosed in the walls of a prison for five months, to see the face of one who has been a friend. It seems to me that my heart will always be more tender after this than ever it was before. My heart bleeds continually when I contemplate the distress of the Church. O, that I could be with them! I would not shrink at toil and hardship to render them comfort and consolation... But trials will only give us the knowledge necessary to understand the minds of the ancients. For my part, I think I never could have felt as I now do, if I had not suffered the wrongs that I have suffered. All things shall work together for good to them that love God.11

In the second letter, sent to the Church at large and to Bishop Partridge in particular, can be found in segments the remarkable revelation known today as Doctrine and Covenants sections 121 and 122. This letter was signed not only by Joseph but by Hyrum, Lyman Wight, Caleb Baldwin, and Alexander McRae.12

It is known that the brethren made at least three attempts at escape, none of which worked out. Early in April the prisoners were forced before another pseudo-court, composed of their enemies and many of the mobbers from Haun's Mill. Asking, after ten days of abuse, for a change of venue to Marion County, the prisoners were instead remanded to Boone County. With four men and the sheriff as guards, they started about the middle of April. Hyrum later declared:

[We] started from Gallatin... and went as far as Diahman that evening... There we bought two horses of the guard and paid for one of them in our clothing which we had with us, and for the other we gave our note. We went down that day as far as Judge Morin's, a distance of some four or five miles. There we stayed until the next morning, when we started on our journey to Boone county, and traveled on the road about twenty miles distance. There we bought a jug of whisky, with which we treated the company, and while there the sheriff showed us the mittimus... without date or signature, and said that Judge Birch told him never to carry us to Boone county, and never to show the mittimus;

and, said he, I shall take a good drink of grog, and go to bed, and you may do as you have a mind to.13

The brethren abandoned their captors and headed east toward Quincy, keeping to the byways in order to avoid the Missouri officers. What little else we know of Joseph and Hyrum's journey, we owe to their mother's spirituality. Several nights following the escape of her sons, Lucy Smith was given a significant vision.

> After falling asleep... I saw my sons in vision. They were upon the prairie traveling, and seemed very tired and hungry. They had but one horse. I saw them stop and tie him to the stump of a burnt sapling, then lie down on the ground to rest themselves; and they looked so pale and faint that it distressed me. I sprang up and said to my husband, "Oh, Mr. Smith, I can see Joseph and Hyrum, and they are so weak they can hardly stand. Now they are lying asleep on the cold ground! Oh, how I wish I could give them something to eat!"
>
> Mr. Smith begged me to be quiet, saying that I was nervous; but it was impossible for me to rest—they were still before my eyes—I saw them lie there full two hours; then one of them went away to get something to eat, but not succeeding, they traveled on. This time Hyrum rode and Joseph walked by his side, holding himself up by the stirrup leather. I saw him reel with weakness, but could render him no assistance. My soul was grieved; I rose from my bed and spent the remainder of the night in walking the floor.14

True to her vision, Mother Smith said, "The next day I made preparations to receive my sons, confident that the poor, afflicted wanderers would arrive at home before sunset."15 The arrival of Hyrum in Quincy was a signal for family rejoicing. One can easily picture the excitement as Mary, with little Joseph F. in her arms, led the entourage of Hyrum's loved ones toward the dock. Moments later, when Hyrum and Mary embraced each other, and then when he had held and kissed little Joseph F. and the rest of his children, renewed strength must have flowed into his exhausted and emaciated body.

However, prison had changed his appearance dramatically. John, Hyrum's seven-year-old son, said, "I... remember seeing my father... when he came home from Liberty Jail. He had a full beard, his hair was long, and he was riding a small bay horse."16

Yet for Hyrum, there was no purpose in looking back on his sufferings, neither was there purpose in looking upon the sight of his family's poverty and starvation. All that mattered at the moment was that the Lord had been kind enough to restore him and his loved ones to each other and had preserved them their health to a degree sufficient that they could immediately begin to establish a new home. And this, too, became a lesson that Joseph F. would learn well.

Joseph F. Smith, Martha Ann Smith Harris (Joseph F.'s younger sister), Mercy Fielding Thompson (sister of Mary Fielding, Joseph F.'s mother), and Mary Jane Thompson Taylor (Joseph F.'s cousin)

CA. 1868

King Collection

6

NOT-SO-BEAUTIFUL NAUVOO

For a moment the Nauvoo Mansion's dining room was so quiet that five-year-old Joseph F. could hear the flies buzzing. It was unusually warm, too, and sultry from the rain that had fallen the night before. The only movement of air came from Dimick B. Huntington who, with a large, hand-held fan, was endeavoring to provide a measure of comfort to those in the room. Joseph's younger sister Martha Ann was crowded fearfully against his side, while his older stepbrother John stood on the far side of his mother, Mary, helping to support her. The stricken young widow was all a tremble, seeming not to know whether to move forward or to stand fast with her children at her side.

Before them, laid out in their finest clothes with white neckerchiefs and shrouds, were the bodies of little Joseph F.'s father, Hyrum, and his Uncle Joseph—the two Smith brothers who had been murdered by a mob the afternoon before, while incarcerated in the jail at Carthage, Illinois.

June 28 had started early and ominously for young Joseph. In the pre-dawn darkness he had been awakened by the staccato sound of distant hoofbeats drawing steadily nearer along Mulholland Street. Then a thin raspy voice had shouted frantically,

"Joseph is killed—they have killed him! --- ---- them! They have killed him!"

Knowing that the desperate, angry voice had belonged to Porter Rockwell, and knowing, too, that his father had accompanied his Uncle Joseph to prison, little Joseph had squeezed closed his eyes and pulled the blanket over his head. But the terror he was feeling would not go away, and a little later, when someone knocked on the window below, he had felt almost resigned to what was coming.

"Sister Smith, ma'am, it's me, George Grant."

Mary Fielding Smith had gone to the door in the gray of first dawn, clutching her dressing gown tightly at her throat while the messenger stood just outside, his hat in his hand. It was obvious that he did not know quite what to say. "They... they've killed them, Sister Smith. Both of them. Your husband and Brother Joseph are both dead, shot and killed by the mob yesterday afternoon."

"It cannot be possible, can it?" Mary's eyes had been wide and staring.

"Yes," Grant had answered gently, "it is true."

Feeling her legs buckle, Mary had steadied herself against a bureau while Joseph F. had watched from his doorway. Grant, hurrying inside, had helped Mary to a chair, where she had begun sobbing uncontrollably. Others had also been awakened by the knocking, and like wildfire, word of the murders had spread throughout the house. Soon crying and wailing could be heard from every quarter, and little Joseph F. was among the mourners.

As he had run to his mother, whose body was still being racked by sobs, the boy had thought of the last time he had seen his father, three days before. He had been standing by the road in front of their home on Water Street when Hyrum and several others had ridden up on horseback. "Son," his father had said, "we have been ordered to go to Carthage to meet with the governor." Then, leaning down from his saddle, he had picked Joseph F. up and drawn him close. "I must leave you now," he had said as he lifted the boy's cap and tousled his hair. "Be a brave boy and help your dear mother all you can."

Kissing and hugging him warmly, Hyrum had then placed little Joseph F. back down in the road. With a last smile he had kicked his horse into motion, and Joseph had not moved until the party of riders, his father among them, had gone from his sight.

Until now, he thought emptily as he stared upward at the two bodies laid out on the table. Now they were here, only they were dead, shot down by wicked men in Carthage!

Such was the darkest day in Nauvoo—and in the life of five-year-old Joseph F. Smith. But it was not the only day in Nauvoo, for in fact all the boy's memories were of that bustling river town on the Illinois side of the horseshoe bend of the mighty Mississippi. And until that day, his memories had been happy. But now, as his little heart beat with pain and sorrow, Joseph F. sensed that he would never be completely happy again—

In April of 1839, after Hyrum and the Prophet Joseph had made their escape from the Missourians and had fled to Quincy, Illinois, to reunite with their families, they were immediately caught up in the Church's need to find another location on which to settle. Among several under consideration, the most favored was a section of land lying twenty-five miles north of Quincy and about two hundred miles northeast of Far West, Missouri. It was on the opposite side of the Mississippi River from the Saints' former enemies and faced a section of land in Iowa known as the "Half Breed Lands." Available for two dollars an acre, the land on the Illinois side was owned by a Dr. Isaac C. Galland, who resided on the site in a frontier trading post he called Commerce.

Within a few days of their arrival, Hyrum, Joseph, and several other brethren rode north to view the proposed community site. As they "topped a promontory, they beheld a landscape falling away to the west in a gradual slope."[1] At the base of the slope the land pushed outward in a sort of peninsula with the Mississippi turning from its normal southerly course and flowing westward around it. The river then turned south and then back toward the east before continuing southward as before, the whole of the watercourse forming a giant horseshoe that half-enclosed the few buildings of Commerce in the center.

By the middle of May, with their scanty belongings piled on lumber wagons, ten-month-old Joseph F. and his reunited parents, with all of their extended "family," were on their way to the baby's first real home.

Hyrum, Joseph and Sidney Rigdon were all able to locate their families in abandoned homes near the river. Sometime in late May or early June of 1839, it was decided to change the name of Commerce to Nauvoo. In explanation, Joseph Smith wrote: "The name of our city (Nauvoo) is of Hebrew origin, and signifies a beautiful situation, or place, carrying with it, also, the idea of rest; and is truly descriptive of the most delightful location."[2]

Mary Smith, her strength restored and again in a home of her own, found herself basking in the joys of motherhood. Finally able to care for little Joseph F., she treasured his happy smile and exulted in his early efforts to stand and take his first halting steps. His teeth were coming in nicely, and she was diligently endeavoring to get him to say his first words. Certainly, it seemed to her, no mother could have been more proud of her firstborn child.

In June Heber C. Kimball received a letter from Mary's brother Joseph, who was still serving a mission in England, which Elder Kimball kindly passed along to Mary. Saddened by its contents, which described her brother's failure in doing missionary work among their own family, she penned an almost immediate reply. Concerning her own experiences and state of mind she wrote:

My very dear brother—

As the Elders are expecting shortly to take their leave of us again to preach the gospel in my native land, I feel as though I would not let the opportunity of writing you pass unimproved...

As it respects myself, it is now so long since I wrote to you, and so many important things have transpired, and so great have been my afflictions, etc., that I know not where to begin; but I can say, hitherto has the Lord preserved me, and I am still among the living to praise him, as I do today. I have, to be sure, been called to drink of the bitter cup; but you know my beloved brother, this makes the sweet sweeter.

You have, I suppose, heard of the imprisonment of my dear husband, with his brother, Joseph, Elder Rigdon, and others, who were kept from us nearly six months; and I suppose no one felt the painful effects of their confinement more than myself. I was left in a way that called for the exercise of all the courage and grace I possessed... I was at least four months entirely unable to take any care either of myself or child; but the Lord was merciful in so ordering things that my dear sister could be with me. Her child was five months old when mine was born; so she had strength given her to nurse them both.

You will also have heard of our being driven as a people, from the State, and from our homes; this happened during my sickness, and I had to be removed more than two hundred miles, chiefly on my bed. I suffered much on my journey; but in three or four weeks after we arrived in Illinois, I began to mend, and my health is now as good as ever. It is now little more than a month since the Lord, in his marvelous power, returned my dear husband, with the rest of the brethren, to their families, in tolerable health. We are now living in Commerce, on the bank of the great Mississippi river. The situation is very pleasant; you would be much pleased to see it. How long we may be permitted to enjoy it I know not; but the Lord knows what is best for us. I feel but little concern about where I am, if I can keep my mind staid upon God; for, you know in this there is perfect peace. I believe the Lord is over-ruling all things for our good. I suppose our enemies look upon us with astonishment and disappointment...

My husband joins me in love to you. I remain, my dear brother and sister [Hannah Greenwood Fielding, whom Joseph had married while on his mission], your affectionate sister,

Mary Smith[3]

In terms of testimony and determination to live the gospel as the Lord had revealed it from on high, young Joseph F.'s father, Hyrum, felt the same as his wife. In a lengthy epistle entitled "To the Saints scattered abroad" he wrote:

Having given my testimony to the world of the truth of the Book of Mormon, the renewal of the everlasting covenant, and the establishment of the Kingdom of heaven, in these last days; and having been brought into great afflictions and distresses for the same, I thought that it might be strengthening to my beloved brethren, to give them a short account of my sufferings, for the truth's sake, and the state of my mind and feelings, while under circumstances of the most trying and afflicting nature...

...I had been abused and thrust into a dungeon, and confined for months on account of my faith, and the "testimony of Jesus Christ." However I thank God that I felt a determination to die, rather than deny the things which my eyes had seen, which my hands had handled, and which I had borne testimony to, wherever my lot had been cast; and I can assure my beloved brethren that I was enabled to bear as strong a testimony, when nothing but death presented itself, as ever I did in my life. My confidence in God, was likewise unshaken. I knew that he who suffered me, along with my brethren, to be thus tried, that he could and that he would deliver us out of the hands of our enemies; and in his own due time he did so, for which I desire to bless and praise his holy name. From my close and long confinement, as well as from the sufferings of my mind, I feel my body greatly broke down and debilitated, my frame has received a shock from which it will take a long time to recover; yet, I am happy to say that my zeal for the cause of God, and my courage in defense of the truth, are as great as ever. "My heart is fixed," and I yet feel a determination to do the will of God, in spite of persecutions, imprisonments or death; I can say with Paul "none of these things move me so that I may finish my course with joy."

Dear Brethren, we have nothing to be discouraged at, if we remember the words of the Savior, which say "in the world you shall have tribulation—If they have persecuted you" [and etc.]. The world has always hated the truth and those who have testified of the same; let us not then think

Joseph Smith's red brick store
at Nauvoo where Endowment
ordinances were performed prior
to the completion of the Temple.

CA. 1885

Church Archives, The Church of Jesus Christ of Latter-day Saints

that these are strange things such as never happened before, but, rather let us take the prophets and saints in ancient days as examples...

To the church in general I would say, be faithful, maintain your integrity, let the principles of truth and righteousness get deep hold in your hearts, live up to those principles at all times, be humble withal, and then you will be able to stand firm and unshaken...

Hyrum Smith.4

These and similar lofty sentiments, expressed again and again by Hyrum and Mary to their children as well as their extended family, began to be assimilated by all of them, and in years to come were to have a profound effect upon the thinking of their youngest son.

As Nauvoo grew, Mary's spirit was "refreshed with new hope and promise. She watched a miracle unfold before her eyes, as the industry of a homeless people transformed the swampy shore line... into a desirable community. Street after street of homes came into being, extending up the slope to higher ground where a Temple was to be built. Nauvoo was to become the largest city in Illinois within the short breathing space permitted the Saints."5 There was a premonition among many that their time there would be short. Early on, Elder Heber C. Kimball had remarked that their stay would be only temporary.6 For a time, however, the Saints were granted peace, and the Church and community grew apace.

On January 19, 1841, the Prophet Joseph received by revelation the first official information the Lord had sent to the Church since his and Hyrum's days in Liberty Jail. Along with instructions to begin building the temple, "for there is not a place found on earth that [the Lord] may come to and restore again that which was lost unto you, or which he hath taken away, even the fullness of the priesthood" (D&C 124:28), significant information was given regarding Hyrum:

> [B]lessed is my servant Hyrum Smith; for I, the Lord, love him because of the integrity of his heart, and because he loveth that which is right before me (D&C 124:15)...
>
> [V]erily I say unto you, [let]... my servant Hyrum... take the office of Priesthood and Patriarch, which was appointed unto him by his father, by blessing and also by right;
>
> That from henceforth he shall hold the keys of the patriarchal blessings upon the heads of all my people,
>
> That whoever he blesses shall be blessed, and whoever he curses shall be cursed; that whatsoever he shall bind on earth shall be bound in heaven; and whatsoever he shall loose on earth shall be loosed in heaven.
>
> And from this time forth I appoint unto him that he may be a prophet, and a seer, and a revelator unto my church, as well as my servant Joseph;
>
> That he may act in concert also with my servant Joseph; and that he shall receive counsel from my servant Joseph, who shall show unto him the keys whereby he may ask and receive, and be crowned with the same blessing, and glory, and honor, and priesthood, and gifts of the priesthood, that once were put upon him that was my servant Oliver Cowdery;
>
> That my servant Hyrum may bear record of the things which I shall show unto him, that his name may be had in honorable remembrance from generation to generation, forever and ever. (Doctrine & Covenants 124:91–96)

The Lord had not only confirmed that Hyrum was to be Patriarch over the whole Church as pronounced by his father but he was also called to fill the position of standing next to the Prophet Joseph, as Associate President of the Church, holding all the keys of power just as Joseph held them. These were weighty callings which required even greater personal sacrifices of Hyrum and Mary, yet they willingly submitted themselves to the Lord's will.

On May 14, 1841, Mary gave birth to her second child, a daughter who was given the name of Martha Ann. The baby was fair, looking more like her father than her mother, and instantly she was the apple of Mary's—and little Joseph F.'s—eye. In fact the boy had a difficult time keeping his hands off the infant as he endeavored to help care for her, and often there were near disasters.

Unfortunately, 1841 also brought tragedy to Mary and Hyrum and their family. In August Don Carlos, Hyrum's and Joseph's younger brother, came down with pneumonia. He was twenty-six years old, married to the former Agnes Coolbrith, and the father of three daughters. Unable to fight the disease, he passed away on August 7TH. Robert B. Thompson, Mercy Rachel's thirty-year-old husband and Don Carlos's partner in a printing business, died of the same cause twenty days later, on August 27. Their untimely deaths left the Smith and Thompson families stunned and bereaved. Both were young men and so left small children to be reared by their grieving widows. Both had promising futures, for they each had exceptional literary talents which they had been using in gospel service, making their deaths a blow to the Church, as well.

Yet life in Nauvoo went on. Joseph F. grew from a toddler to a bright little boy, fun-loving and inquisitive. As the son of one of Nauvoo's two notables, he was known by all, and therefore pampered and fawned over and probably even spoiled. He developed many friendships and loved to play about his yard and neighborhood. Yet overall he was like his father—quiet, thoughtful, even introspective, with a sense of duty and responsibility toward his parents and younger sister that did nothing but increase as he grew older.

New revelations received by the Prophet Joseph Smith kept the Church pointed to new heights and zeal. Among numerous other items and events, on Wednesday, May 4, 1842, Hyrum bid Mary goodbye and retired to Joseph's office in the upper room of his store. During the several hours that followed, the Prophet explained that he felt a strong need to proceed with what he intended, despite the fact that the temple was not yet complete. He then instructed the brethren present in the procedures and rituals of the Holy Endowment.[7]

While this was indeed a wonderful blessing for the Saints, the forces of Satan immediately began to rage and to make renewed war against them and their Prophet. By the spring of 1842 it was becoming clear to Mary and Hyrum that serious trouble was brewing, both at home and back in Missouri. Not only had officials in Missouri renewed their efforts to bring Joseph back to stand trial, but there was evidence of plottings from within their own community. As he had in Kirtland, the devil would find apostates from within the ranks of the Saints to lead the charge.

And so it turned out, though a little time yet remained. Late in August of 1843 Joseph moved his family into the just-completed Mansion House, and Hyrum and Mary purchased brick to begin their new home, which would be located across Water Street from where they then resided. Hyrum had also been put on the Temple Committee and was very much involved in overseeing the daily work of building the temple, raising money, and gathering supplies and materials. It was also during this period that Hyrum, at the instigation of his prophet/brother, asked the widowed Mercy Rachel to be his plural wife.

Nauvoo Temple   *N.D.*

Church Archives, The Church of Jesus Christ of Latter-day Saints

Once again the two sisters found themselves contemplating living under the same roof and sharing the same table. What would be new for them, and very difficult, would be sharing the same family and husband. The practice was so contrary to their sensitivities and convictions that it proved a difficult trial—a divine test of each of their souls. Yet at length each received her own powerful witness of the Spirit that plural marriage was of the Lord, and shortly thereafter, Mercy Rachel and Hyrum were married by the Prophet. Because Mercy Rachel had been sealed eternally to her deceased husband, her marriage to Hyrum was for time only.

In December 1843 a grand Christmas party was celebrated in the home of the Prophet Joseph. Among other guests was little Joseph F. Years later, while standing in that same room, he recalled to young Preston Nibley, "My mother brought me and sat me down on the fiddler's platform in the corner of this very room... He then related that while the dancing was going on, he noted the confusion caused by a man trying to get in at the door. He saw the Prophet make his way through the crowd and take the man to his heart." What Joseph F. didn't know until years later was that the man at the door was a bedraggled Porter Rockwell, who had just arrived in Nauvoo after nearly a year's imprisonment, without conviction, in Missouri.[8]

In January of 1844 a delegation of Pottawattamie Indians visited Nauvoo in order to meet with Joseph Smith. Hyrum and little Joseph F. attended the meeting, held in the courtroom, where one of the chiefs (Keokuk) stated that the Great Spirit had told them he had raised up a great Prophet chief and friend who would tell them what to do. Joseph, much affected and shedding tears, then arose and told them, among other things, to cease their warfare and killing and to live in peace. Joseph F. was also much affected by the scene and would remember it all his life.

On Thursday evening, June 20, 1844, at the Mansion House,

Joseph read Hyrum and others a letter from conspirator Robert D. Foster declaring to another conspirator, John Proctor, that there were "thousands of armed men ready now and thousands more coming from Missouri and the country around" to attack Nauvoo. Lowering the letter, Joseph asked Hyrum to take his family on the next steamboat to Cincinnati. Hyrum instantly declined, saying, "Joseph, I can't leave you." Turning to those who were present, Joseph breathed, "I wish I could get Hyrum out of the way, so that he may live to avenge my blood, and I will stay with you to see it out."9

Rumors and more rumors flew about the city during the next two days, so that Mary and Mercy scarcely knew what to do or what to think. They were worried sick about Hyrum and Joseph; they were just as fearful about themselves and the little ones. Consequently they did their best to keep their children close. Yet the smaller ones such as Joseph F., now five and an half years old, were continually escaping to get on with their play. It was a terrible and foreboding time, with the future looking darker than ever.

On the evening of Saturday, June 22, as threats against the Saints mounted, Joseph determined to take Hyrum and depart for the West. " 'The way is open,' [he declared joyfully]. 'It is clear to my mind what to do. All they want is Hyrum and myself; then tell everybody to go about their business and not to collect in groups, but to scatter about. There is no doubt they will come here and search for us. Let them search; they will not harm you in person or in property and not even a hair of your heads. We will cross the river tonight and go away to the West.' "10

About midnight Joseph and Hyrum, both having said good-bye to their families and with tears flowing freely, entered into a leaky skiff manned by Orrin Porter Rockwell to begin their flight to the west. For the purposes of this narrative, what followed for the next few days can best be described by Mercy Rachel, who was an observer.

[Joseph] called at his brother Hyrum's to take leave of the family previous to their crossing the Mississippi River, intend[ing] to go west to the Rocky Mountains to seek out, if possible, a place of peace and safety for the Saints. His parting words to my sister Mary, as she wept at their going, were these: Sister Mary, don't feel bad, the Lord will take care of you, and He will deliver us, but I do not know how. The two brothers then started to cross the river, not knowing whether they would ever see their home again, or not. But on account of the feelings expressed by some of the brethren, who should have been their truest friends, and by their urgent request, sent after them, the brothers returned to Nauvoo the following day. Watching from a chamber window I saw them being rowed in a skiff across the river until they landed, and walked up the river bank to Hyrum's house, where they entered, Joseph seating himself, while Hyrum made some changes in his clothing, when they went on to the Mansion. Although I did not know that the brothers had returned home to be taken as "lambs to the slaughter," my feelings were indescribable, and the very air seemed burdened with sorrowful forebodings. The awful scene at Carthage followed in a few days, and here all men must draw the veil, for until all the truth concerning these good men, and this black deed of their murderous foes, can be told and understood the history of this time will not be written. But the day will come when God will speak, and the martyrs and their history will be made known.11

When the skiff carrying Joseph and Hyrum came near the Nauvoo shore the following day, Sunday, June 23, little Joseph F. was playing on the bank. Later he declared that he watched the skiff pass a sandy spit which extended far into the river, and when the men departed the boat and he at last recognized his father, he felt a surge of joy.

Joseph F. recalled that Hyrum took him by the hand and walked with him and Joseph to their home, where his father warmly greeted the family, most of whom were busy preparing for daughter Lovina's wedding that same afternoon. While Hyrum changed and commenced shaving, the Prophet chatted with Lovina and then sat and took Joseph F. onto his lap. For a few moments the Prophet and the boy played and laughed together, with Joseph observing his young nephew closely. Speaking to Hyrum, Joseph said, " 'This boy of yours, Hyrum, is pale, too much milk in his diet.' " Hyrum replied, " 'He should have more solid food.' "12 Joseph F. was then placed back on the floor, and the two brothers departed for the Mansion.

The tragic events that followed, both in Nauvoo and again at Carthage, will not be detailed in this volume. Suffice it to say that through treachery, deceit, and careful planning that extended from the former Latter-day Saint conspirators to the highest office in the state of Illinois, early in the evening of June 27, 1844, the jail at Carthage was attacked. "When the roar of muskets had ceased and the fiends in human form with painted faces had fled into the woods... the two key men of the Dispensation of the Fullness of Times lay dead in... pool[s] of their own blood. Two witnesses had been taken to bear testimony at the throne of God that they had done all they could to carry out the divine plan."13 Meanwhile, their widows were left behind to raise their children in righteousness as best they could and to keep them in remembrance of the diligence and sacrifice of their fathers.

Through the interminably long day that followed the news of

Illustration by Robert T. Barrett

Tragedy at Carthage

Joseph and Hyrum's deaths and the wounding of John Taylor, Mary and her family suffered terribly. Writing later in her life, Joseph F.'s younger sister Martha Ann, who was afflicted at the time of the tragedy with a severe case of measles and congestion in her lungs, recalled that the crying and agony " 'and the anguish and sorrow that was felt can be easier felt than described. But... it will never be forgotten by those who were called to pass through it.' " 14 There can be no doubt that Joseph F. felt the same.

At about 3:00 p.m. on June 28, the procession of two wagons carrying the murdered brothers arrived at Nauvoo. The wagons, driven by Dr. Willard Richards, who had miraculously escaped the martyrdom, and a Mr. Hamilton, were accompanied by a guard of eight soldiers who had been detached for that purpose, in Carthage, by General Deming. The bodies had been aced in rough pine boxes, one to a wagon, and once loaded, the boxes had been covered with boughs and leaves to shade them from the hot sun.

Though Joseph F. and his family did not leave their home to meet the wagons, many others did. To the Smiths it was reported that the wagons had been met on Mulholland Street, about a mile east of the temple, by the Nauvoo Brass Band, the city council, the Nauvoo Legion's lieutenant general's staff, Major-General Jonathan Dunham and staff, acting Brigadier-General Hosea Stout and staff, commanders and officers of the Legion, the town sheriff, and about eight thousand of Nauvoo's mourning citizens.

Once at the Mansion, the bodies had been carried quickly inside, and even the families of the brothers were kept away. Telling the vast crowd outside that the Prophet and the Patriarch could be viewed beginning at 8:00 the next morning, William Marks and Dimick Huntington closed the doors and began washing and cleaning the bodies, after which they had dressed them for burial.

Only when Joseph and Hyrum's bodies had been cleaned and

dressed properly were Emma and Mary's families finally allowed into the room.

Following Emma, Mary entered with Joseph F., Martha Ann, John, and one other of her children in tow. Trembling at every step and nearly falling, she at last reached Hyrum's body. Kneeling beside him and clasping his head in her arm, she drew his lifeless face to her bosom.

"Oh, Hyrum, Hyrum!" she wailed plaintively while Joseph F. and the others stood with tear-streaked faces, gazing on. "Have they shot you, my dear Hyrum—are you dead? Oh! speak to me, my dear husband. I cannot think you are dead, my dear Hyrum."[15]

Her grief then consuming her, Mary fell forward across Hyrum's body, her sobs filling the room. Some of her children still clung to her, wailing in their anguish. But little Joseph F., standing alone, felt someone lift him so that he could gaze down into the face of his father. The bullet-riddled face—for Hyrum had been shot once in the side of the nose and once just beneath his chin, a ball which had then angled upward—looked peaceful and even slightly smiling, as if in victory. It was a sight little Joseph F. would never forget.

Joseph F.'s grandmother, Lucy Mack Smith, then entered but shrank immediately back. Finally she made her way to the bodies, where she stood between them, resting a hand on each. She later wrote:

> I had for a long time braced every nerve, roused every energy of my soul and called upon God to strengthen me, but when I entered the room and saw my murdered sons extended both at once before my eyes and heard the sobs and groans of my family and the cries of "Father! Husband! Brothers!" from the lips of their wives, children, brothers and sisters, it was too much; I sank back, crying to the

Lord in the agony of my soul, "My God, my God, why has thou forsaken this family!" A voice replied, "I have taken them to myself, that they might have rest..."16

While little Joseph F. stood watch, Lucy and some of the others were again helped from the room. The doors were then opened and dozens of extended family and close friends came through, paying their last respects to the slain brothers.

Early the next morning, again while young Joseph F. watched protectively, the bodies of Joseph and Hyrum were placed on the soft, white cambric linings of coffins covered in black velvet and studded with brass nails. Squares of glass in the lids protected the faces but allowed mourners a last fond look at their Prophet and Patriarch.

At 8:00 the doors to the Mansion were opened, and between then and 5:00 p.m. an estimated 10,000 mourners filed past the brothers. It was another day that Joseph F. would long remember, in part because it went so slowly and in part because the vast assemblage of people, all sorrowful and teary, was somberly overwhelming.

At 5:00 p.m. the doors swung shut, and Mary led Joseph F. and her other children in for a last look at their slain father and uncle. When at length they, Emma and her children, and Grandma Lucy were ushered from the room, the cadence abruptly changed. Joseph's head still carried a price in Missouri, and rumors had already circulated that some were intent on finding the prophet's body and beheading it in order to collect the bounty. Accordingly a group of brethren lifted the coffins from their outer pine boxes and carried then into a small bedroom to the northeast. They quickly replaced the bodies with bags of sand, and Dimick Huntington then drove the sand-filled coffins to a public funeral.

At midnight, while Joseph F. and his family either slept or

grieved alone, the same men took the two coffins containing Joseph's and Hyrum's bodies out of the Mansion and to previously dug graves in the open basement of the still-unfinished Nauvoo House. In the darkness they filled in the graves, replacing stones and debris and endeavoring to make the ground look natural. A few moments later a heavy rain commenced, and by morning no sign of graves remained in the basement of the Nauvoo House to entice the bounty-hunting mobs.

LEAVING FOR A NEW LIFE

"Mary, I shall speak boldly, for I know that is how our dear departed Hyrum would have us deal with this dilemma."

For a moment Mary regarded the man without reply. True enough, he was the only living brother of her deceased husband. Of six sons, only one remained alive to give help and comfort to Mother Smith in her old age. Alvin had died while the family was still in New York; Don Carlos had died of pneumonia three years ago now; Hyrum and Joseph had been murdered in Carthage; and Samuel had died less than a month later, of exposure suffered while fleeing from the same mobs that had slain his two brothers. Now only William remained alive—poor, wayward William—

"Speak however you may wish, William; boldly or otherwise. I shall most certainly listen."

"Very well." William Smith smiled, no doubt to put her at ease, and Mary couldn't help but notice that his expression somehow lacked the sweet luster of her husband's smile or the beautiful radiance of Joseph's. Instead there seemed to be a darkness in his countenance, a shadow that obscured whatever inner light the man might have remaining.

But that could not be much, Mary knew, not since he had been excommunicated from the Church several months before. Always arrogant, and infused with jealousy over Joseph's appointment from the Lord, William had attacked his older brother many times through the years, occasionally even physically. In Kirtland William's stormy temper and outbursts against Joseph, and even peace-loving Hyrum, had been famous, even among non-family members such as Mary and her sister Mercy Rachel.

One such incident, which had festered unresolved for several months during 1834, had to do with a series of debates being held between Joseph and others, which Joseph usually won. Finally, when someone had suggested that the debates be halted, William had lost his temper and physically attacked Joseph, Jared Carter, and others, meanwhile shouting that the debates continue. Joseph had rebuked William in the name of the Lord. In speaking of the incident later, Hyrum let Mary know that he was perfectly satisfied with the course Joseph had followed. Yet, he had added, he had been wounded to the very soul by William conduct; and although he had the tender feelings of a brother toward him, he considered William's conduct an abomination in the sight of God.

Such behavior had continued in Missouri, Mary knew, just as it had in Nauvoo and in the East, where William had taken his family to serve a mission. There Elder Pratt and others had discovered him teaching false doctrines and sanctioning immoral practices and had ordered him back to Nauvoo to be cut off from the Church.

Yet, now he was here—

"The family is worried, Mary, that you appear to have thrown in with Young, Kimball, and the other members of the Twelve whom they have deceived into following them."

"Are they, really." It was a statement, not a question, and Mary made it only because she was so astounded by the man's effrontery that she could think of nothing else to say. Besides, she could hear movement upstairs, and she knew that Joseph F., now seven years old and very curious, was listening at the heat flue. More than likely Martha Ann was beside him, and for a moment she worried about what it was they were hearing.

"They are, indeed!" William was declaring. "Don't you see, Mary, that such men have become enemies of the cause we have all given so much for—of Joseph's and Hyrum's church?"

"Interesting," Mary replied quietly while she watched the man. "And here all along I have thought it was the Lord's church we are a part of."

"You know d--- well what I mean!" William shouted, suddenly angry and unable to control himself. "Don't you forget, Mary, that I'm an apostle, too!"

"You were, until you were cut off for apostasy and rebellion."

"And I've cut off Brigham Young, Heber Kimball, Parley Pratt, and Willard Richards for the same thing! Just you remember: the church is with the Smiths, Mary, and it always will be! Moreover, I'll fight to the death to see that it is so! What do you say to that?"

"I say, do what you are of a mind to do, William, and allow the rest of us the same privilege."

"That isn't going to do, Mary; it isn't going to do at all!" William took a deep breath. "However, I'm here to offer assistance, not to fight with you. If I can have your word of honor that you will not follow Brigham Young and his dupes in the Twelve, then I am authorized to promise you and your children both peace and protection."

"And how would this be granted?"

"Many in the mob are reasonable men, Mary. They didn't all kill Joseph and Hyrum, you know. Such men have united with the killers strictly for financial gain, for they see great opportunity here in this place. They already have Emma's promise that she will not be following Brigham, and so they have given me their word that neither she nor her family and property will be touched. Without difficulty I can obtain the same promise for you."

Sadly Mary shook her head. "I am sorry, William, but my answer is no. I am not interested. My husband gave his life for the Church, including its proper organization and direct line of authority. After Christ's death, only the Twelve had authority to continue the Church; it is no different today. Hyrum taught me that, just weeks before he died. Therefore, his family and I will continue to follow the Twelve!"

"But he was wrong!" William thundered, his anger instantly back again. "I know he was wrong! This church belongs to the Smiths, Mary! Can't you see that? Joseph, Hyrum, the rest of us! Jerusha's son John is the eldest of either Joseph's or Hyrum's posterity—the one who by right should lead this church until Emma's boy Joseph is old enough to take over. Then John will take his rightful place as patriarch, and young Joseph as prophet. As an apostle I would tutor them in their duties, too. Fact is, I'd be tutoring John right now, if only you hadn't allowed him to be spirited away by Young and Kimball!"

Mary smiled. "Yes, William, I did allow John to accompany Elders Young and Kimball when they crossed the river in February. He was near fourteen and wished to go, neither the brethren nor their company had objections, and so I gave my permission. I am his mother, you know."

"Stepmother!" William seethed, his agitation still showing as he clenched and unclenched his fists in a renewed effort to control his voice. "And don't you forget it, Mary Fielding! You and your high-sounding English accent and pompous airs. Why, if it hadn't been for that fool visionary Joseph, Hyrum would never have married you, not in a hundred years! You... you're nothing more than the milkmaid daughter of a dirt-poor English tenement farmer, for all your uppity ways!"

"And proud of it," Mary replied sweetly.

"Yes, I'll just bet you are!" William's sneering voice lowered. "Whatever, you get John back here, Mary Fielding, and you get him back fast! Do I make myself clear?"

"Very! And I hope I am being just as clear, William Smith, when I tell you that I will do no such thing! Brother Joseph branded you an apostate before he was slain, my dear Hyrum agreed with him wholeheartedly, and now I see what they meant. Your spirit is darkness to me, William, and I feel more thankful by the moment for the privilege of preparing to take Hyrum's children into the howling wilderness after Elders Young and Kimball and of leaving you and your associates to wallow in your own mire."

"Now, see here, Mrs. Smith," William thundered bombastically, "I will not—"

"Stay another moment?" Mary finished for the irate man, rising in the instant to her feet. "Neither am I disappointed to see you go. There is the doorway, Mr. Smith. I beg you not to darken it again."

And with a determined toss of her head, Mary Fielding Smith turned away.

Following the death and burial of Joseph and Hyrum, the mobs temporarily withdrew. This was either because of fear over the deed they had done and its possible recriminations or in order to better observe the rapid collapse of Mormonism. This brief reprieve gave little Joseph F. as well as the rest of the saddened and bewildered Saints the time they needed to regroup.

The death of the Prophet Joseph had left the Saints bewildered and uncertain as to who the new leader should be.

There was danger of the Church breaking up completely as small factions developed behind men ambitious to be the new leader. It was a critical time. However, the order of succession was well understood by the Quorum of Twelve and the crisis passed. The Twelve, united under Brigham Young, the president of the Quorum, were sustained as the presiding officers of the Church by the uplifted hands of the Saints in an assembled body. The Quorum, eventually, would appoint a new Church president."1

While there were many things to consider, including missionary work and what to do with the resulting influx of converts from England and elsewhere, Brigham Young and the Twelve focused for a time on more temporal matters. Nauvoo at the time had a population of between 15,000 and 20,000, with 2,500 homes including 500 in the suburbs. If these people were to remain fed and clothed, then life, and the business of work in all its varied forms, needed to continue. The mobbers had brought much of that to a halt, but during the uneasy peace following the deaths of the prophets, the Brethren urged everyone back to work.

There was also the temple on the hill, which almost all felt an urgent need to complete. Hyrum had been in charge of the building's construction, and many, including Mary, were donating time and whatever financial means they could. Most knew of the blessings available in the Temple, and all these desired such blessings before they were forced to leave the city.

By spring of 1845 the mobocrats, having seen no noticeable dissolution of the Church, recommenced their work of intimidation and destruction. Among the outlying settlements they began burning, pillaging, kidnapping, beating; and the terrified Saints began fleeing for safety to Nauvoo.

Determined to drive the Saints from Nauvoo as well as

An engraving of Nauvoo after the
Saints had departed and before the
last wall of the Temple was leveled

CA. 1850's

Church Archives, The Church of Jesus Christ of Latter-day Saints

Illinois, the mobbers held a mass meeting in Quincy on September 22. There a resolution was drawn up asking the Mormons to leave the state as quickly as possible. Brigham Young replied that the Saints were willing to remove themselves to some remote place, but he asked that they be given until the next spring to do so. He pleaded for relief from vexatious lawsuits and also asked for help from the non-Mormons in assisting the Saints to dispose of their property fairly and equitably. The persecutors agreed, knowing full well that anything they refused to buy, they would get anyway once the Mormons were gone.

Through the fall and winter of 1845–1846 the Saints worked feverishly, seeking out dry goods, groceries, good oxen, beef cattle, horses, sheep, wagons, teams, yokes, harnesses, and anything else that might be a fair exchange for their property. Work also increased on the temple, and it was completed to the point that the October 1845 General Conference was held in it. By December, ordinance work had commenced, and such work continued day and night for the next six or seven months.

From the first day of temple ordinance work, both Mary and Mercy Rachel were called to assist. Though Mary and Hyrum had received their endowments in 1843 under the hand of Joseph Smith, she, along with her brother Joseph, was called back into the temple on December 10, 1845. At 4:25 p.m. that day, Elders Brigham Young and Heber C. Kimball commenced administering the ordinances. The work continued until 3:30 a.m., during which time thirty persons, including Mary, were endowed or re-endowed. The next day Mother Smith and Mercy Rachel were endowed, and from then on both Mary and Mercy Rachel remained in the temple assisting others.

Because of their young children, this was a challenge for the sisters. However, it was solved by having the children accompany them, even going so far as to live for a time on the premises. Mary's daughter Martha Ann remembered that her mother "worked in the Temple for three weeks. I was with her all the time."[2] Mercy adds: " 'I remained with my sister until the Temple was finished so far that the ordinances of the holy priesthood could be administered there, when I was called by President Young to take up abode there to assist in the female department, which I did laboring night and day, keeping my children with me.' "[3] After the first three weeks, while Mary returned home to prepare her large group of dependents for departure from Nauvoo, Mercy Rachel remained in the temple, laboring until the work was over.

On another front, as "the Saints prepared to leave Nauvoo, many widows were married as plural wives to Church leaders. Mary married Heber C. Kimball and became one of thirty-eight women for whom he assumed responsibility. But she made her own way."[4]

Because of the rapidly mounting hostility in and around Nauvoo, the Saints began leaving as early as February 4, 1846. On the 6TH, Bishop George Miller and his six wagons crossed the Mississippi, and from then on, the work of ferrying went on almost day and night. On February 14TH Elder Parley P. Pratt departed, and the next day President Brigham Young, Willard Richards, and George A. Smith, with a large company, crossed on the ice. They traveled about nine miles into Iowa, where a temporary camp was established on Sugar Creek to gather in the fleeing refugees.

For Mary and her family, however, leaving Nauvoo was no easy matter. Not only were there a great many who were depending on her to get them away, but the pressures from William and others were tremendous. Forces to keep her from joining with the westward moving body of the Saints seemed combined against her. But not only had William and his associates taken the wrong approach; they had also underestimated Mary and found her impossible to intimidate. Worse for William, while he was heaping abuse on the widow of his murdered brother, her young son Joseph

F. was listening in an upstairs chamber into which ran the pipe of the living room stove below, thus enabling him to hear his uncle distinctly. Joseph F. wished that he were bigger so that he could protect his mother and give William what he deserved for his words. He couldn't, but he never forgot the incident, or the spirit of darkness and apostasy the man carried with him.5

Despite their troubles with William, Mary and her family were close to the Smiths. They adored Grandmother Smith, who publicly expressed a desire to go west with the body of the Church.6 Though she never did emigrate, she wholeheartedly supported Brigham Young and the remainder of the Twelve.7 Mary also had tender regard for the four living children of the late Samuel H. Smith and his widow, Levira. When a difficult childbirth while visiting her parents left Levira unable to return to her three eldest children in Nauvoo, Mary took them into her already crowded home, and there they lived through the winter of 1845–1846.

Mary B. Smith Norman, one of the girls, remembered Mary thus: " 'I will give a pen picture of her. She had a fine personality, was at that time tall and rather slender, fair in complexion, and a perfect type of English gentlewoman. To complete my story — Aunt Mary took care of us until we were otherwise provided for.' "8 Mary B. Smith's brother Samuel H. B. Smith, nearly the same age as young Joseph F., would later become Joseph F.'s missionary associate and lifelong friend.

As the Saints continued to leave Nauvoo through the spring of 1846, young Joseph F. watched them eagerly. Because his home was right on the river, and the wharf was close nearby, the boy was part of it all. One day, Joseph F. remembered, soon after Brigham Young's company had crossed over on the ice, a stranger rode up on a large bay horse with a fine saddle and bridle. "He asked the boy, Joseph, where the Mormons had crossed the river on the ice.

Joseph pointed out the place. The man, in a gruff voice, declared: 'By G—, if the Mormons can cross on the ice, I can, too.' He started over in the gathering darkness. Later, when the ice had melted, the horse with the saddle and bridle still on was found down the river on a sand bar. There was no trace of the man."9

One more lesson learned, and for Mary Fielding Smith's only son, they kept on coming. Already familiar with teams in harness, Joseph F.'s observations were now giving him a growing knowledge concerning handling large, bulky wagons, as well as multiple teams pulling wagons in tandem. Perhaps without any intention, the eight-year-old boy was learning to be a teamster.

There is no doubt that he longed to be on his way, like his older brother John. However, his mother waited, apparently unable to afford sufficient equipment to make the journey. Her brother Joseph Fielding was having the same difficulty. According to his journal:

> But to return to Nauvoo where I spent the summer for want of means to get away. I sold my house and 20 acres of land for 200 dol's in trade, taking 2 horses a waggon [*sic*], a coat---cloth, and a few (4½ dol's) in cash. The land was in good cultivation; 120 rods of good rail fence; a frame house 16 feet by 24 filled in with bricks; a pretty garden; a number of apple trees and peach trees just ready to bear fruit; and an excellent well 21 feet deep, not 2 miles from the Temple. I paid for the land in its wild state 160 dol's, built a house, etc., so that the price of the whole would not near pay the cost... One of the horses I took for the place I soon found to be balky [*sic*], and I only got in trade for her a small yoke of young oxen...
>
> Soon after I sold my place I removed my family and goods to the house on my sister's farm called Brother

Hyrum's where my sister thought of planting grain but we found it to be useless, and I did not so much as plant the smallest garden stuff.₁₀

As summer waned, Mary was finally able to dispose of her property for $700 (Hyrum's eldest daughter Lovina and her new husband, Lorin Walker, also received $200), which Mary used to begin putting together an outfit. She required at least six wagons, for she had to transport eighteen people as well as all they owned in the world. She also needed teams for this many wagons. Wagons and teams were in short supply, however, and she couldn't seem to find all of what she needed.

Meanwhile the mobbers grew ever more determined to see the Saints gone, no matter what. Finally, seeing no safe alternative, Mary led her large family across the river, trusting that there she would be enabled to finish her preparations. Concerning what occurred next, her brother journalized:

Not long after this... the mob began to collect and to threaten us with extinction, first at Golden's point to the number of 200 or 300 from which they dispersed in fear, but soon began to gather again near Carthage where they lay encamped a number of weeks to the number of 900 as far as I can gather until early in September. They marched into Nauvoo; my two sisters Smith and Thompson and myself with our families had just got over the River Mississippi with all our goods except two boat loads before they came in contact with the citizens. They came and camped on the farm that I had just left. They took this course to avoid any ambushment that might be laid for them. From there they sent balls into the city but before they came near the Temple they were met and repulsed but

I shall not attempt to record the whole scene of outrage. The poor Saints had to flee, sick as well. They hastened to the river but the citizens judged it not best to let them leave when they were so much needed, but the sick and the women and children got over as far as they could. I went down to the bank of the river and found many of the Saints in distress. Some had left their husbands. In the battle the cannons roared tremendously on both sides for several days.11

The scenes of turmoil and terror in Nauvoo during what was called the Nauvoo War left an indelible impression on young Joseph F. and the other children in Mary's group. Never would they forget their fear, anxiety, and sadness in having to abandon their beloved home. According to Martha Ann, " 'We left our home, just as it was, all the furniture, in fact everything we owned. The fruit trees were loaded with rosy peaches and apples. We bid goodbye to the loved home that reminded us of our beloved father everywhere we turned. We crossed the Mississippi River on a skiff in the dusk of the evening. We bid goodbye to our dear old grandmother, Lucy Mack Smith. I can never forget the bitter tears she shed when she bid us goodbye for the last time. She knew it would be the last time she would see her son's family... in this life. We did not realize this so much at that time as we have since."12

It was the evening of September 8 (9), 1846, when Mary's company made their way across the river, barely ahead of the destruction of Nauvoo. Mary " 'had succeeded in getting provisions, bedding, wagons, ox-teams, her husband's big white horse, and a few other necessities, loaded on a flat boat and taken across the Mississippi River to Montrose, Iowa. The children were taken across in a skiff and they and their mother spent the night in their camp on the banks of the river listening to the bombardment of the city of Nauvoo.' "13

For the next several days Joseph F., his mother, and the others remained encamped on the river bank without enough teams to move forward, listening to the canon bombardment of the mob and keeping a wary eye on their abandoned home across the water.

Still, Mary "could now breathe easier, for she was out of reach of the ruthless mob that had taken possession of Nauvoo. The tension of the last frenetic days, while the mob came closer and closer, had mounted to the breaking point. Knowing what the wretches had done and were capable of doing had filled her with righteous anger. She had again felt their hot breath, as they camped on what had been her farm, then pressed near to her abode. The fiends of hell found the old home deserted.

"They had killed her husband; had forced her from her property; had caused her new mental anguish, but she had escaped them. She chose the dangerous way of the wilderness rather than live near and among the unregenerate. She now emerged into the sun. Her gratitude knew no bounds."14

Nevertheless, she and the rest of Nauvoo's poor and sick had no shelter, very little food, and no means to move away from their desperate location. The weather was getting colder, and all about them the suffering of the refugees was beyond imagination. Together Mary and Mercy donated eighteen dollars 15 to try and assist those who surrounded them on the banks of the river, but it did little to help. For some time almost everyone in the camp had been living on boiled corn, for it was all they had. Then came a ten-day stretch when all that was left, for any of them, was parched corn. That seemed to be the final straw.

The shock of being dispossessed, deprived of their homes, personal dignity, and subjected to extreme want, left many in a state of stupor and despair. Empty stomachs, constant weariness, red eyes, colds, and general lassitude, combined to sear and debilitate their spirits. Wretchedly, the aged huddled about the camp fires, hypnotized into blank, empty staring by the flicking flames. The cruel ordeal, the inhumanity, the crude flight, the exposure day and night, the cold earth, and the elements took their toll in sickness and death.16

Finally the Lord intervened. As Joseph Fielding later described it:

Here the Lord sent upon them, as it were, a shower of quails. They came in vast flocks. Many came into the [shelters] where the Saints were, settled on the tables and the floor, and even on their laps so that they caught as many as they pleased. Thus the Lord was mindful of his people, and it was truly a matter of astonishment.17

At length help also arrived from Brigham Young, George A. Smith, and Heber C. Kimball, who were already at Winter Quarters, several hundred miles to the west. Somewhat strengthened emotionally, and borrowing sufficient rolling stock and teams to move all they had a few miles inland, which took going back and forth from the river several times, Mary next took young Joseph F. and made her way to Keokuk, Iowa, nine miles down the Mississippi. There she completed the purchase of sufficient wagons and teams of her own, as well as what foodstuffs she could find for sale, to begin her family's big journey. She and young Joseph F. then drove everything back to Montrose. At last, Joseph F. and his courageous mother knew, the extended family of Hyrum Smith was ready to face the wilderness.

Brigham Young   CA. *mid 1800's*

LESSONS ON THE FRONTIER

"Ma! Oh, Mama!" Quickly growing impatient, young Joseph F., almost nine years old and thinking himself quite mature, allowed the sound of his frustration to creep into his voice. But he also decided, even as he opened his mouth for a second holler, that it would be better to address Mary Smith by a more proper and appropriate title. "Mo-ther!"

It was a cold morning, and despite the fact that the sun was long up, he was soaked to the skin with heavy dew and so cold his teeth were practically chattering. Since daybreak he and his uncle, Joseph Fielding, had been searching through the tall prairie grass for their best yoke of oxen—without success, he thought sourly. They had even left them yoked together the night before, to keep them from straying into a herd of beef cattle that were bedded down on the other side of a creek about a mile away. Yet, with daylight the oxen had been missing; now it was practically noon, and Joseph F. was certain the oxen were gone for good.

"Mother!" he called again as he rounded the corner of one of their heavily loaded wagons. "Moth—" Abruptly the boy closed his mouth and stopped. His mother had not replied for the simple reason that she was engaged in conversation with another—with the Lord, as a matter of fact. Mary Smith was kneeling beside the wagon in prayer, and interrupting her at prayer was the last thing young Joseph F. ever wanted to do!

Quietly, carefully, the boy moved back behind the high, spoked wheel of the wagon. There he stopped, waiting patiently for his mother to finish her prayer. Sometimes her prayers seemed long to him, especially her silent ones when she seemed to actually be visiting with the Lord. Joseph F. couldn't understand that, at least not exactly. But his Uncle Fielding had explained that very righteous people could do that—have literal conversations with the Lord—and the boy no longer worried about it. His mother was righteous, he knew that without a doubt, and so she and the Lord could take as long to visit as they wished. He, meanwhile, was content to wait.

In the distance the beef cattle were bawling, and for a moment Joseph F. watched the men who were herding them. By now he would have thought they would be gone. Since they were still there, he found himself wondering if maybe they had also lost some animals. Perhaps to Indians, who had also stolen his mother's oxen? It was an intriguing thought, no doubt brought to the fore because of the Pottawattamie Indians on whose lands many in Winter Quarters had been staying. For a few moments Joseph F. allowed his mind to play with it—

Two weeks earlier he, his mother, and his Uncle Fielding had left Winter Quarters bound for St. Joseph, Missouri, a hundred and sixty miles away. They had taken two empty wagons with two teams each, for his mother's goal was to purchase sufficient flour, corn, bacon, clothing, and other dry goods to carry the family through the winter as well as the trek westward during the coming spring.

It had been rainy and cold all the way from Winter Quarters to St. Joseph, with muddy roads and poor camps making the journey even more unpleasant. Still, they had finally arrived, his mother had purchased all she had hoped to, and they had even stopped with their precious cargo at Savannah during their return to have their corn ground. Now they were encamped on an open prairie on the Missouri River bottom, only a few days away from Winter Quarters and the small cabin they called home.

Nearby, a small spring creek chuckled past on its way to the Missouri River, about three-quarters of a mile distant. Even standing on the ground rather than up on the wagon bench, Joseph F. could see the river plainly in the southwest, as well as every foot of ground in between. He could also see the bluffs to the northwest and the distant line of timber which skirted the prairie both to his right and to his left. In short, the entire country was plainly visible and seemed to hold no hiding places. Moreover, neither had he nor his Uncle Fielding been able to find any such places where the lost oxen might have wandered.

Which was why, he thought grimly, the idea of thieving Indians made sense—

His mother's voice was coming to him now, still praying, and he could hear her pleading with the Lord not to suffer them to be left in such a helpless condition, but to lead them to recover their lost team so that they could continue their travels in safety. For a moment or so she paused, and as she concluded her prayer, Joseph F. stepped back around the wheel to deliver his news.

Instead, however, he stopped again in his tracks. On Mary Smith's face was a lovely smile, the first he had seen in weeks on the perpetually worried woman. Instantly Joseph F. was filled with renewed hope and assurance, and all thoughts of his negative report fled from his mind. Things were going to be all right! They would find their oxen, and then—

In that instant Joseph Fielding came around the wagons, and it was obvious to young Joseph F. that his uncle was as wet, cold, and discouraged as he had been. "Well, Mary," he grumbled as he removed his hat and lowered himself onto a wagon tongue, his appearance the epitome of despair and self-pity, "the cattle are gone!"

"Never mind," Mary Smith replied in a voice that fairly rang with cheerfulness. "Your breakfast has been waiting for hours, Joseph, and while you and Joseph F. are eating, I will just take a walk out and see if I can find the cattle."

Staring at his older sister, Joseph Fielding held up his hands in blank astonishment. If the Missouri River had suddenly turned up stream, Joseph F. thought wryly, his uncle could not have appeared more surprised. Neither, for that matter, could he. Even after her smile—

"Why, Mary!" Uncle Fielding exclaimed. "What do you mean? The boy and I have been all over this country, all through the timber and through the herd of cattle, and our oxen are gone— they are not to be found! I believe they have been driven off. It is useless for you to hunt for them."

Mary's smile only grew softer, more gentle. "Never mind me," she said as she pointed to the mess chest, upon which she had spread their much-delayed meal. "Eat your breakfast, and I will see."

Turning, she started down the small creek toward the river, not hurrying, but not deviating much at all from her set course. With a shake of his head, Joseph Fielding turned to eating, dismissing thoughts of his sister from his mind. But not young Joseph F. He watched, wondering, and before his mother was out of speaking distance he saw the man who was in charge of the herd of beef cattle, ride up from the opposite side of the creek.

"Madam," he called loudly from the back of his horse, "I saw your oxen over in that direction this morning about daybreak." He then pointed in the opposite direction from the one Mary Smith was taking.

To Joseph F.'s surprise, his mother continued forward, ignoring the man completely. She did not speak, she did not even turn her head in his direction. Instead she continued walking, her long skirts and petticoats making an audible swishing in the tall grass.

For a moment the cattle drover seemed perplexed, not knowing exactly what to do. But then, when it had become obvious even to him that Mary Smith was not to be diverted from her course, he wheeled his horse and rode off rapidly toward his herd. Soon the cattle were being driven through the timber and toward the road leading to Savannah, and within another few moments both men and cattle had completely disappeared.

Mary Smith, meanwhile, held her course along that small spring creek, not turning or stopping until she stood almost on the bank of the Missouri River.

"Uncle," Joseph F. muttered as he stared after his mother's distant form, "Ma's waving. I reckon she wants us to come."

"You can still see her?"

"I haven't lost sight of her, even once. She's beckoning us to come."

Instantly Joseph Fielding rose from the mess chest. "Well, then," he said with a wide grin, "we ought not to keep her waiting. Bet I can beat you in a footrace, young man!"

"Bet not!" Joseph F. shouted in reply, and with a whoop he was off across the prairie, his uncle following closely behind.

"What...is it, Ma... I mean, Mother?" Joseph F. gasped moments later as he approached her still form, some fifteen seconds ahead of his laboring uncle. "Did you find the oxen, huh? Did the Lord show you where—"

Turning to where his mother was pointing downward, young Joseph F. was not at all surprised to see their oxen, still yoked together, tied to a clump of willows growing in the bottom of a deep gulch. The gulch had been washed out of the sandy bank of the Missouri River by the little spring creek and was perfectly hidden from the view of their camp.

"Well," Joseph Fielding breathed heavily as he came to stand beside his sister, "if that doesn't beat all I ever saw."

"The Lord showed her where they were," Joseph F. declared excitedly as he started down the bank to free the errant oxen. "He did, Ma, didn't he!"

"'Mother,' Joseph F. I'm your mother, not your ma, and I would appreciate being addressed by the appropriate title."

"Yes'm." Joseph F. stopped, his eyes on the ground. "Mother. But he did, didn't he! The Lord showed you, when you were praying back there by the wagon! That's how you knew right where to come!"

Mary Smith smiled tenderly. "Yes, Joseph F., he did. He gave me to know exactly where the oxen had been tied, and he gave me to know just as clearly how those men with the cattle were trying to steal them in order to keep us from joining with the Saints in the valleys of the mountains. The Lord loves us, Joseph F., and when we keep the commandments as well as we are able, he is perfectly capable of giving us all we ask for—lost oxen included. Do you understand?"

"Yes'm," Joseph F. muttered easily.

"Good. Now, why don't you fetch the oxen up, and we can all be on our way."

The circumstance of finding those oxen on the banks of the Missouri made a deep impression upon young Joseph F. Years later he declared, "'It was one of the first practical and positive demonstrations of the efficacy of prayer I had ever witnessed. It made an indelible impression upon my mind, and has been a source

Joseph Fielding,
uncle of Joseph F. Smith

N.D.

of comfort, assurance and guidance to me throughout all of my life.' "1

While this adventure with the oxen occurred after Joseph F. and his family had arrived in Winter Quarters, several events transpired prior to that, that should be addressed. Even though the adults found the 1846 trek across Iowa terribly difficult but largely uneventful, to Joseph F. every day was an adventure and every mile a new experience. He quickly learned to help with harnessing and unharnessing the teams of horses and even to yoke and unyoke the oxen. He spent hours seated on the wagon benches handling the reins, or walking beside the oxen with his stick, prodding them and shouting "gee" or "haw" when he wished them to turn one way or the other. He also labored as herd boy and spent many days trailing the loose stock, which comprised, in addition to the teams, twenty-one loose cattle and forty-three sheep.

The caravan, or wagon train, they traveled with, which all referred to as Mary Smith's, was composed of nine wagons, six belonging to Mary, one to Mercy Rachel, and two to Joseph Fielding. In Mary's group were eight men, five single women, and a sister in the Church who came with her four children, making a total of eighteen in addition to Mary and her four youngest children. Mary's stepson John had gone ahead with Heber C. Kimball's company, and her stepdaughter Lovina was of course with her husband, Lorin Walker, and his family. In Mercy Rachel's group were herself and her little daughter, Mary Jane. Joseph Fielding's family consisted of two men, two women, and five children.2

Many years later Joseph F. stated, "'I can remember my mother in the days of Nauvoo [1839–46]. I remember seeing her and her helpless children hustled into a flat boat with such things as she could carry out of the house at the commencement of the bombardment of the city of Nauvoo by the mob. I remember the hardships... on the way to Winter Quarters, on the Missouri River, and how she prayed for her children and family on her wearisome journey.'" 3

> There was no faltering, no doubts or discouragements too great amidst all of these trials for Mary Fielding Smith. She had put her hand to the plough, and could not turn back. Moreover, all that she did was with the pure and sacred knowledge that she was serving the Lord, her God. Each day as she journeyed along she sought Him in prayer; and each day the prayer was answered with the comforting assurance which was borne in upon her soul and impressed upon her heart, that He would not forsake her, and in the end she should triumph, if not in this life, then in the glorious life to come. Therefore, in faith and knowledge that she was doing the will of God, she and her dependent flock [made] their way, wearily, tediously, hungry, and only partly sheltered and clothed.4

At about 150 miles from Winter Quarters, the Smith caravan met some travelers headed east, and to everyone's surprise one of them was John Fielding, Joseph F.'s older stepbrother. There was much rejoicing in the family, for John had heard the others were coming and had set out to meet them.

It soon became evident to all that Mary's decision to "allow John to go west had been no mistake. As heir to the patriarchship of the Church, he belonged with the body of the Saints. Although only fourteen years old, he was robust, mature, and large of stature. He brought back with him an air of western sophistication. For a boy, he had had a great adventure. He imparted to [Joseph F., his mother, and the others,] a feeling of security and comfort through intelligence of the trail ahead and conditions at Winter Quarters.

John piloted the company the rest of the way and brought the wagon-train safely to the camp of the Saints."5

On October 21, 1846, long after dark of a lengthy, grueling day during which they had crossed the Missouri River into present-day Nebraska, the Smith wagon train pulled into Winter Quarters. Uncle Joseph Fielding commented that "the lights of the camp of the Saints as we saw the lights at a distance were interesting. It reminded us of Israel of old in the wilderness...there were few houses; nearly all were in their tents upon about a square half mile."6

Because the entire camp was divided into wards, little Joseph F. and his group were called to attend the 13th Ward. Brother Rolf was bishop, and he called Uncle Joseph Fielding as one of his counselors. All in the ward were tithed, but inasmuch as Mary and Mercy Rachel, who were widows, were also caring for three other widows as well as numerous children, it was judged that they were already paying tithing enough and should forgo any extra.

The first order of business, once they had been assigned a ward, was to erect a more permanent sort of shelter. According to Joseph F.'s uncle, with much hard labor on the part of all, including Joseph F., who dragged in logs by ox team from nearly two miles away, they erected for the Smith family a double home of logs, sod, and clapboard, each half being sixteen feet square, with a log lean-to on the back for Mercy Rachel and her daughter. All had dirt floors with chinking between the logs to keep out the winter winds. Joseph Fielding built for his own family a smaller version of the Smiths' home a little distance away.7

For that winter and the following spring, which was 1847, Joseph F. and the rest of the Smiths, the Thompsons, and the Fieldings remained at Winter Quarters, doing their best to survive. Despite the dirt floor and rough interior of their home, Joseph F.'s mother:

...made it habitable. It was a haven of peace and rest. It was a place of good cheer enhanced by the play and laughter of children, the whetting of appetites by newly baked bread or the savory aroma of a stew cooking in the iron kettle at the fireplace. Despite the rusticity of the cabin, it had sanctity of atmosphere engendered by a pilgrim humility and refreshment of spirit rooted in the reading of scripture, verse, and the perusal of learning in a few precious books. There were hymns, also, Mormon and Methodist.

Mary presided with calmness, all home activities centering in and revolving about her. The prayer of faith, uttered in gratitude and love, was a ritual night and morning. At bedtime she tucked the children in and gave them a goodnight caress. They arose in the morning to a breakfast she had waiting for them. They looked for her when they returned from work or play. If she were absent, they were crestfallen. They would look about and call: 'Mama! Mama! Where are you?' She was mother in all that the word meant—long-suffering, hard-working, God-loving, and dutiful. She made the crude cabin a home. It became hallowed—the prototype of a house she would build out of adobes one day when she reached the mountains.8

"'Do you not think that these things make an impression upon the mind?" Joseph F. asked rhetorically some years later. "Do you think I can forget the example of my mother? No; her faith and example will ever be bright in my memory. What do I think! Every breath I breathe, every feeling of my soul rises to God in thankfulness to Him that my mother was a Saint, that she was a woman of God, pure and faithful, and that she would suffer death rather than betray the trust committed to her; that she would suffer poverty and distress in the wilderness and try to hold her family together rather than remain in Babylon. That is the spirit which imbued her.'"9

Early in 1847 George Mills, the old nonmember soldier who had been with Hyrum and Mary Smith through so much, departed with Brigham Young's company on the initial trek into the valley of the Salt Lake. In June of that same year, Mercy Rachel and her daughter joined with J. Lawson's party, and they set out for the west. Meanwhile, Mary and her brother set about preparing for another winter as well as their own ultimate departure from the banks of the Missouri, still a year away.

More than anything else they needed supplies, for they were ragged and foodstuffs were scanty. During the summer and fall of 1847, to alleviate that problem, Mary and Uncle Joseph Fielding, taking young Joseph F. with them, made two trips to St. Joseph, Missouri—the nearest supply post. There Joseph F.'s mother, using the money she had realized from the sale of her properties in Nauvoo, purchased provisions sufficient for what remained of her large household. It was during one of these two trips that the incident with the lost oxen occurred, as described at the beginning of this chapter.

The winter of 1847–1848 was a terrible one for the people of Winter Quarters. Because of their poverty and primitive mode of living, as well as their diet being sorely deficient and out of balance, the resistance of many of the refugees was very low. The trials and suffering of the Saints at Winter Quarters were reflected in the 600 graves that were dug during the terrible sojourn. Somehow no one in Joseph F.'s own family died, by spring most who had survived were doing a little better, and all of them were preparing with mounting excitement for their coming exodus to the valleys of the mountains. But Joseph F. recalled that " 'Winter Quarters was a most sickly hole, and was being deserted by the Saints.' "10

Early in the spring of 1848, as his mother and uncle were preparing for their immediate departure, young Joseph F. finally got his fill of Indians. He described his harrowing experience as follows:

One bright morning in company with my companions, namely, Alden Burdick, almost a young man grown, and very sober, steady boy, Thomas Burdick, about my own age, but a little older, and Isaac [Ike] Blocksome, a little younger than myself, I started out with my cattle, comprising the cows, and young stock, and several yoke of oxen which were unemployed that day, to go to the herd grounds about one and a half or two miles from the town (Winter Quarters). We had two horses, both belonging to the Burdicks, and a young pet jack belonging to me. Alden proposed to take it afoot through the hazel and some small woods by a side road, and gather some hazel nuts for the crowd, while we took out the cattle and we would meet at the spring on the herd ground. This arrangement just suited us, for we felt when Alden was away we were free from all restraint; his presence, he being the oldest, restrained us, for he was very sedate and operated as an extinguisher upon our exuberance of youthful feelings. I was riding Alden's bay mare; Thomas, his father's black pony, and Isaac, my jack. On the way we had some sport with "Ike" and the jack, which plagued "Ike" so badly that he left us with disgust, turning the jack loose with the bridle on, and he went home. When Thomas and I arrived at the spring we set down our dinner pails, mounted our horses and amused ourselves by running short races, and jumping the horses across ditches, Alden not having arrived as yet. While we were thus amusing ourselves, our cattle were

Illustration by Robert T. Barrett

feeding along down the little spring creek towards a rolling point about half a mile distant. The leaders of the herd had stretched out about half way to this point, when all of a sudden a gang of Indians, stripped to the breach-clout, painted and daubed and on horse-back, came charging at full speed from behind this point, towards us.

Thomas Burdick immediately started for home, crying "Indians!" "Indians!" Before he reached the top of the hill, however, for some cause he abandoned his pony, turning it loose with bridle and rope, or lariat attached. My first impression, or impulse was to save the cattle from being driven off, for in a most incredible short time, I thought of going to the valley; of our dependence upon our cattle, and the horror of being compelled to remain at Winter Quarters. I suited the action to the thought, and at full speed dashed out to head the cattle and if possible turn them towards home. I reached the van of the herd just as the greater number of Indians did. Two Indians had passed me, in pursuit of Thomas. I wheeled my horse in almost one bound and shouted at the cattle which, mingled with the whoops of the Indians and the sudden rush of a dozen horses, frightened the cattle and started them on the keen run towards the head of the spring, in the direction of home. As I wheeled I saw the first Indian I met, whom I shall never forget. He was a tall, thin man, riding a light roan horse, very fleet; he had his hair daubed up with stiff white clay. He leaped from his horse and caught Thomas Burdick's, then he jumped on his horse again and started back in the direction he had come. While this was going on the whole gang surrounded me, trying to head me off, but they did not succeed until I reached the head of the spring, with the whole herd under full stampede ahead of me, taking the lower road to town, the road that Alden had taken in the morning. Here my horse was turned around at the head of the spring and down the stream I went at full speed till I reached a point opposite the hill, where other Indians had concentrated and I was met at this point by this number of Indians who had crossed the stream to head me off. This turned my horse, and once more I got the lead in the direction of home. I could outrun them, but my horse was getting tired or out of wind and the Indians kept doubling on me, coming in ahead of me and checking my speed, till finally, reaching the head of the spring again, I met, or overtook, a platoon which kept their horses so close together and veering to right and left as I endeavored to dodge them, that I could not force my horse through. I was thus compelled to slacken speed and the Indians behind overtook me; one Indian rode upon the left side and one on the right side of me, and each took me by an arm and leg and lifted me from my horse; they then slackened their speed until my horse run from under me, then they chucked me down with great violence to the ground. Several horses from behind jumped over me, but did not hurt me. My horse was secured by the Indians and without slacking speed they rode on in the direction from whence they had come. About this moment a number of men appeared on the hill with pitchforks in hand, whom Thomas had alarmed with the cry of 'Indians!' These men were on their way to the hay field, and at this juncture, as the men appeared on the hill, an Indian who had been trying to catch the jack with corn, made a desperate lunge to catch the animal and was kicked over, spilling his corn, which in his great haste to get away before the men could catch him, he left on the ground. The jack cooly turned and ate the corn, to the amusement of the men on the hill as well as my own.

At this point I thought I better start after Thomas, and as I reached the top of the hill I saw him just going down into the town. The Indians having departed, the men returned with the pitchforks to their wagons and I continued on to the town. When I arrived a large assembly was counseling in the bowery, Thomas having told them of our trouble. My folks were glad to see me, you may be sure. A company was formed and on horses started in pursuit of the Indians, and a second company on foot with Thomas and myself to pilot them, went in pursuit of the cattle. We took the road we had traveled in the morning and went to the spring. In the meantime Alden had arrived at the spring, found nobody there, dinner pails standing as we had left them, became alarmed, took the herd by the lower road and drove them home. We who did not know this, hunted most of the day and not finding our cattle we returned home disheartened, and I was filled with fears that we would not now be able to journey to the valley. When we returned home we learned that Alden had found the cattle and they were all home, safely cared for, and so this trouble was soon forgotten. Thomas' horse was recovered, but the one I was riding was not found. It cost the Indians too much for them ever to part with it. I was at this time about nine years of age.[11]

THE WIDOW'S MIGHT

It was the sound of approaching hoofbeats that first got Joseph F.'s attention. Looking up from his seat by the fire, he quickly ascertained that the two riders were Elder Heber C. Kimball, his stepfather, and one other whom he had seen on occasion but did not know' a venerable old gentleman with flowing white hair and beard. Because his mother had stood at their approach, so did he, dropping the harness he had been mending as he did so.

It was the morning of June 5, 1848, and Mary Smith's company of seven wagons, seven adults, and five children had made it exactly two miles yesterday during their first day of travel from Winter Quarters. Neither, Joseph F. thought with disgust, did this day look to be much of an improvement.

Despite his personal heroics with the Indians a few weeks before when he had helped save the camp's cattle, Joseph F. knew that his mother's own livestock had been decimated by the two hard winters spent in Winter Quarters. Eleven of her thirteen horses had died, and she had left only one real ox that had been trained to the yoke. They had been forced, therefore, to use half-wild cows and young oxen that had not been broke for either leader or driver. Worse, because there were not even enough wild cattle to make sufficient teams, he, his brother John, his Uncle Fielding, and a Brother Terry, whom his mother had hired to assist as a driver, had also been forced to hook and drive the wagons tandem, which was difficult for even the most seasoned teamster.

Joseph F. was still shaking his head at the memory of their first day. Besides being required to yoke and unyoke certain of the green teams all by himself, a large task for a nine-year-old boy, he and John had taken turns either herding the loose stock or driving two such teams yoked to two wagons, hooked tandem. On the flats they had moved fairly well, but at the least sign of a hill they had been forced to separate the wagons and take only one to the top. Unhooking the two yokes of green cows and oxen, they had led them back down the hill so they might pull the other wagon up to the first. Finally hooked in tandem again, they had proceeded down the far slope as best they were able.

Which had been an especially tragic comedy, the boy thought ruefully. In fact, the whole day had been one long series of the most amazing and trying circumstances. Several times the heavy wagons had mired in mud when the teams had bolted off the trail, requiring even more doubling up of green teams; on the downslopes of the numerous hills the young and half-wild cattle had fled at ungovernable speeds from the wagons rattling along behind them, ultimately crashing on every occasion and breaking wagon tongues and reaches, snapping lines, and fracturing one almost irreplaceable axle.

Thus in the entire day they had made two paltry miles, which left them twenty-five miles to go before the Elk Horn River and Heber C. Kimball's waiting company. Twenty-five miles, daylight of their second day was burning, and they still had not completed all of their repairs!

"Sister Smith," Elder Kimball smiled as he halted his horse and dismounted, sweeping off his hat as he did so. Despite the fact that she was one of his plural wives, he always called her Sister Smith. "Good morning to you. I am pleased to see that you have made a start. I assume, therefore, that Brother Eagan found you?"

"Good morning, Elder Kimball," Joseph's mother curtsied politely. "Yes, Howard Eagan brought us word of your desires that we join you, despite our poor preparations, and so we have acted accordingly."

"You started late in the day, then?"

"No, we traveled all through the day."

"Hmmm. Interesting." Elder Kimball looked around at Mary Smith's ragtag outfit, his sharp eyes missing nothing. "Well, most companies must have a day or so of shakedown before they can settle into the business of travel. No doubt yours will do better today."

"We pray so."

Elder Kimball smiled and then looked at Joseph F. "Good morning, young master Joseph. I see that you are repairing lines this morning. See that your stitches are tight, and you will repair them far less often."

Silently Joseph F. nodded. His mother had given him the same advice only half an hour before, and all along he had been pulling the fool stitches as tight as was humanly possible—

"Sister Smith," Elder Kimball continued, turning back to Joseph F.'s mother, "this is Cornelius P. Lott. He is captain of the group in which I have assigned you to travel. You will report to him as required, and he will see to it that you and your people have the assistance you need to make it to the valley."

"Widow Smith." The portly old man bowed, sweeping off his hat as he did so.

"Captain Lott." Mary Smith again curtsied, this time only slightly.

"Brother Lott had the good fortune of enjoying the esteem of the Prophet Joseph," Elder Kimball enthused. "Once the Prophet even dined at his table."

"Yes," Mary's smile was thin, "I have met Captain Lott before, and on occasion my husband, Brother Hyrum, also spoke of him."

"Well, good. Good. I'm pleased that you are acquainted. I'll be on my way, then, and you and the good captain can work out the details of your travel." With a fluid movement Elder Kimball swung into his saddle. "Good day to you, master Joseph. Good day to you also, Sister Smith. It is good to have your company with us! Give my regards to your brother!"

For a moment the three stood in silence, watching the apostle ride away. Joseph F. was aware, for the first time, that the rest of his mother's company had gathered behind the wagons and were silently watching his mother and Cornelius Lott. Widow Aunty Grinnels was holding Martha Ann; Widow Jane Wilson was in the act of using her despicable snuff; Widow Margaret Brysen was holding Sarah's hand; his teenage brother John and sister Jerusha were standing together; Brother Terry was far in the background holding one of the horses; and Joseph F.'s Uncle Fielding was standing beside his wife, Hannah, but looking as if he were ready to charge forward to his sister's aid, though he was not moving a muscle. In fact the whole moment seemed frozen, and young Joseph F. was certain he would remember the scene for the remainder of his life.

Well he knew of his mother's unhappy opinion of Cornelius Lott, a pompous, arrogant old man who did little work but liked to impress others with his association with the Prophet Joseph. The trouble was, his mother didn't impress very easily, especially as regarding that topic; and even the least shred of pride and arrogance, in herself or anyone else, made her angry as a stepped-on hornet. The venerable Cornelius Lott affected her in just that way, and Joseph F. found himself wondering why in the world Elder Kimball had assigned him to be their captain. Of all the men in the company that Elder Kimball could have picked, why—

"You're almighty late in arriving, Widow Smith."

"Yes, Captain Lott, we are late."

The old man looked around. "Your wagons look to be poorly used and in mighty sorry shape."

"Yes," Joseph F.'s mother agreed quietly, "that is also true. May I remind you, however, that it is difficult to find good rolling stock in this country."

Captain Lott did not so much as glance at her. "Your teams look even worse than your pathetic wagons, Widow Smith. How do you expect green and yearling stock to haul a sorry, rawhide outfit like yours all the way to the valley?"

Surprised by the man's tone of voice as much as he was by his words, Joseph F. stared at him. Nobody spoke to his mother in that tone of voice! Nobody!

"Again," Mary Smith responded calmly, "it's all we could obtain, Captain Lott."

"Who are your teamsters, if I might ask?"

"Brother Terry, my brother Joseph, my sons John and Joseph F., and myself."

Captain Lott laughed harshly. "You and your little boy, teamsters? Come, Widow Smith; be reasonable. Besides, you have seven wagons, and yet you named only five—"

"We pull six of the wagons tandem," Mary Smith responded icily as she placed her hand on Joseph F.'s trembling shoulder. No doubt his rising anger at the man's effrontery was obvious to her, and she wanted to stop him from doing something foolish. Joseph F. knew this, and yet with all his heart he wanted to—

"I drive the seventh wagon," his mother was continuing, "which I am perfectly capable of doing, and both John and young Joseph do just fine with their outfits, thank you!"

The captain continued to chuckle while Joseph F. seethed. "Of course they do," the old man sneered. "Let's see, now. The register says you have in your company, in addition to your children and brother and wife, three other widow women."

"Yes, and as I mentioned, Brother Terry has come with us as a teamster."

"I don't wonder that you took him on. The thing is, Widow Smith, your company is not only very poorly equipped but essentially helpless. Instead of useless widow women you should have brought more grown men, for only with such full-grown help will you ever be up to the task of journeying to the valley."

The old man clapped his hat on his head, not even noticing that the woman now had both hands on her small son's trembling shoulders. "To be perfectly honest, Widow Smith, your best hope is to turn around right now and go back to Winter Quarters. Perhaps if you will remain there another year, others will come along who will help you. I fear that I cannot."

Gathering up his reins, the man dragged his fleshy body up onto his horse. He was just starting to ride away, assuming his business with the troublesome woman was completed, when Joseph F.'s mother spoke again.

"Captain Lott," she said, her voice still quiet and unruffled.

"What is it?" he growled as he reined his horse back around.

"We are not going back to Winter Quarters!"

"But...you can't stay here!" The harsh old man looked astounded. "And you surely can't go on—"

"Oh, but we can go on, sir." Mary Smith's voice was adamant. "And we will!"

"No, you won't!" Cornelius Lott thundered, his anger getting the best of him. "Why, if you start out in this manner, you will be a burden on the company the whole way, and I will have to carry you along or leave you on the way!" With that, he again turned his prancing horse.

Joseph F. felt the grip of his mother's fingers tighten on his shoulders as she held him down. "Father Lott," she declared boldly, abandoning forever the title of captain as it had applied to him, "I will beat you to the valley and will ask no help from you, either!"

"Humph!" the old man replied as he swung his anxious horse back around. "You can't get there without help, Widow Smith, and I tell you, the burden will be on me!"

"We shall see," she replied quietly as the white-haired man spurred his mount away. "We shall see."

Once the man had ridden away, Mary Smith turned and knelt before her youngest son, who was still trembling with anger.

"Joseph, I know you are angry at the way that man has abused me. I'm thankful that you love me so."

"He's an old fool, Mother! He... he deserved to be kicked, or hit in the eye with a dirt clod, or... or something!"

Mary Smith smiled. "Perhaps. But had it been you who did it to him, my son, it would also have been you who had the problem with your temper. Because you remained still, the problem is now his, and the Lord will deal with him in his own due time. Besides, did you notice how foolishly red his nose and ears got when he became so angry?"

Joseph F. found himself chuckling at the memory; his mother joined him, and after a quick hug she released him and rose to her feet. "Remember, Joseph, I never once heard your father's voice raised in anger; or saw temper take away his reason. Your father was a mighty man of God, Joseph, dear, and if you wish to be like him, as I know you do, then you must be the same.

"Now," she declared brightly as the family gathered near, "if you, John, and Brother Terry will finish our repairs, my brother and I have some business we must attend to back in Winter Quarters—"

Illustration by Robert T. Barrett

Joseph F.'s mother and Uncle Joseph Fielding, upon their return to the Missouri River that June day, were finally able to borrow or hire additional oxen which could be used for teams. "'I can remember,'" Joseph F. said later, "'all the trials incident to our endeavors to move out with the Camp of Israel, coming to these valleys of the mountains without teams sufficient to draw our wagons; and being without the means to get those teams necessary, [Mother] yoked up her cows and calves, and tied two wagons together, and we started to come to Utah in this crude and helpless condition, and my mother said—"The Lord will open the way;" but how He would open the way no one knew.'"1

A day later Elder Kimball sent Howard Eagan back to Mary with two additional yoke of seasoned oxen, and by late in the afternoon of the 6th of June, with the still-chaffing Cornelius Lott watching nearby but not helping, the Smith caravan had almost caught up with Elder Kimball's large train.

At that time Indians somehow slipped up on Howard Eagan's party, which had not gone far from the Smith caravan, and made off with Eagan's own teams. Eagan and others went in pursuit of the thieves, and a skirmish ensued. This incident, happening so close to Joseph F.'s wagons and to the men who had just befriended his mother, affected not only the boy but everyone else in the scattered wagon train. All knew they had now entered dangerous country and that they must start taking precautions against further trouble.

About 3 o'clock [that same afternoon] the camp commenced moving off the river, as it was considered wisdom to leave the timber as soon as possible, and all wagons being over, which had arrived, so that the people should not be in so much danger from attacks of Indians, who it is pretty certainly ascertained were the Omaha and

Ottoe tribes, and from every circumstance were undoubtedly in the neighborhood for the purpose of plundering the traveling Saints of cattle, etc. Brother Cornelius P. Lott, Joseph Fielding, sister Mary Smith and families had been expected at the "Horn" soon after dinner, and as it was known that they were not far distant some anxiety was felt for their safety, after the camp had moved 2 miles and the encampment had been formed. President Kimball sent back 10 footmen, well armed to meet Brother Lott and company, and about 5 o'clock they arrived all safe, with the exception of having a broken axle tree, and being very short on teams. The wagons were soon ferried across, the chains attached to the raft taken up, the raft made fast, and the last of the wagons composing this company on their way to camp, and before dark the brethren had the satisfaction of seeing about 110 wagons formed in one corral, preparatory to their proceeding on their long journey west. Those who were wounded felt as well as could be expected after the short journey.2

By daylight the next morning the vast wagon train was lined out and moving westward into the deep plains, Mary's seven wagons included. Joseph F. knew Cornelius Lott was watching them; no doubt he was pleased to have Joseph F.'s mother assigned to his company, for now he could control her and prove that she should have remained behind for another year. She would be a burden, he was certain, and would be dependent upon help from him. "In this he, no doubt, gloried, for he was going to see that it was fulfilled."3

Yet that morning, nothing could take away from Mary Smith's joy. She and her loved ones were finally on their way to a place of peace and rest, and she had been prepared to take them there. First she had traveled from Kirtland to Missouri with her dear husband, learning from him the intricacies of travel on the long trail. That had prepared her to lead her loved ones over the plains of Iowa, gathering supplies and living from one day to the next while they made their escape from Nauvoo. And that journey had prepared her for this—a thousand-mile trek into a dangerous, openly hostile wilderness without adequate teams and wagons. Yet she would prevail, she knew it! Then, once in the valley, she would find peace for herself and would be allowed to assist in fulfilling Joseph Smith's prophecy that the Saints would become a mighty people in the Rocky Mountains. These things Mary Smith knew, and day after day she spoke of them to her children, imbuing in them, through one tiny lesson and example after another, the same faith, the same dauntless courage in the face of overwhelming adversity, that was keeping her going.

Westward they continued, Mary in her light spring wagon, John and Joseph F. working as teamsters, and the girls helping their brothers herd the loose stock. According to Uncle Joseph Fielding:

> We seemed to improve in our traveling and our cattle improved in their condition until we crossed the Platte River. We overtook Bro. B. Young's company at Loup Fork and it was an interesting sight... to behold in the morning a string of oxen reaching from one side of the river to the other about a mile from Brigham's company coming to assist us in crossing for the wagons sunk into the sand and it was hard drawing for the cattle, so we put our cattle to the wagons and put on extra teams to each and got through well.4

According to family tradition, when the Smiths crossed the mile-wide Loup Fork, Joseph F.'s mother tied both him and Martha Ann "to the back of her husband's big white horse, 'Old Sam.' They all crossed safely; however, clothing, bedding, and provisions got wet making it necessary to camp and dry out the wet things."5

In the meantime, cool relations existed between the Smith party and Cornelius Lott, for the journey was turning into "a unique race across plains, hills, and mountains to the Valley of the Saints."6 And it was at the Loup Fork of the Platte where that usually quiet animosity next made itself manifest.

Jane Wilson, who was traveling with Mary's group, had finally run out of snuff. It happened, however, that her mother, an old lady who was traveling with Bishop Newel K. Whitney's company, had plenty and to spare. Upon their arrival at the Fork, and seeing her mother's company in the distance, Jane Wilson started out ahead on foot, expecting to return to her own train of wagons in the evening. The companies were so near Jane thought they would both camp together that night.

[K]nowing that Jane had gone ahead, [Captain Lott] concluded to camp in the middle of the day, and the result was that the advanced company pulled further away as they traveled during the afternoon. Late in the afternoon Captain [Lott] came into the center of the circle of the camp, and called the camp together, and when all had assembled he inquired in a very excited and noisy manner, "Is all right in the camp!" This he repeated several times and then asked each group if all was right with them, and each answered "Yes." Then, turning to Widow Smith, he asked if all was right with her. She answered, "All is right with me." When she spoke he exclaimed: "All is right, is it, and a poor woman lost!"7

According to Joseph F., his mother replied:

"Father [Lott], Jane is not lost, she has gone to see her mother, and is quite safe." At this the captain was very much enraged, and replied, "I rebuke you, Widow Smith, in the name of the Lord! She is lost and must be sent for at once!" Mother replied, "All right, she shall be sent for." Accordingly, my brother John, only a boy, was sent off to overtake the company ahead, traveling in the night through droves of ravenous wolves, fierce for the flesh of dead cattle strewed along the road, howling and even snapping at him on every side, their eyes gleaming in the dark. When he did reach the camp, that had made a good half-day's travel, he found Jane all snug and comfortable with her mother.

After this... we moved smoothly until we reached a point about mid-way between the Platte and Sweetwater, when one of our best oxen laid down in the yoke as if poisoned and all supposed he would die.[8]

As the ox spasmed in what seemed to be the throes of death, and as the entire train ground to a halt, Widow Smith looked on in consternation. So did Captain Lott, for he knew as well as she that the death of the animal would also be fatal to Widow Smith's progress to the valley. Joseph F. related that "Father [Lott] came up and seeing the cause of the disturbance he blustered about... as if the world were about at an end. 'There,' said he, 'I told you you would have to be helped and that you would be a burden on the company.' But in this he was mistaken."[9]

Obtaining some consecrated oil, Mary Smith asked her brother and James Lawson "if they would please administer to the ox just as they would do to a sick person, for it was vital to her interest that the ox be restored that she might pursue her journey. Her earnest plea was complied with. These brethren poured oil on the head of the ox and then laid their hands upon it and rebuked the power of the destroyer just as they would have done if the animal had been a human being. Immediately the ox got up and within a very few moments again pulled in the yoke as if nothing had ever happened. This was a great astonishment to the company."10

They hadn't gone much further before a second ox fell as had the first. It, too, received the ministrations of the holy priesthood, and it, too, arose and began pulling as before. Moments later a third of the Smith oxen fell as if dead, and again by administration this animal was fully healed. "This brought great chagrin to the countenance of the captain of the company."11

Onward the company pressed, experiencing no further oxen troubles, until at the last crossing of the Sweetwater, three of Captain Lott's best oxen, as well as his finest mule, all laid down near the campground and died. This was a sore trial to Captain Lott and:

a very great loss, as he was obliged to get help for himself before he could proceed. I [Joseph F.] heard him say, "It looks suspicious that four of my best animals should lie down in this manner all at once, and die, and everybody's cattle but mine escape!" and he then insinuated that somebody had poisoned them through spite. All of which was said in my presence and for my special benefit, which I perfectly understood, although he did not address himself directly to me. It was well for him that I was only a stripling of nine years of age, and not a man, even four years would have cost the old man dearly regardless of his age, and perhaps a cause of regret to me. My temper was beyond boiling, it was "white hot," for I knew his insinuation was directed or aimed at my mother, as well as I know that such a thing was beyond her power even had she been capable of such a deed. All of which he knew as well as I, and all the camp. At this moment I resolved on revenge for this and the many other insults and abuses he had heaped upon my mother, and perhaps could have carried out my resolutions had not death come timely to my relief and taken him away, while I was yet a child.

One cause of his spite at mother was because she would not allow me to stand guard at nights and perform all the duties of a man. To [working as a man] she had no objections, and I did faithfully perform many duties that should have been reserved for one of mature years in the day time; but mother, in my interest, would not consent to me acting as a guard at night. I yoked, unyoked and drove my own team, and took my turn as day guard with the men. I feel, too, that I was equal to the best, which was more than reason could demand, or than any other child in camp of my age was asked to do.[12]

Of his partners in his teamster duties, later in his life, Joseph F. declared:

My team consisted of two pairs, or yokes, of oxen. My leaders' names were Thom and Joe—we raised them from calves, and they were both white. My wheel team were named Broad and Berry. Broad was light brindle with a few white spots on his body, and he had long, broad, pointed horns, from which he got his name. Berry was red and bony and short horned. Thom was trim built, active, young, and more intelligent than many a man. Many times while traveling sandy or rough roads, long, thirsty drives, my oxen, lowing with the heat and fatigue, I would put my arms around Thom's neck, and cry bitter tears! That was all

I could do. Thom was my favorite and best and most willing and obedient servant and friend. He was choice![13]

Despite the difficulties of the journey, Cornelius Lott chose to keep up his persecution. One night, according to Joseph F., after everyone had retired and were sleeping, the man "'raised a false alarm of "Indians!" coming directly to the big carriage where my mother, my little sister and myself slept; shaking it terrifically and in a loud hoarse whisper shouting "Indians! Indians! Get up quick, Widow Smith! We're beset by Indians!" Mother replied, "Why don't you arouse the men, I don't see what I can do." At this he went to the next wagon where some of the family were asleep, shaking it rather mildly, and then slinked off, not wishing to carry his alarm any further.'"

"During the entire length of the journey of one thousand miles this man who claimed to have faith in the Gospel, and who should have had in his heart the spirit of his religion to teach him to care for the widow and the fatherless, never lost an opportunity when the occasion presented itself, and when it could be manufactured, to annoy and harass Widow Smith. His superior officer in command was traveling on in the advanced company and did not know of these little petty annoyances and, at times, grave insults which the widow of the martyred Patriarch Hyrum Smith, was constantly receiving."[14]

And so they pressed on. Joseph F.'s mother

was the moving spirit of the fatherless family. She was flawless in her surveillance and a stickler in caring for details. There could be no miscalculating nor anything left to chance. Wheels were watched for the need for axle-grease. The shoulders of her oxen received special care and attention to ward off soreness; also, their feet to avoid dropping of shoes and to replace one when necessary. She looked out for her children's comfort stops. Each had his assigned tasks. John and Joseph F. became expert bull-whackers. All the children walked barefooted most of the way, Jerusha, Sarah, and Martha helping with the loose stock. The women cooperated in the preparation of the food and putting things away after everyone had finished. It was a poignant scene at supper time. Brave, fatherless family, but they were doing well.15

Slowly and with constant toil the summer of 1848 passed away. In the evenings following meals, the "strains of a new hymn were frequently sung which stirred a responsive chord and buoyed the spirits of the weary travelers. The words 'All is well! All is well!' gave them courage to go on."16 And in the darkness after the fires had burned to a few glowing embers, as howling wolves and yapping coyotes, hooting and screeching owls, and even plaintive cries of killdeers that might just as easily have been Indians, interrupted their exhausted slumber, the promising refrain whispered on in their weary minds; All is well! All is well!

To the Bear River they came in early September, past Jim Bridger's ramshackle fort, and then down Echo Canyon with its towering cliffs and strange, hollow sounds. Fording the Weber River they crawled upward again through the thick timber, winding up the east side of East Mountain. Worn-out animals slowly dragged the creaking wagons upward until they finally reached the top. And then wonder of all wonders, the valley of the Latter-day Saints, the Promised Land of a people who thought of themselves as modern Israel, lay spread out below them. Still many miles away, the valley was, nevertheless, gloriously beautiful in the afternoon sun. "'It was a most delightful sight to us,' said Joseph F."17

It was the 22ND of September, and their first view of the valley "filled Widow Smith and her little flock with renewed zeal and determination, their long-sought-for goal was now in sight. Thus far she had come without asking help of anyone, except of the Lord, who [had come] to her rescue in [every] dark hour when it seemed all earthly help would fail... One more day and they would, if all signs did not fail, pitch their little camp in the coveted valley of refuge that lay before them."18

Immediately Captain Lott ordered all teams to be turned out, loosened from their wagons, and driven down the canyon. "The hind wheels of the wagons were all rough-locked with chains, and were thus dragged down the mountain slope with one yoke of oxen. In this way the company came to the foot of Little Mountain, where they were ordered to make camp for the night. And what a happy night! On the morrow the journey would come to its weary end! Peace and some degree of comfort awaited the weary band, for this was to them the land of promise, and while it did not flow with 'milk and honey' as did the land of Palestine when possessed by ancient Israel, it at least held out the hope of peace and rest free from the interference and persecutions of man's worst enemy—his fellow man."19

Who knows how young Joseph F. slept that night? Perhaps excitement kept him awake, as it often does for nine-year-olds, even today. On the morrow he knew they would drive into the valley! On the morrow they would see his beloved Aunt Mercy Rachel Thompson and his cousin Mary Ann, and then for certain he would know that their long and tiresome journey would be over. But perhaps Joseph F. merely slept the weary sleep of the exhausted, for his work had not let up until the last animal had been cared for, the last length of wood cut and stacked for the morning fire.

However he slept, when morning came "there was consternation in Widow Smith's camp. The Captain, remembering the prediction she had uttered that she would beat him to the valley, had in the night taken steps to forestall the fulfillment of any such prediction. He was smarting under constant defeat along the way. His [own] predictions had thus far failed; but he was determined that they should not fail in the final test at the end."20

Joseph F., remembering that terrible morning years later, told the story as follows:

To our consternation, when we gathered up our cattle, the essentia part of our means of transportation, for some reason had strayed away, and were not to be found with the herd. ...[John] obtained a horse and rode back over the road in search of the lost cattle. The captain ordered the march to begin, and, regardless of our predicament, the company started out, up the mountain. The morning sun was then shining brightly, without a cloud appearing anywhere in the sky! I had happened to hear the promise of my dear mother that we would beat the captain into the valley, and would not ask help from him either. I sat in the front of the wagon with the teams we had in hand hitched to the wheels, while my brother was absent hunting the others. I saw the company wending its slow way up the hill, the animals struggling to pull their heavy loads. The forward teams now had almost reached the summit of the hill, and I said to myself, "True enough, we have come thus far, and we have been blessed, and not the slightest help from anyone has been asked by us." But the last promise seemed to be now impossible; the last hope of getting into the valley before the rest of our company was vanishing in my opinion.

You have doubtless heard descriptions of the terrific thunder storms that sometimes visit the mountains. The pure, crystal streams a few moments before flow gently down their channels; but after one of these rains, in a few minutes they become raging torrents, muddy and sometimes bringing down fallen trees and roots and rocks. All of a sudden, and in less time than I am taking to tell you, a big, dark, heavy cloud rose from the northwest, going directly southeast. In a few minutes it burst in such terrific fury that the cattle could not face the storm, and the captain seemed forced to direct the company to unhitch the teams, turn them loose, and block the wheels to keep the wagons from running back down the hill. The cattle fled before the storm down into the entrance into Parley's canyon, from the Park, into and through the brush. Luckily, the storm lasted only a short time. As it ceased to rain, and the wind ceased to blow, my brother, John, drove up with our lost cattle. We then hitched them to the wagon, and the question was asked by my uncle of mother: "Mary, what shall we do? Go on, or wait for the company to gather up their teams?" She said: "Joseph... they have not waited for us, and I see no necessity for us to wait for them."

So we hitched up and rolled up the mountain, leaving the company behind, and this was on the 23RD day of September, 1848. We reached the Old Fort about 10 o'clock that Saturday night. The next morning, in the Old Bowery, we had the privilege of listening to President Brigham Young and President Kimball, Erastus Snow, and some others, give some very excellent instructions. Then, on the afternoon of that Sunday, we went out and met our friends coming in, very dusty, and very foot-sore and very tired!

The prediction of the widow was actually fulfilled; we beat them into the valley, and we asked no help from them either!21

10

HOME IN THE VALLEY

With the heat from the wood stove, as well as the winter afternoon sun boring in through the west-facing window, the temperature in the schoolroom had become unbearable. It was all fifteen-year-old Joseph F. could do to keep his eyes open, and even then it wasn't possible to focus on the teacher's droning words. Thank goodness the warmth had also aroused a couple of hibernating wasps. At least he could be entertained by them and would not be caught napping by the insufferably boring teacher.

At the moment the long-legged insects were buzzing slowly about the rafters, but every now and again one of them would swoop down near the students, causing a mixture of consternation and mirth as hands frantically flailed the air. Nearby students did their best to laugh silently at these antics, while the offending wasp was finally driven off. Yet the threat of future forays remained constant, as did the entertainment, and so Joseph F. was feeling good.

School, after all, was not his favorite place, and the teacher was dryer than an Egyptian mummy, with even less of importance to say. Strange, he was thinking, that his younger sister would find it so enjoyable. Was that like his mother had been, he wondered? Or his father? Joseph F. didn't know, though he supposed it might have been like both of them. But now that they were both dead, and he and Martha Ann were orphans—

Glory, but the man in front of the school was boring! His voice was nasal and monotone; he would forget, even in the midst of a sentence, what he was endeavoring to say; his balding dome and curiously wrinkled forehead made his eyebrowless eyes look too small, like pig's eyes, and this was further compounded by the dark, fleshy bags beneath them. In short, the teacher was like a caricature of a man rather than a man himself, and it was all Joseph F. could do to pay him even a modicum of respect.

And all this was made worse, Joseph F. felt, by the man's arrogant attitude. He was a tall man, rather fleshy, and he used his size to intimidate and bully his pupils. He was always right, his students were always wrong, and at even the least mistake he would growl and threaten horribly. Worse, he carried a leather belt in his hand, mostly rolled around his fist, which he used to whack desks and students both. It was his attention-gainer, his means of enforcing his will on the pupils who cowered before him. Strangely, he seemed to delight in using his belt, especially on the girls and smaller children, for his eyes literally gleamed as he did it. Yet Joseph F. disdained him for it and found himself quite often comparing the man unfavorably with his mother.

Until her death she had been his and his sisters' only teacher, presenting her lessons daily in the warmth and security of their home near Mill Creek. How Joseph F. missed those winter days, laboring beside Martha Ann, Sarah, and Jerusha at household tasks as their mother presented her lessons. She believed work to be the best training and discipline for young folk, so even while they studied their letters and figures they were knitting and spinning, carding and weaving, shelling nuts and grinding corn and wheat, churning butter, mixing and kneading dough for baking, and any of a hundred other tasks that their mother required of them. And never, ever, had she whipped or otherwise demeaned them—

"Eeeeek!"

Startled, Joseph F. brought his mind back to the present and saw that one of the wasps had swooped down to land on the back of his thirteen-year-old sister's neck. Martha Ann had reacted about as one might have expected, with a squeal both of surprise and fear. Now she was off her bench and hopping about, flailing at her neck and bunned hair with both hands, though the wasp was obviously long gone—either that or it had crawled for its life down the back of her dress.

Abruptly the whole class was in commotion, either trying to assist or simply laughing, as was Joseph F., at the spectacle.

"What's the matter, Martha Ann?" one of the older boys quipped. "Saint Vitus' dance got ya?"

"Or ants in your pants?" someone else snickered.

Martha Ann suddenly stopped her frantic movements to look around, and as she realized what sort of show she had been putting on, her face turned bright red.

"It's gone, Martha Ann," one of the girls beside her mumbled quietly.

"Yeah, you got that old wasp first swing," a younger boy agreed with a grin. "See? It's over there, in the corner."

Ducking her head, Martha Ann quickly retook her seat, her ears and the back of her neck still red enough with embarrassment that Joseph F. could see it clearly. Which was too bad, he was thinking. She was already so terribly sensitive about what others thought of her—

"Martha Ann Smith, you have disrupted this class!"

Instantly all eyes were on the teacher, who, in the excitement of the moment, had been forgotten.

"You most certainly know better than to make such a disruption!" the man thundered angrily. "Why, I should throw you out of here on your ear!"

"But... it was a wasp," Martha Ann gasped in both surprise and fear. "I... I'm sorry, Sir, but it was on my neck—"

"I care not a fig what it was or where it was!" Dramatically the man began unrolling the belt that was coiled around his hand. "Young lady, I have changed my mind. You are not only a disruption, but I will not tolerate one who argues. Stand up and hold your hands out before you!"

Joseph F. was stunned. The teacher was going to whip his sweet younger sister. In front of everyone in the room, he was going to whip and humiliate her—

"Stand, I tell you!" the man ordered as he moved toward Martha Ann, his belt swinging menacingly. "Stand and hold out your hands, both of them, or your whipping will be so much the worse for you, I promise you that!"

"Please, Sir... I—"

As rage began boiling within him, Joseph F.'s mind filled with the image of the day a couple of summers before when he had, with one blow, laid out his mother's hired man. His older brother John had been teasing the man mercilessly, an angry chase with a pitchfork had ensued, and Joseph F., made strong with a lifetime of work and already large for his age, had stopped it with one angry blow. For perhaps a moment the hired hand had lain unconscious in the straw of the dugout barn, and for the first time in his life, Joseph F. had become aware of his own strength. Now, despite the lifetime of warnings his mother had given him concerning his anger and temper, he was thinking of that strength again—

"Don't you touch her with that belt!" he ordered, his voice breaking with a pubertal squeak. Then, when the teacher turned to come at him, his belt swinging wildly, Joseph F. eagerly pushed himself up from his bench.

"I'll teach you to sass your betters!" the man snarled as he raised his hand and charged forward.

"We'll see about that," Joseph F. replied as he felt the old anger surging within him—the burning desire to stop injustice in its tracks. Without difficulty he ducked the first swing of the belt. Then, before the teacher could reset himself, Joseph F. lashed out with his fist, hitting him on the mouth and splitting his lip.

"Why," the man snarled in surprise as he wiped away blood, "you are an insolent young pup, no better than your dead mother—"

The teacher never uttered another word, at least from on his feet. His anger now an all-consuming rage, Joseph F. threw one punch and then another, fast and furiously. Quickly the sound and sight of students shouting and screaming became a blur, and he watched the startled look on the face of the teacher turn to fear. Still Joseph F. pummeled him, his rage white-hot, pounding until the man went down between the benches and the offending belt fell from his unclenched hand.

Breathing heavily the young orphan stopped, looked at the whimpering and moaning man on the floor, looked next at the stunned and silent faces surrounding him, saw the look of horror on Martha Ann's face, and finally his reason returned and Joseph F. realized what he had done. Somehow his anger had taken over once again, and he... and he...

"I... I didn't mean to hurt him," he breathed to no one in particular except, perhaps, his departed mother. "I... I reckon I lost my temper—"

"He deserved it!" someone growled.

"Yes, but I... I shouldn't have... Oh, Mother, what have I done?" And then, with a choking cry of his own, the only son of Hyrum and Mary Smith fled in bitter tears from the room.

In the minds of most, journeys, particularly long and difficult ones, end with the peace and comfort of home, a motel, or at least some place where we can rest our weary bones. For Joseph F., his mother, and the rest of her large family, the Old Fort in the Salt Lake Valley provided no such respite. Yes, Aunt Mercy Rachel and her daughter were dwelling in a small adobe apartment where they were welcome to visit, and other friends offered the same scanty conveniences, which were gladly accepted. Yet as the winter of 1848–1849 closed in around them, the Smiths found that their nightly accommodations were to remain the unheated beds of their wagons. They did erect a small cooking shack so that meals could be prepared and taken out of the weather, but that was the best they could do. Quite literally, there was nothing else available. Yet life's difficulties had prepared them for such eventualities, and all, even Joseph F. and the other children, accepted them without much complaint.

Besides Mercy Rachel and her daughter, the Smith family at that time consisted of Joseph F.; his twenty-year-old brother, John; Hannah Grinnels; and Joseph F.'s sisters, sixteen-year-old Jerusha, fourteen-year-old Sarah, and nine-year-old Martha Ann. And all of them, as well as occasional others, were under the wonderful care and tutelage of his widowed mother.

Though sealed to Heber C. Kimball in Nauvoo after the death of her husband, as she had done on the plains, she "made her own way."[1] Mary Fielding Smith "was a delicate girl who had been raised in an English village, conditions foreign to all that she was called upon to endure after coming to America and joining the Church. In the valley of the mountains, she could retire at night assured that she would not be disturbed by mobs; but there were the cares of the farm-life she had taken upon herself. These were arduous and severe. Yet she toiled on day by day striving to make a living for her little flock…'Where men were going about seeking charity, and asking for a day's work at the hands of the Church, this indefatigable woman gathered enough to leave her family in comfortable circumstances. She was the soul of thrift and economy, of industry and tireless energy. She worked early and late, and she taught others around her, no matter how small her children might be, the lesson of frugal and constant toil.' "2

Like mother, like son. "On the journey across the plains Joseph Fielding Smith, a lad in his tenth year, [had driven] two yoke of oxen all the way. He had performed similar service in 1846 across the plains of Iowa to Winter Quarters. This was no small task for a boy, but it was accomplished successfully without the loss of wagon or cattle or other mishap of any kind. Surely his mother could be proud of him. Never in his life had he been given the advantages which come to most boys. There was never any time to play. Robbed of his father's earnest counsel, and forced by necessity to labor as soon as he was able to assist, nay, even before the ordinary boy could have given assistance, he grew up in the midst of trials and tribulations. So constant were these tribulations that the boy came to look upon them as the ordinary events of life. Now, at last, his mother had arrived in the Salt Lake Valley. Now that the journey was over would there be time for relaxation and a time to play? Naturally in the heart of every boy there is the desire to associate with companions and have some measure of innocent fun. The journey's end did not bring, however, this time of recess from daily toil. His mother was forced to set about at once to provide a home and shelter for her growing family and the dependents who looked to her for help,"3 and it was required of Joseph F., as well as his brother and three sisters, to do all in their power, to assist.

Soon after her arrival, Mary saddled Old Sam and set out to explore the valley. She and her brother Joseph had both been assigned town lots on the city plat, but Mary wanted a farm, some acreage where she and her family could earn a living. She found what she wanted in an area called Mill Creek (now Sugarhouse), which at the time was a wilderness, "impenetrable in places adjacent to the creek and branching streams." Finally,

> her reconnaissance brought her to a delightful crystal streamlet. Following it along, she came to a number of natural springs gushing forth to form a pool at the base of a hill rising gently to the east. The spot was lovely—the crystal, cool water, pouring up through the clean sand, a delight. This was it—the place for her. She would have those springs and the surrounding land. She got both— good, pure drinking water in sufficient quantity for household needs and for irrigation and, in addition, forty acres of land.4

Before much home building could be accomplished, however, winter was upon Joseph F.'s family and everyone else in the valley. Thinly clad because of their poverty, and with no place to replenish supplies, all in the valley suffered. Joseph F.'s uncle, speaking of both his own and Mary Smith's families, said:

> The tent I borrowed for a week or two, but we were compelled to keep it at least 4 months, the ground being covered with snow about 12 weeks. This length of winter was very unexpected, and took us by surprise and unprepared, and in fact it has been a time of much suffering to the Saints in the Valley...
>
> Our children have gone barefoot almost entirely through a long and severe winter, and many times have I been grieved to see their naked feet in the snow, and many a cry have they had.5

Foodstuffs were every bit as scanty as were shoes and clothing. In January, 1849, Church leaders took inventory of food on hand in the valley and discovered that there would be slightly less than a pound of flour per person if they rationed it to last until July, when they estimated the first crops of 1849 might be harvested. Rationing was instituted, and for the rest of the winter the Saints seemed to live mostly on faith, though there is evidence that Mary's foresight had provided adequately for her family. Again from the pen of Uncle Joseph Fielding: "I have taken my breadstuff in corn chiefly on my shoulder 2 miles to the mill, and in the latter part of winter I have had corn of my sister Mary Smith by the bushel, but at this time it is likely I can have no more. We have also had a few bushels of wheat the same way, which I intend to return to her with interest."[6]

And, "it is now the 11TH of May... and the ground is covered with snow, and snow is falling. There is no sign of Spring. The cows and the cattle are poor, and many of the Saints find it very difficult to draw their fuel with their oxen. The wolves have killed some few, but not so many as last year."[7]

It is difficult to imagine such a winter: the children without shoes and adequate clothing, yet forced by necessity to traipse about in the snow, no matter. As he had on the trail, necessity required that Joseph F. help his brother John care for the hungry livestock, milk the cows, chop wood for fuel and carry it into the cooking shack, help empty corn and wheat from his mother's commissary wagon so it could be ground at the nearest mill, and at least twice a day trudge with his mother and sisters to and from their sleeping accommodations in the wagons. And when weather permitted, particularly after the days began to warm, he and everyone else scoured the countryside for anything that might be edible. Yet Joseph F.'s mother's faith and foresight provided well for her extended family, and they were blessed.

Looking back, Joseph F. declared, "We never lacked so much as many others did; for while we found nettle greens most acceptable when we first came to the valley, and while we enjoyed thistle roots, segoes and all that kind of thing, we were no worse off than thousands of others, and not so bad off as many, for we were never without corn-meal and milk and butter, to my knowledge."[8]

The long winter finally passed, and with spring, the Smiths and Fieldings were hard at work on their acreage out at Mill Creek, clearing a site for a home not far from the springs. Adobes were made from dry grass and the compact soil underfoot, and lumber was cut in the canyons and dragged to the mill by their oxen. Once cut it was hauled to the site in wagons, and soon construction was underway on a two-room house.

But if they wanted to eat during the coming year, there were also fields that needed to be cleared of trees and brush, plowed, harrowed, furrowed, planted, and irrigated, as well as seemingly endless ditches to dig if water was going to reach the thirsty soil. Joseph F. was involved in it all: digging ditches; driving teams ahead of their three-corner plow and iron-spiked wooden harrow; planting corn, wheat and potatoes; furrowing with a cultivator; irrigating, or "taking the water" as they called it; hoeing out the voracious weeds that would suck all the moisture away from their thirsty crops; and in every way possible nursing the first crops to be grown in the virgin soil.

Work also continued on the house, hauling in rock for the foundation, slaking lime, mixing mortar, and laying up adobes. The structure Joseph F.'s mother designed for Mill Creek was to face south toward the springs, one of which was curbed with stones so it would form a deep basin from which they could draw their water. Immediately to the north and a short distance to the east of the house was a low hill. In the side of the hill a warm dugout barn was built of rocks for the animals.

The house, when it was finally finished in 1850, was 14′ x 28′ on the outside, divided by a center portion into two good-sized rooms. A ladder was built up the center wall to the attic, where

Joseph F. and John slept. A fireplace was built into the north wall of the living room, and the other room was used for storage and sleeping accommodations for Mary and her daughters.

Besides helping with all the family's home building activities, Joseph F. had his own particular responsibilities. A sober boy who had rarely since his father's martyrdom had time for play, he spent day and night caring for the cattle, accepting the responsibility with a spirit of integrity and devotion. From 1846 through 1854 he was so occupied, not losing a single "hoof"[9] by death or straying away through neglect or carelessness.

At that time, large wolves were numerous, and occasionally they attacked the Smith's sheep at night, taking one or two. They also killed a fine colt one night, almost within a stone's throw of the Smith home, and left another severely bitten and wounded the same night. Those were the sum of livestock losses sustained during Joseph F.'s herding days. It was a record he felt justifiably proud of. Once one of their cows had calved out on the range. Though the weather was extremely cold and it was late in the day, Joseph F. did not desert the animal. "Exerting all his strength, he carried and pushed the calf until he reached home, a pack of wolves following him and making the night hideous with their howling. Had he left the calf it would without question have been devoured by this hungry pack."[10]

Joseph F. was often out on the range after dark, where he could hear the wolves' ferocious howls. "This was the nature of the amusement accorded to... [him] at an age when most boys like to play and engage in athletic sports."[11]

The early years in the valley were difficult, but Joseph F. and his family prospered. Their stock increased, and the few cleared acres produced abundantly well. The best tenth of their increase was taken personally by Mary and her children to the Tithing Office, where they were well known. Mary Smith "was diligent in paying her tithes and offerings and earned the reputation of being honest with the Lord."12

For instance, early in the spring of 1851 Mary determined to open her potato pits so that she, John, and Joseph F. could take a load of their best potatoes to the Tithing Office. There a clerk, William Thompson, came out and said, " 'Widow Smith, it's a shame that you should have to pay tithing.' "

Instantly his mother turned upon the clerk, saying, as well as Joseph F. could remember, " 'William, you ought to be ashamed of yourself. Would you deny me a blessing? If I did not pay my tithing I should expect the Lord to withhold His blessings from me; I pay my tithing, not only because it is a law of God but because I expect a blessing by doing it. By keeping this and other laws, I expect to prosper and to be able to provide for my family.' "13

Of his mother, Joseph F. declared:

> Though she was a widow, you may turn to the records of the Church from the beginning unto the day of her death, and you will find that she never received a farthing from the Church to help her support herself and her family; but she paid in thousands of dollars in wheat, potatoes, corn, vegetables, meat, etc. The tithes of her sheep and cattle, the tenth pound of her butter, her tenth chicken, the tenth of her eggs, the tenth pig, the tenth calf, the tenth colt—a tenth of everything he raised was paid... She prospered because she obeyed the laws of God. She had abundance to sustain her family.14

Despite the fact that his mother was teaching her children through her own obedience to God's laws, Joseph F. was not always a whole-hearted supporter. Time and experience were to be required of him before Joseph F. would comprehend his mother's wisdom and greatness. He adds:

> When William Thompson told my mother that she ought not to pay tithing [with her best potatoes], I thought he was one of the finest fellows in the world. I believed every word he said. I had to work and dig and toil myself. I had to help plow the ground, plant the potatoes, hoe the potatoes, dig the potatoes, and all that sort of thing, and then to load up a big wagon-box full of the very best we had, leaving out the poor ones, and bringing the load to the tithing office. I thought in my childish way that it looked a little hard, especially when I saw certain of my playmates and early associates of childhood, playing, riding horses and having good times, and who scarcely ever did a lick of work in their lives, and yet were being fed from the public crib... Well, after I got a few years experience, I was converted, I found that my mother was right and that William Thompson was wrong. He denied the faith, apostatized, left the country and led away as many of his family as would go with him.15

In other ways, also, Joseph F. was a typical boy:

> One day... at the age of nine, [he] was out with his air-gun. His sister Martha, wearing many petticoats and a dress to her ankles as they did in those days, saw Joseph. Greeting her brother, she provokingly said, "I dare you to shoot me Joseph, I dare ya! I dare ya!" Whereupon, she turned her back to him, stooped over and held her dress and petticoats around her ankles. Young Joseph, being a remarkably fond brother, took her at her word and her double dare. He pointed the gun at her and shot her in the lower back, at

which she let out a terrific howl and went running to her mother.

When her mother removed Martha's clothing, the pellet dropped out from the folds of her petticoats. Then Mother Smith directed her attention to Joseph.

"You weren't trying to shoot your sister were you?" she asked.

"I knew it wouldn't hurt her," replied Joseph. "She double dared me, and because of her quaint position—well I knew it wouldn't hurt her anyway," explained the lad.

When it was found out that the pellet had made only a small pink dent in her daughter's skin, Mary breathed a sigh of relief. It taught Martha Ann the lesson: never jest unless you want to take the consequences.16

Perhaps three years later, as Joseph F. was in the midst of his pubertal growth spurt, came the incident with his mother's hired man. Joseph F.'s older brother John "was a great tease. He teased the hired man so unmercifully one day that the latter took after him with the pitchfork. Around and through the barn they ran, John laughing and the hired man seething with rage. Joseph F., who was large and strong for his age, became alarmed fearing that John might get hurt. As the two came running by, Joseph swung at the man. The blow dropped him and ended the race. However, the impact to the man's head fractured a bone in the back of Joseph F.'s right hand. It was not properly set, and he had a lump there the rest of his life."17

There is little doubt that Mary Smith did her best to use that broken bone as another lesson for her growing son. She could see clearly his wonderful potential to become a mighty man in Zion; but just as clearly she could see that his greatest weakness—his anger and terribly fragile temper—might easily keep him from it.

Heber C. Kimball

CA. *about 1853*

Church Archives. The Church of Jesus Christ of Latter-day Saints

She knew that Joseph F.'s heart was tender and soft toward others, but it was so very easy for Satan to twist that compassion into a rash anger that would destroy him. How she must have pleaded with her son, endeavoring to help him see and understand why he must overcome.

Joseph F. himself would speak of the months immediately following her passing as "perilous times... I was almost like a comet or a fiery meteor, without attraction or gravitation to keep me balanced or guide me within reasonable bounds."[18]

Heber C. Kimball was of great help, keeping a protective eye on the Smith children, and performing necessary ordinances for them. "The youngest, Martha Ann, wrote: 'I was baptized in 1849 by Heber C. Kimball, who was my stepfather.'"[19] Of his own baptism at the hands of Heber C. Kimball, which was performed on May 21, 1852, in City Creek near the northeast corner of Temple Square in Salt Lake City, Joseph F. declared:

> I felt in my soul that if I had sinned—and surely I was not without sin—that it had been forgiven me; that I was indeed cleansed from sin; my heart was touched, and I felt that I would not injure the smallest insect beneath my feet. I felt as if I wanted to do good everywhere to everybody and to everything. I felt a newness of life, a newness of desire to do that which was right. There was not one particle of desire for evil left in my soul. I was but a little boy, it is true, when I was baptized; but this was the influence that came upon me, and I know that it was from God, and was and ever has been a living witness to me of my acceptance of the Lord.[20]

Until 1852 Mary Smith was a well-known citizen, a vital part of life in the Salt Lake Valley. "She witnessed the wilderness take on cultivation and beauty. She saw the [gold seekers of 1849] stream through on their way to California gold fields. She beheld an industrious people establish a frontier city in a mountain fastness."21

It was in her children, though, that Joseph F.'s mother took her greatest satisfaction. Lovina and her husband, Lorin Walker, had finally found their way to the valley; John was a man grown and was known for his strength and determination to do right; Jerusha, Sarah, and Martha Ann were becoming well-trained spiritually as well as in the womanly arts of homemaking; and in Joseph F. she could see the same stirrings of greatness that had been so evident in her dear husband and his prophet/brother.

Yet the tremendous stress of her life was wearing on Joseph F.'s mother. Though she still had the friendship and invaluable assistance of Aunty Hannah Grinnels, the grueling hardships of frontier life were hard on both of them. Joseph F., watching his mother, saw streaks of gray appear in her dark hair. He realized that lines had appeared in her forehead and around the corners of her mouth and that her shoulders and back had slumped a little and were now resting wearily forward. "Her eyes had a squint as from long gazing across sagebrush flats. Her hands—hands of toil—hands of character—were now showing thickened joints. The strong thumbs appeared flat and shortened. Her whole person bore a suggestion of great fatigue and the need of rest or getting away from all her labors for a while—a relaxed vacation—a trip to England to which [Mary Smith's] thoughts often turned."22

Then, at a public function in 1852, Mary came down with a bad cold. Feeling too ill to ride all the way to Mill Creek, she retired to the home of Heber C. Kimball where she sought a blessing, after which she thought she would soon recover. Instead, for two months she dwindled in poor health, with complications making things even worse.

Then thirteen years of age, Joseph F. with his brother and

sisters gathered around her, exercising great faith for their mother's recovery. Yet it was not to be, for their mother, having given all she had to establishing for her family a home of peace and safety in the wilderness, passed away on September 21, 1852, at the age of 51. "It was said that she died of a tired, broken heart...

"The grief of her large family at her passing was overwhelming. 'Martha's sorrow was so intense that she went out away from the house and prayed to the Lord that she might die. The shock to Joseph [F.] was so great that he turned deathly pale and fainted and some of the others had to work with him for hours to keep him alive.'" 23

At her funeral, President Heber C. Kimball said:

As regards Sister Mary Smith's situation and circumstances, I have no trouble at all, for if any person has lived the life of a Saint, she has. If any person has acted the part of a mother, she has. I may say she has acted the part of a mother, and a father, and a bishop. She has had a large family and several old people to take care of, and which she has maintained for years by her economy and industry.24

The Deseret News reported:

The deceased was truly a "mother in Israel," and her name and deeds will be had in everlasting remembrance... Possessed, in a superlative degree, of those peculiar qualifications that support and invigorate the mind in adversity, she endured afflictions and overcame difficulties with a degree of patience and perseverance worthy of imitation...

She has entered into rest, and may the example she set, during her sojourn on earth, not be forgotten by those she

George A. Smith

CA. 1867

Church Archives, The Church of Jesus Christ of Latter-day Saints

has left behind to follow after.25
Now orphaned, Mary's children determined to do just that. Having learned independence, they continued to live in their home near Mill Creek. Aunty Grinnels stayed with them because they were truly her family, and so in a sense there remained an adult in their home. Yet responsibility for the family's support now rested solely upon Joseph F. and John. They carried on as best they could, harvesting their crops, shepherding their livestock, and putting everything in readiness for the coming winter—as well as for the remainder of their lives—building on the firm foundation their mother had laid for them.

Despite being both fatherless and motherless, Joseph F. was not altogether friendless. Brigham Young, Heber C. Kimball, and his father's cousin George A. Smith remained close. "These were men, Joseph F. declared [later], 'whom I learned to love as I loved my father, because of their integrity and love of the Truth.'"26

Until the spring of 1854, when the incident with the schoolteacher occurred, Joseph F. had charge of the family's livestock, "and he assumed that responsibility with a spirit of integrity and devotion which was commendable."27 And during his quiet times, in the saddle following the cattle, taking the water turn in the fields, or lying sleeplessly at night, Joseph F. thought almost constantly of his mother.

He had seen the Spirit of the Lord rest upon [her] on numerous occasions and heard her predict the future in which the family was concerned, and never at any time did one of her predictions fall to the ground unfulfilled. He had seen her devotion; her faithfulness to the restored Gospel and the Church. He knew that she had endeavored by example and by precept to instruct her children in paths of righteousness. He had watched her with an abiding confidence and faith in her ability to care for her tender flock. He knew of her loyalty to her friends and her prayerful spirit and testimony of the divinity of the work the Lord had revealed. He had seen her many struggles against the overwhelming odds which constantly confronted her and her unwavering determination through it all to press on against all obstacles no matter how insurmountable they appeared to be. He had seen her tired and weary by her constant toil and struggle against these overwhelming forces, when she would gladly have taken a rest; but the circumstances of the times would not permit that blessing to come to her. Through it all he had learned almost to worship that noble, God-fearing, patient, prayerful mother. Did ever a boy have such a mother as he! He [had been] constantly at her side, willing and ready to lend a helping hand, [ever since] his earliest childhood. The Lord had endowed him with a tender love which is seldom seen and never surpassed. To him his mother was an angel, pure and undefiled, sent from the mansions above. To him she returned when her work was done, just as pure, just as holy, just as worthy, to the mansions of the blessed. It was an hour of the deepest trial... Joseph knew that it could be said of his mother that she was one of those "which came out of great tribulation, and have washed their robes, and made them white in the blood of the Lamb." There was no bitterness in his soul when thinking of his mother's departure from this life but there filled his bosom a strong determination that, come what may, he would live as she taught him to live so that when he should go to meet her and his worthy martyred father, he could say to them, "I am clean."[28]

Is it any wonder, then, that so shortly after his mother's death, Joseph F. found himself weeping bitter tears because of his angry whipping of the schoolteacher? Despite the unjust provocation, the young man knew that it was he who had done wrong—he who had gone against all his beloved mother had taught him, all he knew for himself to be true!

Years later he declared:

> In my childhood... I was instructed to believe in the divinity of the mission of Jesus Christ. I was taught by my mother, a Saint indeed—that Jesus Christ is the Son of God; that He was indeed no other than the Only Begotten of God in the flesh, and that, therefore, no other than God the eternal Father is his Father and the author of his existence in the world. I was taught it from my father, from the Prophet Joseph Smith, through my mother who embraced the gospel because she believed in the testimony of Joseph Smith, and she believed in the honor, integrity and truthfulness of her husband; and all my boyhood days and all my years in the world I have clung to that belief; indeed, I have never had any serious dubiety in my mind, even in childhood.[29]

Having been taught with such clarity, Joseph F. must have wondered with anguish as he fled from the schoolhouse that early spring day in 1854, what in the world he was going to do about his anger—his temper? How could he overcome this weakness that had been so displeasing to his mother, that seemed only to be growing more severe the older he grew?

MISSIONARY TO THE ISLANDS

"Well, Joseph, from word coming out of Salt Lake, being a Mormon is mighty hard doings these days, don't you think?"

Joseph F., on his way home following nearly four years of missionary work in the Islands, glanced out across the Mojave Desert. From his seat on the wagon bench where he was handling the lines to the teams, he then turned to look at George Crisman, his new employer. He had been blessed indeed to obtain work of a sort that did not strain his body, which was still weakened from the three months of fever he had endured on the island of Molokai. Of a truth he had thought he was dying, and likely would have, too, if it hadn't been for the tender care of a young native couple. Of course the woman, Ma Manuhii, had provided the bulk of the labor in his behalf. She had indeed lived up to her name—tender mother. He would never forget her, he knew that! And oh, how he prayed from day to day that the Lord would bless her for her goodness—

"Joseph, are you all right?"

"I'm sorry, George," the young man responded easily. "My mind was back on the Islands. Still doing missionary work, I suppose."

"Well, it's no wonder! You've been at it long enough."

Joseph F. nodded. "It's a great work, though—worth every minute. Still, I suppose that's why it seems so strange to be going home. Not only have I changed some little bit, but no doubt so has everything at home. Why, most everyone but me is married; even my younger sister Martha Ann, who was twelve when I left, is now a happily married woman. Of a truth, I hardly know what it is that I am returning to."

George Crisman grinned. "You'll do all right, Joseph. From what I hear, you did just fine in the Sandwich Islands. Wasn't it three districts you presided over, the first when you were only sixteen? And now you're what? Eighteen? Nineteen? To the world you're still wet behind the ears. But look at you; you're full grown, and Brother Partridge says you're full of valuable experience and mature with wisdom far beyond your years. You'll do well once we get to the valley; I'm sure of it."

Soberly Joseph nodded, feeling uncomfortable with the heady praise. Certainly he had held positions of leadership, but he had always felt humbled by them, woefully lacking in maturity or wisdom, either one. Time and again the Lord had blessed him, causing him to think of things to do or say that were right for the situation but far beyond his own ken or understanding. On the other hand, his whole life up to his mission had been of such a nature that he had known only responsibility, work, and privation. Yet if anything, his missionary experiences had been even more difficult. All together, his stress and sorrow-filled lifetime had somehow advanced him in his thoughts and actions far beyond the ordinary young men of his age. Joseph F. understood this and even acknowledged it privately; but hearing it discussed by others continued to cause him discomfort.

"Yonder about half a mile is a fine spot for camping," George abruptly declared, interrupting Joseph F.'s reverie. "It's a bit early, I admit, but there's feed and water aplenty, so we'll turn in there for the night.

Statue of Ma Manuhii

As his employer rode away to pass the word to the other teamsters, Joseph F.'s mind continued rehearsing past events. Released from his missionary labors on the 6TH of October, 1857, he, his cousin Silas Smith, Edward Partridge, Sixtus Johnson, Ward Pack, Smith Thurston, and William King had done odd jobs on the Islands until they had earned sufficient for passage back to the mainland. Finally sailing on the Yankee for San Francisco, they had taken quarters in the hold because they could afford no better.

Joseph F. grimaced as he thought of how terribly disagreeable the odor in that hold had been—the smells from the below-deck, uncleaned stalls of beef cattle, sheep, and poultry, intensified multiple times by the foul tobacco smoke from sailors' nasty pipes. Even the memory of it caused him to shudder! But as he took a deep breath of the clear desert air, the young returning missionary thought wryly that it was better to possess experience than to gain it, for experience was like a bruise—it felt better after it quit hurting!

In San Francisco it had been winter when they had arrived, and being lightly clothed, he and the other missionaries had practically frozen. Elder George Q. Cannon had given both he and Edward Partridge good overcoats and a pair of blankets between them. Thus equipped, they had started down the coast to Santa Cruz County, where they had met a company of Saints on their way to the Salt Lake Valley. The missionaries had joined them, and they had traveled together until they had come to the Mojave River. There the two missionaries had separated from the company and gone on to San Bernardino, where they had both found work. By mid-winter they had earned sufficient to procure clothing to travel the rest of the way to the valley, and it was at that point that they had hired on with George Crisman, a faithful member who was hauling a wagon train of supplies to assist the Saints in their coming war.

As he turned his teams off the rough road toward the wide, sandy creek bed where George Crisman had said they would camp, Joseph F. finally found himself pondering the man's first question, the one he had never answered. At the moment, being a Mormon was hard doings, indeed! Word seemed to have spread everywhere, even in California, that the Saints had begun a rebellion and that U.S. President James Buchanan had sent an army westward to quell it. Of course no one knew any details of what was going on or what was to be expected, but since so many had gone through the terrible persecutions in Missouri and Nauvoo, it didn't take much for them to draw some frightening conclusions.

Nor did such conclusions seem unjustified. For years the government had been antagonistic toward the Saints, and this latest embroglio, which involved lying government officials as well as the tragic and too-real Mountain Meadows massacre, had seemed to give license to a number of men scattered about the entire country who had murder in their hearts and were bragging that they would not hesitate to kill "Mormons" wherever they might be found.

Thus far Joseph F. had encountered no such men personally, though he had most certainly heard stories —

"Joseph, pull over here beside my wagon, and we'll camp together."

Looking up, Joseph F. smiled and nodded to Edward Partridge, and in a matter of moments the heavy wagons were parked side by side and Joseph had his teams unharnessed and was leading them to water.

"Well," Edward smiled after Joseph F. had staked his animals to graze and had come back to the wagons, "Old George picked a fine camp tonight, didn't he. And for a change we're alone here, with no antagonistics wandering about."

"Should be peaceful, all right."

"You think there'll really be a war back home, Joseph?"

Joseph F. shook his head. "I hope not, Edward. My father was killed in the last one, in Nauvoo, and the burden of his death ultimately killed my mother." For a long moment he stared off into the distance. "No," he finally responded, "I think this is a time for faith, not fight. Live righteously, I say, and let the Lord fight for us. Did George approve fires for tonight?"

Edward grinned. "He did. Reckon we'd best be gathering a little firewood and get one built up."

Together the two young men walked into the brush and trees that lined the creek, joining others that were already on the hunt. But even as he filled his arms with dry limbs and branches, Joseph F. was thinking of what was now being called Johnston's Army, a federally commissioned army that was presently encamped for the winter at Fort Bridger but was preparing to attack the Saints as soon as the snows in the canyons melted in the spring.

What would the Saints do in the face of such an attack? How would the Lord want them to respond? Joseph F. didn't know, but as he stepped back down into the creek bed and started for his wagons, his arms still full of wood, the returning missionary found himself approaching a company of drunken men who had thundered up on horseback.

"Who's in charge of this hyar outfit?" one of them was growling loudly. "We're God's destroying angels, by ---, and we're here to destroy every --- ---- Mormon we can find!"

Looking around, Joseph F. realized that he was standing alone. All the others were either still hunting firewood or had slipped back into the brush at the mob's first appearance.

The young man's first thought was to do the same. He had no desire for a confrontation, and the way these men were waving their guns about, it looked as though it would be far more serious, even, than that!

"Speak up!" the bearded leader threatened, swearing profusely as his horse pranced anxiously about. "Where'n bloody ---- is everbody? Are ye all a bunch of Mormon cowards? Speak up, I tell ye!"

Realizing that he had not yet been seen, Joseph F. was about to turn, when the thought came to him, unbidden: "Why should I run from these fellows?" With that thought in mind he started instantly forward, marching boldly up to where the fire would be built. There he set down his load, straightened, and faced the angry, blustering leader.

"You, there," the man shouted, at the same time pointing one of his pistols at Joseph F. "We're here to exterminate every --- ---- Mormon we meet; every --- ---- last one! Are ye a Mormon?"

Fully expecting to receive the charge from both of the man's pistols in his chest, Joseph F. squared his shoulders and looked the ruffian straight in the eye. "Yes siree!" he answered boldly. "Dyed in the wool; true blue, through and through!"

"Well," the man responded, completely disarmed and bewildered by the straightforward answer, "you are the --- ---- pleasantest man I ever met! Shake, young fellow! I am glad to see a man that stands up for his convictions!"

With that he holstered his pistols and reached out his hand to shake Joseph F.'s, while he paid him a few more profanity-laced compliments. Then, still at the head of his band of blustering mobbers, he turned and rode away, leaving Joseph F. alone and wondering that he wasn't lying there dead.

One thing he did know, he thought as he knelt to kindle the fire: the dream he had been given early in his mission was still in force. Despite his youth he was a man; he had been called and chosen by the Lord's servants to do a work for the Lord, and so long as he was doing it the Lord would protect him and he need have no fear!

Illustration by Robert T. Barrett

Despite his uncertainties about returning to a home where so much had changed, Joseph F. had felt far greater uncertainty about going on his mission in the first place. And with good reason. Almost from the moment of his departure from the Salt Lake Valley he had encountered one sort of opposition after another, so that at times he despaired of even seeing the Islands in the first place, let alone serving a mission there.

For all practical purposes, Joseph F.'s mission began when his name was read from the pulpit during the April conference of 1854. And that, of course, occurred after he had whipped to a fare-thee-well his and Martha Ann's schoolteacher, thus incurring the concern of his stepfather (Heber C. Kimball) and Church President Brigham Young. Quickly endowed and set apart, Joseph F., with several other missionaries and Church leaders, made his way south through Cedar City, Santa Clara, and on across the desert toward San Bernardino, experiencing various misadventures along the way.

Concerning one of those, when they ran completely out of food because they had been feeding starving Indians, Presiding Bishop Charles W. Nibley once said:

> I have heard [Joseph F.] tell how, journeying down through the southern country to Los Angeles... [with a party of missionaries, they]... were followed by a band of hungry Indians... They were down on the desert, this side of Los Vegas [sic], and these Indians became a little troublesome. Joseph F. Smith and one other of the party... were a little slow in getting their horses saddled, and the others of the company rode off or drove off, leaving these two behind. The Indians became more bold when the larger part of the company went on, and as [Joseph F.] was saddling his horse, pulling up the strap, he looked into the barrel of his own gun. An Indian had grabbed his gun from the saddle

and pointed it at him. The boy, who was strong [as] an athlete, smiled merely; but quickly getting under his horse's neck, he grabbed that Indian, who pretended at first to play, and in the tussle, wrenched the rifle from his hands.1

Finally arriving in San Bernardino on the 9TH of June, all of the missionaries ended up taking several odd jobs in order to earn their way to San Francisco, which they reached on July 10TH. There Elder Parley P. Pratt had purchased a sailing vessel, which, according to Joseph F., "they intended to ply between the islands and the Pacific Coast, for the purpose of gathering the Saints, taking the Elders to and from their fields of labor, etc."2

An old sea captain was employed, and "the missionaries were to constitute the crew. All went well until the sea captain, who was a gruff old tar, tried to assert his prerogatives as a captain of a vessel, as understood in that day... Many of the things this raw 'crew' of missionaries were to do, its members considered below their dignity and unbecoming to ministers of the Gospel, no matter how much they were under the necessity of securing a passage across the Pacific to the Hawaiian Islands. Violence was narrowly averted."3

As it turned out, the vessel soon proved to be unseaworthy, and it was forced to return to San Francisco. There, after taking all things into consideration, it was considered best to dispose of the ship for whatever they could get. Unfortunately this left the missionaries penniless once again, and so back to work they went, again earning the money for their passage to the Islands. They accomplished this by early September, and on September 27 Joseph F. and eight other missionaries arrived in Honolulu.

Assigned to labor on the islands of Molokai and Maui, Joseph F. experienced all the difficulties common to adapting to a new culture: new food, new language, and mostly unresponsive listeners. First, he was stricken with a high fever just as he was departing from Honolulu. After reaching Maui he was nursed for most of the next month by Sister Mary J. Hammond, wife of Elder Francis A. Hammond and the only white woman laboring in the Islands at that time.

Weakened by sickness and discouraged because he seemed to be experiencing so much opposition, the young missionary was then assigned to labor in Kula, which meant in Hawaiian "country near the base of a mountain."4 His field of labor consisted of some scattered and impoverished mountain villages, the closest one some eighteen miles from the city of Wailuku, one of the chief cities of Maui.

"'I felt for him,' President Hammond wrote, 'knowing what he has to undergo in preaching and in residing among the people... Brother Joseph is the son of Hyrum Smith, the martyred prophet. He is not yet 16 years old, but bids fain to make a mighty man in this Kingdom.' President Hammond blessed Joseph F. that 'a mighty man in council should he be, and the spirit of his father Hyrum the martyr should rest upon him.'"5

Joseph F.'s life up until then had been nothing but hard work, and so that was how he approached his labors. The first task he assigned himself was to master the native language, which he saw as a requirement for carrying the message of salvation to the people. To that end he began spending every possible moment with the Islanders, ignoring their poverty and filth and ignoring, too, those missionaries who felt their work was only for the whites. Thus he began exercising his faith with great energy and dogged determination.

One hundred days after his arrival in the Islands, despite the terrible setback imposed upon him by his sickness, Joseph F. had learned the language so well that Elder Reddick N. Allred, one of the old missionaries on the island, declared that the young elder "spoke the language well enough to do missionary work wherever he was called to labor."6 At the very next meeting, Elder Smith named the hymn to be sung, opened the meeting with prayer, and before it had closed spoke fluently, all in the native tongue.

As President Hammond had understood, Joseph F. was compelled to make his home with the native people, which made it necessary for him to accept their diet and other unique hospitalities. That diet consisted mainly of poi, which was made from taro root that was baked underground, mashed on a large wooden platter with a stone pestle, and then mixed with water until a thick paste had formed. This paste was left to ferment until it soured, and it was eaten with the fingers.

At first nauseated by the smell of it, Elder Smith again applied dogged determination to adapting to poi as a food of choice, once more mixing his determination with the simple faith taught him by his mother. And as he entered into the spirit of his work, and mingled with the people, poi gradually acquired a sweetness in his mouth. It was for him as it had been for Elder George Q. Cannon a year or so before, who had written:

> [I]n traveling among the people I soon learned that if I did not eat "poi" I would put them to great inconvenience; for they would have to cook separate food for me every meal. This would make me burdensome to them, and might interfere with my success. I, therefore, determined to learn to live on their food, and, that I might do so, I asked the Lord to make it sweet to me. My prayer was heard and answered; the next time I tasted it, I ate a bowlful and I positively liked it... it was sweeter to me than any food I have ever eaten.7

Very quickly Joseph F. "learned to love these native islanders for their loving, kindly hearts. He discovered that they were always willing to share their last morsel of food even if they did not know from whence more was to come. The best they had was reserved for the Elders and they would place themselves at any inconvenience in order to make the brethren comfortable who were called to carry the Gospel message unto them."8

Laboring with a native companion named Pake, Joseph F. said of his first actual missionary tour, " 'We had one horse between us, and we would "ride and tie" [one missionary rode while the other tied himself to the horse's tail]. It is 125 miles around east Maui, from Kula around to Kula again, and we then had small branches at numerous places. I had then been in the islands only a little over three months, but I could say anything in the Hawaiian language, and took my turn with Pake in preaching. I was only a little more than fifteen years and 9 or 10 months old.' "9

Joseph F.'s "labors on the island of Maui continued for one year and an half, and during this time he made the circuit of the island repeatedly, visiting all the branches, living in the homes of the natives, partaking of their hospitality, eating their food and blessing them with the inspiration of the Gospel which he possessed in great abundance. These labors were not always pleasant. Sometimes there were difficulties to be settled, grievances to be adjusted, jealousies to be overcome, a task that was not easy even for one of more mature years. However, young as he was, he was old in experience and judgement and the natives as well as the missionaries looked up to him with respect for his sober-mindedness and sound judgement. Although his education had been meager, yet he was a natural student, always seeking knowledge and a better way to express himself."10

At the same time, Joseph F. was also seeking to grow spiritually. He relates:

On my first mission I began to learn something for myself;
I had hitherto believed the testimonies of the servants of
God whom I had heard converse and preach, as well as the
instructions I received from a most kind and affectionate
mother, as also what I could comprehend through reading
the Book of Mormon, the Doctrine and Covenants, and
the Bible. But in the ministry, where I labored earnestly, I
began to comprehend more fully, through the inspiration
of the Holy Spirit, what I had read and been taught, and so
they became in my mind established facts, of which I was
as absolutely certain as I was of my own existence.11

Among the difficulties that helped young Joseph F. to grow and
mature in this spiritual growth was contact with evil and unclean
spirits, "for the spirits of Satan were frequently present attempting
to overcome or retard the progress of the work. [Yet] the Lord
blessed him abundantly with the gift of discernment, knowledge
and the power to heal by faith."12 In fact he tried to emulate the
mission of the Lord Jesus Christ, of whom it had been recorded by
Nephi:

> And I beheld multitudes of people who were sick, and
> who were afflicted with all manner of diseases, and with
> devils and unclean spirits... And they were healed by the
> power of the Lamb of God, and the devils and the unclean
> spirits were cast out. (1 Nephi 11:31)

" 'Of the many gifts of the Spirit which were manifest through my
administration,' " Joseph F. recorded, " 'next to my acquirement of
the language, the most prominent was perhaps the gift of healing,
and by the power of God, the casting out of evil spirits which
frequently occurred.' "13 One such incident, the first of that kind

for the youthful Elder, took place one night while he was earnestly engaged with a native family in the study of the language. "[T]he wife of the man of the house was suddenly seized with evil spirits. She went through all manner of hideous contortions. Her husband was overcome with fear and crouched in a corner trembling as a leaf in the wind. At first Joseph F. was also seized with fear at this new and unexpected demonstration of the power from the unseen world of evil spirits. Praying inwardly, he says, the fear suddenly left him and the power of the Spirit of the Lord came upon him in great abundance. He stood upon his feet and faced the writhing, distorted woman and said: 'In the name of the Lord Jesus Christ I rebuke you.' No sooner had he uttered these words than the woman fell limp to the floor and became as one dead. Her husband then began to wail and pronounced her dead; his actions the youthful missionary rebuked, and the rebuke quieted the husband and restored peace in the home. Presently the woman recovered her strength and her normal attitude and was able to pursue her duties in the home."14

Buoyed by such clear manifestations of the Lord's Spirit, Joseph F. wrote to those at home:

> I well know that I am young and inexperienced at present, therefore I wish to be humble, prayerful before the Lord, that I may be worthy of the blessings and love of God to protect me at all times... I am happy to say that my whole soul is free to do all in my power for the advancement of this work; I feel anxious to see the cause of truth speed forth to earth's remotest bounds, and I hope that I may become an instrument in the hands of the Lord in doing much good in helping to spread righteousness.15

In July, 1855, Joseph F. was called to preside over the island of Maui, with Sixtus E. Johnson and Simpson A. Molen as his assistants. At this time he was sixteen years old. "This was a grave responsibility for one so young, nevertheless he was greatly respected by his brethren and all with whom he came in contact... To him life was real and earnest, and with it all, he had obtained the firm conviction of the Truth... His labors on Maui under this appointment took him to all parts of the island and frequently also the island of Lanai, where he was called to advise and counsel with men much older than himself."16

Despite the arduous work, Joseph F. enjoyed much about the Islands, including the beauty of the people. On one occasion he recorded, " 'In the evening we seen a sight that was worth all other "sights" that I ever seen. It was composed of three native girls engaged in a hawaiian dance. It is more than I can describe.' "17

Late in July of 1855 a ship arrived from Australia carrying a company of Saints bound for Utah. Unfortunately the ship was no longer seaworthy, and the Saints were marooned for a time in the Islands. Two of them, Fred W. and Charles Clemment Hurst, the latter but a boy, entered the mission field in Hawaii and continued to labor there for some time.

"At that time the missionaries laboring on the islands of Maui, Lanai, Hawaii and Molokai were using the church store house at the settlement of Palawai, on the island of Lanai, as a place where they stored their trunks and all that they possessed which was not then needed in their respective mission fields. On the third of June, [1856], this store house and the meeting house were burned through an accident on the part of young Charles Clemment Hurst, and the Elders who had placed their trunks and other belongings in this place lost all they had, including clothing and journals."18

Among the items lost by Joseph F. were clothing, copies of the first European edition of the Book of Mormon, and the Doctrine

TO ALL PERSONS TO WHOM THIS LETTER SHALL COME:

THIS CERTIFIES, That the bearer, ELDER *Joseph Smith* is in faith and fellowship with the Church of Jesus Christ of Latter Day Saints, and by the General Authorities of said Church, has been duly appointed a mission to *the Pacific* to preach the Gospel and administer in all the ordinances thereof pertaining to his office: And we invite all men to give heed to his teachings and counsels, as a man of God, sent to open to them the door of Life and Salvation; and assist him in his travels, in whatsoever things he may need. And we pray God the Eternal Father to bless Elder *Smith* and all who receive him, and minister to his comfort, with the blessings of Heaven and Earth, for Time and for all Eternity, in the name of Jesus Christ; Amen.

Signed at Great Salt Lake City, Territory of Utah, *U S April 18th* 1854 , in behalf of said Church.

Brigham Young
Heber C. Kimball } First Presidency.
J M Grant

Church Archives, The Church of Jesus Christ of Latter-day Saints

Joseph F. Smith's missionary
certificate which survived the fire

and Covenants, "which had been given as a present to the Patriarch Hyrum Smith. In one of these books Elder Joseph F. Smith had placed his Elder's certificate. When the house was destroyed with its contents, Elder Smith's trunk, and every article in it was reduced to ashes except his missionary certificate. In some remarkable manner it was preserved intact, except that it was scorched around the edges, but not one word was obliterated even though the book in which it was contained was entirely consumed."19

This fire so reduced Joseph F. and his companion that they were forced to share, for a time, the one suit that remained between them. While one ventured out to meetings wearing the suit, the other remained home in bed. "Then the scene was reversed and the brother who went to meeting went to bed while his fellow companion went to meeting. Of course this did not continue but for a short time, but it was one amusing story that was frequently told in later years, when time had removed the suffering Elders far from the scene of their embarrassment and difficulties."20

Joseph F.'s next assignment was to preside over the islands of Hawaii and then Molokai. On January 1, 1857, as he prepared to leave Hawaii to go to Molokai, he wrote to President Heber C. Kimball, his stepfather and the man who had engineered his call to the mission field:

Dear Sir: I have for some time had an inward desire to write you a few words, although I have no doubt that you are well posted in regard to the prosperity of the mission upon these islands and the labors of the brethren.

I am happy to say that my health is good and that I enjoy all the blessings that could be desired in all circumstances under which I have been placed. I have tried with all my might to be a good boy since I left home; how far I have succeeded is not for me to say...

We never tire in well doing; it is true we get leg weary a little sometimes, but in the most adverse circumstances when the clouds of oppression, slander and ridicule darken and frown upon us in the most frightful manner, and in the discharge of our most arduous and fatiguing labors, just one thought upon the glorious hope and faith we cherish dispels every cloud, strengthens our nerves, invigorates our minds, and makes all thoughts of fatigue and weariness vanish like the morning dew before a cloudless sun...

May the "little stone roll forth" till it has done its work among the nations, and it alone "shall stand and fill the whole earth;" and may the Prophets of the Lord live long to guide Zion's ship heavenwards and to see their children do a mighty work, is the constant and most earnest prayers of your obedient servant.

Joseph F. Smith [20]

"Forged in adversity, Joseph F.'s testimony [grew] strong and powerful, a testimony that endured with the same passion and commitment to his dying day. Near the end of his mission, he wrote his favorite childhood cousin Josephine Donna Smith [who had left the Church, and wrote and lived under the penname of 'Ina Coolbrith':

Do you not know that Mormonism is the foundation upon which I have built? The Life of my soul, the sweetest morsal of my existence, the heighth of my pride and ambition? it is! Tuch it, and you tuch the apple of my eye, the fiber of my existence!—because I know,—hear it ye worlds!—I KNOW IT IS TRUE!... Mormonism I love. Not with that

"Boyish love" that lasts for a time, and changes with each new phase, but with the devotion of Man-hood!... Let me expire in and for the Cause, for which my Fathers died. I love their hallowed names, and cherish in honor the remembrance of their Noble Spirits... A radiant smile from the Parants who gave me Birth, will thrice pay me for an hundred deaths!22

A few months later, on Molokai, Joseph F. became desperately ill for the second time on his mission. For three long months he was ministered to by a young native woman who not only saved his life but "filled this motherless boy's need for tenderness."23 Never would he forget his loving Ma Manuhii, and never would she forget her beloved Iosepa.

"Years later, as President of the Church, he visited Hawaii where the Saints greeted him with leis and music. Holding a few bananas as a gift for the distinguished visitor, a frail ninety-year-old blind woman approached, calling 'Iosepa, Iosepa!' {Hawaiian for 'Joseph.'} Presiding Bishop Charles W. Nibley describes this emotional reunion."24

"Instantly, when he saw her, [Joseph F.] ran to her and clasped her in his arms, hugged her, and kissed her over and over again, patting her on the head and saying, "Mama, Mama, my dear old Mama!" And with tears streaming down his cheeks he turned to me and said, "Charley, she nursed me when I was a boy, sick and without anyone to care for me. She took me in and was a mother to me!"25

Shortly after his illness, at the next conference which was held in Honolulu, Joseph F. and the other missionaries who had gone to

Joseph F. Smith in Hawaii

CA. 1909

Church Archives, The Church of Jesus Christ of Latter-day Saints

the Islands in 1854 were released by special letter from President Brigham Young. Partly this was because they had all served for nearly four years, and partly they were released because word had come to the valley that an army was marching toward the Saints, apparently with the express purpose of destroying them and their way of life.

After once again obtaining odd jobs and earning sufficient money for passage to the mainland, the missionaries set sail from Honolulu on the 6TH of October, 1857. Arriving in San Francisco the group split up and commenced earning their various ways eastward toward home. It was during Joseph F.'s journey eastward that the experience portrayed at the beginning of this chapter occurred. It should be pointed out that never again in their journey to the valley was Joseph F.'s company troubled by men such as those who had threatened with such bluster to kill the young returning missionary and his companions.

Looking back on his mission years later, Joseph F. summarized his experience by declaring:

> My four year mission to the Sandwich Islands restored my equilibrium, and fixed the laws and metes and bounds which have governed my subsequent life. I shall always thank God and Pres. Heber C. Kimball for that mission, altho' it was the hardest one I ever performed.26

Joseph F. arrived in Salt Lake City on February 24, 1858, having been absent from his home since May 8, 1854. It was now time, he was certain, to settle down and begin a life of his own.

MUSKETS, MARRIAGE & A MISSION

"Halt! Who goes there?"

Joseph F., in the unaccustomed position of holding a musket in his hands rather than his scriptures, pointed the weapon out into the darkness. "Who goes there?" he repeated, this time more forcefully. "If you don't sing out, I'll fire!"

"You have good ears, Mister," a voice called from perhaps fifty yards out.

"Maybe. Who are you?"

"Peace commissioners. From Washington. We're unarmed."

"How many are you?"

"Two, and two soldiers who are back with our horses. Can we come in?"

"Yes," Joseph F. replied as other members of the militia, including its leader, Orrin Porter Rockwell, silently gathered with their weapons at the ready. "Come in, all four of you. But do it slow, and keep your hands empty and in sight!"

It was early June, and though the nights along the Weber River at the mouth of Echo Canyon were only moderately cool, Joseph F. had still not acclimated from his years on the Hawaiian Islands and so was cold almost all the time. Yet he had been recommended by Brigham Young to do his part in this war with the States, and he would not shirk his duty—

"What do you reckon peace commissioners are?" someone mumbled from behind him.

"Probably just another government trick," somebody else growled from nearby. "Good work, Joseph. I hadn't heard a thing when you sang out, but you can bet I'm ready now!"

"You know, boys, maybe the government has had enough, and these fellers are real." The sotto voice belonged to Orrin Porter Rockwell, and because he spoke so rarely, all strained to listen. "Think about it. Them army fellers have been starving and freezing there at Bridger's burnt-out fort and on up Black's Fork since way last November, and not one of them has been able to pass through our defenses without our say-so. Now old Governor Cummings has had his heart softened by Brother Brigham and the Holy Spirit; Colonel Kane has been our friend forever; and just maybe they've managed to persuade that fool Buchanan what a horse's road apple he's been, sending his sorry army against us in the first place."

"Could be you're right," one of the men voiced for the others. "Was it me, I'd sure have given up!"

"Maybe, but these fellers had better have the proper credentials, no matter!" another breathed, and then all grew still as the sounds of moving horses drifted in from the darkness.

The Mormon War, Joseph F. thought with disgust as he held his musket and waited. Wouldn't the Gentiles ever have enough of fighting against the Lord and his people? Wouldn't there ever be enough of persecution, murder, and mayhem?

Though he'd known nothing of it at the time, this particular conflict had started several years before—as usual with greedy and self-serving men who wanted either that which was legitimately owned or controlled by others or impunity from the law for their

Illustration by Robert T. Barrett

immoral and self-aggrandizing lives.

Trouble began in 1852 with lies from federally appointed and now "runaway" government officials, followed by false reports from government justices. This was followed by outright lies by mail contractor W. M. F. McGraw, who with John M. Hockaday had lost a government mail contract to Mormon bidders. In anger, McGraw managed to convince President James Buchanan that Utah was without law and that the lives of all in the territory were in danger from Brigham Young and a few fanatical Church leaders.

Meanwhile, in 1856, certain congressional leaders in Washington had linked polygamy and slavery, calling them the "twin relics of barbarism." Soon Mormonism was being referred to as "an ulcer on the body politic" which needed to be cut out, and with popular backing generated by such slogans, combined with all the outright lies being proffered by so many, in 1857 President Buchanan dispatched 2,500 troops to put down the supposed rebellion in Utah.

Upon learning of the army's approach, the Mormon community, which had twice before fled before the effects of mobocracy, stiffened in its mountain retreat, drew in its outlying colonies to consolidate its strength, and defied military approach. Members of the Nauvoo Legion hastened to the plains of Wyoming and began defensive operations, destroying forage along the army's route, stampeding its livestock, and burning its supply wagons.

Apparently as a result of divine aid to the Mormons, winter snows had then come early, and soon the army found itself short of rations and almost snowed in on the barren and desolate plains of Wyoming—miles from Salt Lake City.

Desperate, General Albert Sidney Johnston led the army on a thirty-five-mile march through winter storms and below-zero temperatures that took fifteen long and grueling days. Men suffered terribly and cattle died by the hundreds before they arrived at Fort Bridger—only to discover that the Mormons had burned the wooden buildings. The stone walls remained, however, providing a modicum of shelter, and there and for several miles up Black's Fork they went into winter bivouac.

Back in the valley Brigham Young and the Saints spent the winter re-strategizing, and early in 1858 they adopted a scorched-earth policy and began moving southward, abandoning their homes in Salt Lake City. Between the end of March and mid-May, some 30,000 settlers from northern Utah moved south at least as far as Provo, leaving behind only enough men to care for fields and crops.

Joseph F. had returned from his mission just in time to witness this mass exodus, but his assignment had not been to move, but to ride to Echo Canyon and beyond, serving as a scout and courier between the forces there and General Daniel H. Wells's headquarters in the valley. Back and forth he had ridden, so many times he had lost count, until finally, weary to the bone, he had been granted picket duty on the Weber River under Brother Rockwell, who had been such a staunch friend of his father and Uncle Joseph during the early days of the Church.

And now, he thought ruefully, he had "caught" these two men who were claiming to be peace commissioners—

"Good evening, gentlemen." The two men in front, more elderly than the soldiers who followed, were clearly not a part of the army.

"Good evening," Joseph F. responded amiably as he lifted his musket a little higher. "Would you halt there, please?"

"Most certainly," one of the men responded with a tired smile. "I am Lazarus W. Powell, young man, former governor and now senator from Kentucky. This is Ben McCulloch, hero of the Texas Revolution and the Mexican War. Are you the fellow who first hollered out?"

"I am. My name is Joseph F. Smith."

In an instant the two had focused their attention on Joseph F. "Are you the son of the great Mormon prophet?"

"No, Mr. Powell," Joseph F. responded quietly, "but I am his nephew. My father was murdered with him while they were illegally incarcerated in Carthage, Illinois."

"Yes," Lazarus Powell acknowledged, "that was a terrible tragedy, just terrible! You could not have been very old when it occurred."

"I was but five, Sir, but my memories of it are very vivid."

"If they are as vivid as your ears are sharp," Ben McCulloch said softly, his Texas drawl much in evidence, "you won't have forgotten a thing. We were between fifty and sixty yards out, Joseph, making as little sound as humanly possible, and were planning on scouting you out afore we made ourselves known. I congratulate you on your astute action."

"Are you in charge here, Joseph?" Senator Powell asked then.

Joseph F. smiled. "No, Sir, that will be Captain Rockwell— Orrin Porter Rockwell."

Almost laughing at the looks of consternation that appeared on the men's faces, for Rockwell's name alone struck fear into men's hearts far and wide, Joseph F. controlled himself and stepped aside as his dark-bearded leader took over.

For the next hour a conference was held at the fire, where it was quickly ascertained that the two men indeed carried a proclamation from President Buchanan that ostensibly offered peace to the Saints. Unfortunately it actually censored them for their spirit of insubordination and urged them to accept the federal officers as well as the nation's laws in order to earn a free pardon for the seditions and treasons heretofore committed.

As this was read aloud, some of the brethren actually chuckled, but when neither Powell nor McCulloch responded in kind, but instead forcefully declared their intentions not to negotiate on any point, but to encourage the Saints to accept the proclamation at face value, the smiles vanished.

"Isn't that gracious!" one of the men growled. "Granting us a full and free pardon just to cover up his own blunder!"

A ripple of grim laughter spread through the camp, and then all was silent.

"Well, boys," Orrin Porter Rockwell declared laconically as he rose to his feet, "since these two 'gentlemen' obviously have their work cut out for them if they intend to convince the Saints of such tommyrot as that, I'd best get them to Brother Brigham mighty soon. Henry, saddle my horse and fetch me my pistols. Joseph F., you'll be in charge until I return."

"Do you intend to ride tonight?" Senator Powell asked in surprise. It was obvious to Joseph F. that he was a talker, and very fast on his feet. It was just as obvious that Ben McCulloch, more reserved, was also more sincere with whatever it was he happened to say.

"I do, Sir."

"Very well, then, I suppose we are ready. May we take our escorts?"

Orrin Porter Rockwell made a show of checking the loads in one of his brace of pistols. "It makes no never mind with me who you take, Sir, since I'll be riding behind you, no matter."

"With your own escort, we assume?"

The famous Mormon scout and bodyguard grinned widely, at the same time spinning his pistol's cylinder. For a moment he eyed it with obvious pleasure, and finally he slipped it under his belt. "These are all the escort I've ever needed," he declared, tapping the butts of both pistols with his hands. Then, once the again-discomfited peace commissioners were mounted and moving out into the darkness behind their two very nervous young escorts, he gave a

Orrin Porter Rockwell

CA. late 1860's

Church Archives, The Church of Jesus Christ of Latter-day Saints

broad wink to Joseph F. and the other smirking brethren, nudged his horse gently, and followed suit.

His spirits buoyed by four years of peaceful pursuits as a missionary, Joseph F. rode into the boiling war-caldron that was Salt Lake City on February 24, 1858. The Army of the United States may have been halted by Wyoming blizzards, but all knew that warmer weather was bound to come, and with it the thousands of men whose one intent seemed to be the total destruction of the Saints. Brigham Young had declared martial law, and the air throughout the settlements was rife with rumor and speculation. A move south had been ordered; all knew that much. But to where seemed a universal question.

Going directly to his deceased mother's home, Joseph F. spent the remainder of that day and evening in renewing acquaintances with his family. The next morning, February 25TH, he repaired to the office of President Brigham Young and reported on his missionary labors, as well as conditions in the Islands when he had departed. That same day he

enlisted in the legion militia to defend ourselves against the encroachment of a hostile and menacing army. From that time until the proclamation of peace, and a "free and full pardon" by President Buchanan came, I was constant-ly in my saddle, prospecting and exploring the country between Great Salt Lake City and Fort Bridger, under the command of Col. Thomas Callister and others. I was on picket guard with a party of men under Orrin P. Rockwell, when Commissioners Powell and McCullough met us near the Weber River with the President's proclamation. Subsequently I was on detail in the deserted city of Great Salt Lake, until after the army passed through the city, and thence to Camp Floyd. After this I assisted my relatives to return to their homes, from which they had fled, going to the south some time previous.1

During this same time, on March 20, 1858, Joseph F. was ordained a seventy and became a member of the 32ND Quorum. He had filled a lengthy mission and as an elder had presided over four districts on the islands of Maui, Hawaii, and Molokai, so the calling was a natural one for him to assume. And meanwhile he continued his labors in the mountains until peace was established and the Saints had returned to their homes.

Joseph F., knowing that he needed work in order to support himself, labored through the summer and fall in the various harvests going on in the valley. He found work putting up hay and straw, threshing grain, shucking corn and chopping silage, and digging potatoes and other vegetables. At nights he was also some-what occupied, keeping company with one of his cousins, the lovely Levira Annette Clark Smith. The daughter of his Uncle Samuel Harrison Smith and Levira Clark Smith, she had been born in Nauvoo on April 29, 1842, and so was three and an half years younger than Joseph F. She was also the younger sister of one of his favorite missionary companions in the Islands—Samuel H. B. Smith. There is little doubt that it was Samuel H. B. who first recommended that the two begin seeing each other.

In December the Territorial Legislature of 1858–59 met in Filmore, which was the capital of the territory. Joseph F. was appointed sergeant-at-arms for the council, which for convenience immediately recessed and moved back to Salt Lake City. In that capacity he labored through the winter, at the same time continuing to spend what time he could courting Levira.

On the 5TH of April, 1859, he and Levira were married in Brigham Young's office, with President Young performing the ceremony.2 Joseph F. was filled with great expectations for making himself and Levira a home of their own. Apparently they began their married life in the house his mother had built, and so Joseph F. put his energies to work on what was considered the family farm, endeavoring to build for himself and wife the same type of security and prosperity his mother had always provided for him.

In October, just before his twenty-first birthday, Joseph F. was ordained a high priest and called into the high council of the Salt Lake Stake of Zion, and he served in that capacity until the following April, 1860, when once again he heard his name read from the pulpit during General Conference. He, along with several others, including Levira's brother, Samuel H. B. Smith, was being called to a second mission, this time to Great Britain.

Though destitute, there was no hesitation on Joseph F.'s part—he would go as requested. The decision was not as easy for his bride, Levira, who had been a wife for barely one year. She had so hoped to be a mother by that time, or at least to be expecting. Yet this blessing had not occurred, and she knew that if Joseph F. left her, she would have no children for another two or three years. To her this was a vital issue; in her mind it was the supreme reason for her creation, why she had married Joseph F. in the first place. Yes, she loved him, but that love could best be expressed as she gave him children—as she created an extension of the two of them. If he was in Great Britain, such giving and creating on her part would be impossible!

One can only imagine the conversations and discussions—and considering Joseph F.'s rather warm temper, perhaps even arguments—that took place over the next two and an half weeks as Joseph F. prepared to depart. In his mind there were no questions: the Lord had spoken, and he would obey. Neither could he fathom that Levira might feel any differently. And she, somehow, could not communicate adequately that she did.

On April 27, 1860, Joseph F., in company with his cousin Samuel H. B., departed from Salt Lake City in Bishop Edwin D. Woolley's wagon company, headed east. A devastated Levira remained behind. Moving back in with her mother, she did her best to deal with her loneliness. Meanwhile, both Joseph F. and Samuel H. B. drove four-mule teams from Salt Lake City to Fort Des Moines, Iowa, for which they obtained their passage and board. "At that place they were able to borrow money to help them on their journey."3

"The weather was stormy and at times very cold, but except for minor accidents and the straying of mules when they were turned out to feed, all went well."4 Upon reaching the Mississippi River, "Joseph F. and Samuel H. B. Smith visited Nauvoo and called upon Emma Smith, who was then the wife of one Major Bidamon. On entering the room where Emma Smith was seated, they were presented to her by her son Frederick G., who said: 'Mother, do you know these young men?' She looked up and said: 'Why, as I live, it is Joseph. Why, Joseph, I would have known you in hell, you look so much like your father.' These were her exact words, said Joseph F., and they made a deep impression upon him as well as giving him a shock at the manner in which they were spoken. She did not appear to recognize Samuel, although he had visited her only about two years before."5

That evening, according to Joseph F., as they were led to their sleeping quarters by Joseph Smith III, he said

on bidding us good night: "John L. (meaning John L. Smith), slept here a while ago and he had a dream. I have had several myself in this room, and I would like you to remember what you dream tonight and let me know." This was but a few weeks after his acceptance of the position he now occupies (i.e., as president of the Reorganized

Samuel H.B. Smith,
cousin of Joseph F. Smith

CA. 1873

Church Archives, The Church of Jesus Christ of Latter-day Saints

Church) at the hands of William Marks and others. He was feeling somewhat zealous and urged us not to go any further on our missions, but stop and reflect, etc. In the morning I asked Samuel if he had dreamed anything. He replied, "No." I then told him my dream as follows: I thought I was standing on a large pine raft, moored at the foot of the street in the edge of the river, and was fishing with a hook and line, and I thought I pulled out the fish almost as fast as I could bait my hook. The water seemed clear, so that I could see into it at a great depth. I stood on the outer edge of the raft, which was large, filling the space opposite the street. Soon I dropped my hook as usual, and no sooner had it sunk below the surface than I saw a huge gar making directly for it. Fearing I would lose my hook, I drew it rapidly out, but the gar was so determined to nab it that he ran out of the water more then half the length of my arm in the vain endeavor to snap it. However, I saved my hook and line and carried away my fish. When I told Joseph my dream he made no reply and the subject dropped.6

While they remained in Nauvoo, Joseph F. and Samuel H. B. were treated very kindly by their Aunt Emma. Upon their departure they also visited their fathers' three sisters, who were living at or near Colchester, McDonough County, Illinois. "At this place there were a few members of the Church and a meeting was held and the two young missionaries delivered inspirational talks to the people assembled, including their three aunts."7

From there Joseph F. and his companion continued on to New York, and on July 14, 1860, in company with eleven other missionaries including Amasa M. Lyman and Charles C. Rich of the Council of the Twelve, they embarked on the steamship Edinburgh for Liverpool. Soon Joseph F.'s mission to Great Britain would begin in earnest.

13

DUTIES ABROAD

"Aren't you doing well again, dear?" Joseph F., finally home from his mission in England, forced open his exhausted eyes, reached, and turned up the lantern.

"I... I'm not doing well at all, Joseph darling." Levira sighed weakly. "I know you've slept hardly at all, but I... I am so everlastingly thirsty! Would you mind fetching me another drink of water?"

"I'll be happy to, Levira, but there's water aplenty there on the stool beside you."

"But it has been sitting for almost an hour, Joseph, and tastes so stale!"

Gritting his teeth, Joseph F. threw back the bed-cover and staggered to his feet. He was so everlastingly tired and exhausted, for only rarely had his wife allowed him to sleep more than a few moments at a time in all the weeks since his return. Of course she was unwell with some sort of nervous condition, and he knew that. But she had ought to know that the water he was now on his way to fetch for her would be ladled from the same bucket that had supplied her previous drinks. He had drawn that bucket from the well around midnight; this would be her fourth glass from it in less than three hours, and thus far she had taken little more than a sip from any of them!

Still, Joseph F. reminded himself, this was the woman he loved! Though it sometimes seemed that he hardly even knew her, this was the woman he had covenanted to stand beside throughout eternity. Therefore, he must not lose his temper over what some might consider her unrighteous demands. Neither must he question her or grow weary or upset when she made such foolish and childish requests—

"Thank you, darling," Levira sighed moments later as he held the glass to her lips and she took a tiny sip. "That's sufficient, thank you. I don't know what it is that troubles me so, but I get to feeling so parched and dry, that I hardly seem able to stand it."

"It's all right," Joseph F. soothed as he placed the drink beside the other one, skirted the bed, thought again of undressing but quickly abandoned the idea, and slid back under the cover. "I hope it helps you."

"I... I am certain that it will. Oh, how thankful I am that you are home from that awful mission! Three years is such a terribly long time, my darling! I... I don't know how I have endured! Oh, promise me, promise me, Joseph, that you will never leave me so again! I could not bear it! I don't know how I have borne this horrible separation, and I am absolutely positive that I could not endure another! Promise me, my darling Joseph? Please?"

With a heavy heart Joseph F. reached out and turned down the lantern. Almost since the day of their marriage, Levira had been pleading for this promise from him, which he felt was so unkind and so unreasonable—

"Joseph, please swear it to me, I beg you!"

"Levira, dear," Joseph F. sighed deeply, "we've talked about it an hundred times, and I can say no more than that which has already been said. I am now nearly twenty-three years old, and since age fifteen I have served seven years of my life on missions. It is highly unlikely that the Brethren will see fit to call me on another—"

"That is not a promise, Joseph, and you know it!" Levira's voice was suddenly strident, angry. "I shall not rest until I shall have of you a promise that you will serve no more missions!"

"Levira, please keep your voice down—"

"Why? So that our precious neighbors will not discover that you have left your wife unfulfilled? Well, Joseph, I care not a fig what they discover! If they don't know by now that I am unfulfilled as a woman—if they can't see that you have left me childless and yearning these three long and painful years, then I hope they do hear! Do you understand? And I hope they hear that you will give me no promise that you will not leave me childless again!" Levira flounced up on the bed so that she could adjust her pillows, not noticing that she had pulled the covering from her husband in the meantime.

"Oh, Joseph, you have no idea what it has been like for me, suffering in poverty and loneliness whilst all my friends and associates have been joyfully idling away their time as their wee ones played about their knees and ankles! Can't you see that?"

"I can see it, my dear. I can, and I am sorry! How many times must I say it? I am sorry!"

Levira folded her arms, her back against the wall, and stared ahead. "If that were true, Joseph, if you were truly sorry, then six weeks ago—no, three years ago, I would have obtained your promise that you would not again leave me, and I would be at peace!"

Shaking his head in frustration, Joseph F. stared upward to where the dim lantern light flickered on the ceiling. For his entire mission to Great Britain this had been his wife's primary theme, written him time and again in a dozen or more different ways. And no matter how many times he had tried to explain to her by return mail that he had had no choice but to respond to the call from their prophet, she just couldn't seem to understand—

"Please, Joseph, take me in your arms! Hold me, my darling, and promise me that you will not leave my side until I am with child—until I am finally fulfilled as a woman!"

"Levira," Joseph F. growled, still doing his level best to control the old temper he could feel churning and rising within him, "for the last time, I cannot give you that promise! What? Do you suppose that I do not want children, that I do not wish for a quiver full of arrows to honor before the Lord? Of course I want children! That is why I sent you little Edward. Even though you were unable to care for him, yet still I love little children with a pure love, and cannot wait until I am holding and bouncing some of my own upon my knee. But I have no say in such a matter, Levira, and you know it! It is God who sends forth children, not a mere mortal such as myself."

Joseph F. took a deep breath. "Can't you see, my dear? If it had been the Lord's will that you be with child before my departure for Great Britain three years ago, it would have been done. Why, had it been his will, you would have become a mother in the year before my departure, for there was certainly time enough. Only, for some reason it didn't happen—"

"Are you implying that I am not worthy to be a mother?" Levira's voice was now a snarl. "You're the always-righteous missionary, of course, so is it my fault, then?"

"I didn't say that, my darling." Now Joseph F. was doing his best to soothe and placate his young wife. "I am only saying that God, in his infinite wisdom, must have a purpose in this, a divine understanding that, for the present, remains hidden. When it is time, then I am certain he will open the heavens and send us children—"

"When it is time? It is time right now, Joseph; time and past time! To become fulfilled, I must become a mother! You have served your missions; that is mine! Why cannot you understand that?"

"Please, Levira—"

"I mean it! Further, I will not allow that awful Brigham Young to draw you away again before it is accomplished!"

"My dear, you mustn't talk so about the Lord's anointed—"

"And why not, I ask you? Don't I have a right to a little happiness? Don't you? Other married couples in this valley are allowed to remain together, Joseph; and yes, to bring forth children, one after another, almost like rabbits! Why cannot the great "Lord's anointed" grant you and me the same privilege? Can't the "much-childrened" Brigham Young see that we need time together if we are to cherish the same blessings that he so bounteously enjoys? That we need our lives? Our family? Are there no other men he can send on these fool missions?"

"Oh, Levira, I tremble to hear you speak so!"

"I mean every word I say, Joseph, and you know it! It is why I demand of you a promise. Neither will I cease pestering you, until I obtain it!"

With another flounce Levira turned onto her side, her back to Joseph F., and grew still as if in sleep. Yet for the young returned missionary, sleep had utterly fled, just as it had fled for so many days and nights before. What was wrong with her, he found himself continually asking? Why could she not understand? It was the Lord who was sending him, not Brigham Young. And it had always been the Lord whom he had served!

Why, Levira was almost as much a child of the prophets as was he. Her father may not have been Joseph or Hyrum, but he was Samuel Harrison Smith, their brother. He, like Joseph F.'s own father, had been one of the eight witnesses to the Book of Mormon and had held and turned the leaves of the golden plates with his own hands. As a matter of fact, it was he who had served the very first true mission for the Church and whose copy of the Book of Mormon had been instrumental in converting Brigham Young—the man his daughter was now calling evil—to the gospel of the Lord Jesus Christ! Moreover, Samuel had died on July 30, 1844, only a month following the deaths of Joseph and Hyrum and was every bit as much a martyr to the cause of truth as were they!

How was it that Levira could not remember these things? How was it that she could not keep in her mind how her father and uncles had given their all, even their very lives, for the Lord's true Church? Why could she not remember how important the work really was? And that, to accomplish it, the Lord seemed to require the sacrifice of all things?

Of what import, then, was a much lesser sacrifice such as a three-year mission? Or two missions, or even three or four if the Lord should desire them? How could he, whose father had set such a perfect example, possibly hold back? Or how could Levira, whose father had done the same?

And then there was Joseph F.'s sainted mother. She had given her life to the cause of truth no less than had his father! How could he possibly let her down? Why, to do as Levira was demanding would be tantamount to turning his back upon both of his parents, as well as his uncle, the Prophet Joseph! It would be to make a solemn mockery of the truths they had died for, the very truths the Lord in his mercy had made known unto him, Joseph F. Smith, through the unspeakable power of the Holy Ghost and which he now knew without doubt were true!

No, he sighed as he, too, rolled onto his side, he could make his troubled wife no such promise, not and remain true to his divinely given witness and testimony. Instead he must continue to exercise his faith that the Lord might heal her—might raise her up and clear her mind so that she would stop feeling so agitated.

Of course, he thought wearily as his eyes closed in troubled slumber, it really was highly unlikely that Brother Brigham and Brother Heber would call him on a third mission. Thank the Lord for that—1

Nearly three years before the above account, Joseph F. and his companions arrived in Liverpool around the 1ST of August, 1860. No longer, however, was Joseph F. a child who would have much to learn before he could become a teacher of the gospel. Though not quite twenty-one, he was both a seasoned missionary and an effective leader, and his coming to the British Isles was noted. In fact, the editor of the *Millennial Star*, the Church's official publication in Great Britain, stated:

> There was much food for thought and for me a precious morsel was the presence of the sons of Hyrum and Samuel Smith and nephews of Joseph, our Prophet. I could not be forgetful of the great dead, or be insensible of the presence of these their natural [offspring].2

One of Joseph F.'s first acts of business was to get a haircut and purchase a new wardrobe. " 'You had ought to see me now,' " he wrote Levira. " 'You would hardly know whether it was Joseph or not. Let me discribe him as he sits. Here he is, hair "shinggaled," tall "stovepipe" hat, stiff collar & in full English Style, all set & in full trim to go forth a regular english mormon preacher!... We stand quite a show even if they did take us to be wilde beasts & monkeys when we first came.' "3

Immediately thereafter, both Joseph F. and Samuel H. B. were assigned to labor in the Bradford Conference, "which was a portion of the pastoral district of which Sheffield, Hull and Lincolnshire formed the parts. Shortly after his arrival Joseph F. Smith was made president of the Sheffield Conference, and later was made pastor of the district, which position he held until the fall of 1862."4

During his labors in Sheffield, Joseph F. became acquainted with a man named William Fowler, and a lasting friendship was formed. William Fowler was employed in the cutlery works of Sheffield as a grinder and polisher, though after he joined the Church, persecutions set in against him and he ultimately lost his employment. Prior to his dismissal, however, and while laboring under the spirit of inspiration, William Fowler penned a hymn which he titled "We Thank Thee O God for a Prophet." Joseph F. was in attendance at the branch of the Church in Sheffield when this wonderful hymn was first sung, and he never forgot the occasion.5

It was also in Sheffield that an epidemic of smallpox broke out, and some of the members of the Church succumbed to the disease. In visiting with the various members who had lost loved ones, on one occasion Joseph F. was "invited to occupy the bed on which the father of the family but a short time before had passed away of smallpox. The poor mother of the family... showed him the bed he was to occupy saying: 'It was on this very bed that my poor William passed away.' In that day vaccination was not generally understood and only a sprinkling among the people had availed themselves of its benefit, although more than a half a century had passed since Edward Jenner had made his wonderful discovery. Fortunately for Elder Joseph F. Smith he had been vaccinated against smallpox, and while the methods employed in that day were somewhat crude, in his case as in thousands of others, it proved a blessing."6

No doubt Joseph F. felt a certain amount of revulsion at sleeping on the deceased man's bed, for he knew it would be filled with the deadly germs. Nevertheless, in deference to the kindness of the poor widow who was offering her all, Joseph F. accepted her invitation. The result was that he came down with a mild form of the

Joseph F. Smith in Liverpool, England

CA. *1861*

Church Archives, The Church of Jesus Christ of Latter-day Saints

disease, which caused him some suffering but did not debilitate him.

Frequently on this mission, just as had happened in the Sandwich Islands, Joseph F. found himself in the position of being required to rebuke and chastise local offenders from the stand. On one occasion he rebuked a local Elder by stating, " 'I wish those who are in the habit of drinking liquor to keep off the stand on the Sabbath, when their breath smells.' "7 Before the end of the day, the offended party returned to Joseph F. his Elder's License and a penny for his *Millennial Star*, writing: " 'I have burnt up my hymn-book and all other works that I have, and will burn the Book of Mormon as soon as I can find it.' "8

Joseph F. commented in his journal:

> Oh! when will men learn that in rejecting their own salvation, ...they themselves alone are the sufferers? What a wonderful influence the devil has over men when they once give way to the wickedness that is in them! That which yesterday was lovely and dear to them, today is hateful and obnoxious. Yet truth is the same forever: it is man that changes.9

It was not in Joseph F.'s nature to be harsh or unkind, and he was "always ready with an outstretched hand to lift up the brother who had stumbled and who showed the spirit of repentance, but under his administration he expected those who had made covenants to serve the Lord to do just that thing with all their hearts. He would not and did not look upon sin among the members of his flock with the least degree of allowance. He frequently declared in the council meetings that he expected the Elders and all who were called to the ministry 'to toe the line,' and taught the members of the Church to 'always set a good example' among all people with whom they came in contact. 'If we wish the people to do right, then we, who minister unto them must do right ourselves, then they will follow us and the example we set before them.' This was constantly his policy... No [one] was more zealous or labored more faithfully in the performance of duty than did Joseph F. Smith."10

During his years in England, Joseph F. had the privilege of meeting and spending time with members of his mother's family. He was treated kindly by all of them, but never was he allowed to preach or discuss his religious beliefs, "as their minds were filled with prejudice based upon the false stories that were rife." In fact, they deplored the "fact that such lovely, virtuous girls as Mary and Mercy R. Fielding and their kind, loving brother Joseph, should be so foolish and ignorant as to be led astray by the 'Mormons.'"11 For himself, Joseph F. admired their devout natures and their faithful performance of the duties connected with their own religious faiths, yet he wept that they had set up stakes (self-imposed limitations), as the Prophet Joseph had once put it,12 and would not progress beyond them.

In March of 1862 Joseph F. learned that Levira had become chronically ill with a nervous condition which it seemed obvious was connected with his long absence from home. Since his departure she had lived with relatives, then had taken in wash and made rag carpets "to support herself and her widowed mother."13 And all the while she was anxiously awaiting her husband's return.

Quickly Joseph F. wrote that he thought he might be home in six weeks. However, he stayed to supervise emigration through the fall, and then the work continued to demand his attention on through the winter. The disappointments of each delay were heartrending for his lonely and childless wife, and her condition grew steadily worse.14

Doing his best to assist his struggling wife, Joseph F. concluded that adoption might be the answer for her. In England he had become acquainted with a four-year-old orphan boy named

Edward, whom he had grown to love. Surely the child would be good for Levira and would lift her spirits by making her a mother. Soon arrangements were made, and the child was sent with an emigrating family to Utah. Unfortunately Levira was unable to take care of herself, let alone Edward, and so the little boy was sent on to live with Joseph F.'s cousin Rachel Fielding Burton.[15]

As his third year in Great Britain rolled around, Joseph F., only twenty-three years old, found himself presiding over a very large part of England. "At no time did his presiding officers lose faith and confidence in him,"[16] and under his direction the Church prospered and continued to grow. It was a day of gathering to Utah, however, and so as soon as a man united himself with the Church, he was urged to gather with the body of the Saints. To make certain all were prepared for that eventuality, Joseph F. taught that

> if a man cannot be honest and deal justly with his fellow-men here (Great Britain) he cannot there (the gathering place of the Saints). And if a man emigrates, who has been thus acting dishonestly, he carries with him the elements of dissatisfaction and apostacy [*sic*], and in a few years such a person may, perhaps, be seen dragging himself back to the States, or somewhere else, where he can find spirits more congenial to his own, for surely he can find none of this kind who are contented to dwell along with the Saints, unless they speedily repent of their sins, and forsake their pernicious ways. On the other hand, those who leave these lands to gather to Zion, engaged heart and soul in the great work, will enjoy the Spirit of God, will leave behind them a good name, and a reputation unsullied and unblamable. They will be found obedient to the counsels of those whom God has placed to guide them; they will prosper on their voyage and while

crossing the plains, and when they get to the end of their journey, they will be satisfied, and continue to prosper and grow in knowledge and wisdom.17

Among Joseph F.'s greatest blessings while serving in England was developing a close personal friendship with Elder George Q. Cannon—a friendship that would continue for the remainder of their lives. Elder Cannon had been called to the Apostleship in April, 1860, the same conference during which Joseph F. was called to England. Soon Elder Cannon had been assigned to serve in Great Britain, and by Joseph F.'s third year, Elder Cannon was presiding in the British Isles and adjacent countries.18

In the fall of 1862, Joseph F. was invited by Elder Cannon to make a tour of the conferences of the Church in Denmark. This was a remarkable experience for the young missionary, for he saw and heard much from which he would be able to learn. Joseph F. also had the privilege of touring Scotland and then visiting Paris and other places with Elder Brigham Young, Jr.19 These journeys, too, contributed to his growing knowledge of the world and its peoples. Once back in England Joseph F. "was given charge of the emigration of four thousand Saints who left for Utah [in 1863], requiring much correspondence with local church leaders, government officials, and steamship lines... [and giving him] ample opportunity to develop administrative skills and leadership abilities."20

Joseph F. was also much loved by the people over whom he had been called, members and missionaries alike.

Elder Jacob G. Bigler, who attended the Sheffield Conference then under the presidency of Joseph F. Smith, wrote to the *Millennial Star* and said: "On the 19TH (Sept., 1862) I went to Sheffield to visit the Saints who compose that Conference, and under the Presidency of Elder Joseph F. Smith, and attended one branch meeting, which was well attended. I took much pleasure with Brother Joseph; he reminded me much, in his appearance, of his father, whose example he seeks to follow. This Conference I consider to be in a healthy, thriving condition"...

Another missionary, Thomas Taylor, also wrote to the *Star* as follows:

"...I find the Sheffield Saints are warm-hearted and full of good works, under the Presidency of Joseph F. Smith, who though young is like a father to them. He is esteemed very highly by the Saints, and by some who have not, for some reason or other, dared to own the Latter-day work by baptism, although they have in every other way."21

In America, meanwhile, a problem was arising that would affect Joseph F. for most of the remainder of his life. In Washington "the first successful anti-Mormon legislation was passed... This was the Morrill Anti-Bigamy Act of 1862. Applying specifically to the Territory of Utah, it levied penalties against anyone practicing plural marriage, disincorporated the Church, and limited the value of real estate which it could hold to $50,000. Any amount of property above that figure could be confiscated by the government.

"Abraham Lincoln signed the bill on July 8 but did not push for its enforcement. He was fair-minded with regard to the Mormon question and tried to steer a middle ground between the Saints and their most vocal opponents... When he was a boy on a farm, he said, there was a great deal of timber that had to be cleared away. Occasionally they came to a log that was 'too hard to split, too wet to burn, and too heavy to move,' so they plowed around it. That, he said, is what he planned to do about the Mormons. 'You go back and tell Brigham Young that if he will let me alone I will let him alone.'... [T]his attitude won him the respect of the Saints..."22 including Joseph F. Smith.

In April of 1863 Joseph F., along with Samuel H. B. Smith and numerous other missionaries, were finally released to return to the valleys of the mountains. Arriving in New York in July, they witnessed the great riots that accompanied the beginning of the terrible War between the States—the conflict prophesied of by his Uncle Joseph so many years before.23

"From the spring of 1854 to the summer of 1863, with the exception of the time spent with the Utah army in Echo Canyon, Joseph F. Smith was engaged in missionary work in Hawaii and Great Britain. He went on each of these missions without means, and returned in the same condition."24 Without funds when he arrived in America, Joseph F. found short-term employment in New York, and soon collected the means necessary to carry him to Florence, Nebraska. There he was employed by a wagon train as "chaplain and 'physician,' "25 and by fall he was home again, ready to go to work for the support and building up of his family.

Unfortunately, upon his arrival on September 27, 1863, he found Levira in a terribly nervous state which required his constant nursing care. " 'For six weeks after my arrival,' " Joseph F. wrote, " 'I did not go to bed, nor take off my clothes to rest. Nor did I have an hour's unbroken rest or sleep during that whole six weeks night or day, but my struggles and faith prevailed. The Lord raised her up.' "26 It is this trying period that is portrayed at the beginning of this chapter.

Perhaps just as unfortunately, Levira did not conceive a child that fall or early winter, and when in February 1864 Joseph F. was called by Brigham Young to serve another mission to the Hawaiian Islands, this one of a more specific nature, there was no way Levira could prevent him from going. Though Joseph F. did not believe he would be gone for as long as he was during his first two missions, it was nevertheless

his duty to go as he had been called—which meant that once again
Levira, and therefore his unborn family, would have to wait.

DEPOSING A "KING"

"Quite a breeze today."

Turning from the approaching shore of Maui to look at William W. Cluff, who was standing next to him in the bow of the schooner Nettie Merrill, Joseph F. nodded his response. In fact the wind was whining through the schooner's rigging in a way that the twenty-three-year-old missionary had never heard, and the sound was making him nervous.

"No sign of storm, though," William Cluff continued, glancing upward at the clear sky.

"The skies may be blue," Joseph F. responded as he continued to watch the shore, "but this wind is a storm indeed, William, and I don't recall ever seeing higher swells in these waters."

"But the sea doesn't seem that rough."

"Not here, perhaps. But look yonder to the breakwater and the reef. That's where you can see the height of the swells. And see how frightfully high the splashes are where the waves are breaking? I've traveled the waters between here and Lanai many times, William, and this is the worst I've ever seen. I do not have a good feeling about landing here—not under these conditions."

William chuckled. "Well, good luck convincing the Brethren.

Only moments ago I heard both of them request of the captain that they be allowed on the first boat to land."

Inwardly Joseph F. sighed. By the Brethren, he knew William was speaking of Elders Ezra T. Benson and Lorenzo Snow of the Quorum of the Twelve, who were the leaders of this particular mission. Elders Cluff, himself, and Alma L. Smith had been called by President Young to accompany the apostles as interpreters, for it seemed that in the past three or four years, an apostate named Walter Murray Gibson had set himself up as Chief President over the members of the Church in the Islands, had deceived a great many, and was growing daily in apostate power. The two Brethren had been called to put an end to such nonsense, with his, William's, and Alma's aid, of course; but already it looked to Joseph F. as though the adversary was endeavoring to stop them in their work.

It was the 31ST of March, 1864; they had left Salt Lake City March 1ST, and for most of that month of travel the journey had seemed more than treacherous. As their stage had crossed the deserts approaching the Sierra Nevada Mountains they had seen a man shot down in cold blood; much of the narrow and precipitous road over the mountains had been slippery with ice and snow; and the drivers, profane and blasphemous, had deemed great speed on the part of the horses as the safest course to follow. Somehow, though, they had all survived to reach San Francisco and set sail for the Islands, but now as they approached the harbor of Lahaina, this storm was threatening—

"Come, Joseph," Elder Snow called from near midships where the boat was already being loaded, "get your things aboard! We're going ashore!"

With another sigh Joseph F. turned and walked back along the deck. He felt loathe to counsel the Brethren in any way, for they presided, but he also knew the seas were too dangerous for landing, at least for the time being. All his life he had been taught that it was wrong to counsel the Brethren, but on this occasion he could see a danger they could not, and he knew that something must be said.

"Elder Snow," he finally blurted out, "with a view to the size of these swells, may I suggest that we wait awhile before going ashore?"

"Wait? But Joseph, why on earth should we do that? The sea seems no rougher than normal. Besides, Captain Fisher is an experienced seaman. Surely he would not be sending us ashore if there were danger!"

"He's right, boy," the captain blustered as he swaggered up. "I wouldn't! Now, what seems to be the problem?"

Joseph F. looked the old captain straight in the eye. "That freight boat of yours is ungainly, Captain, and with the seas so high and coming together there at the breakwater as they do, I sense great danger."

Abruptly the captain laughed. "You sense danger? And who are you, boy? Are you a pilot, perhaps? Show me your papers, boy, and perhaps I'll give a listen!"

"I have been in these waters before, Captain, and I don't think—"

"There's the truth of it!" the old man growled. "You don't think. That's my job, boy, thinking! That's what captains do! Now, I say there is no danger here—none whatsoever! In fact, I am so certain of it that I intend going ashore myself!" Turning, the captain glared at all who had gathered. "All the rest of you landlubbers who are going ashore, let's be about loading this boat—"

"What is it, Joseph?" Elder Benson had just arrived on the scene. "What's wrong?"

"He senses there might be danger at the breakwater," Elder Snow responded before Joseph F. could reply. "He is encouraging us to wait until the seas go down."

"What does the captain say?"

"That there is no danger. In fact, he seemed very scornful of Joseph's concern and intends to accompany us into the harbor."

Elder Benson looked thoughtful. Finally, though, he clapped his hand on Joseph F.'s shoulder. "Don't worry about it, Joseph. The captain is an old salt and knows what he is about, so I believe we should respect his experience and follow his orders."

"But...Elder Benson, it is too dangerous right now! I'm certain of it!"

"Joseph," Elder Snow admonished quietly, "we're going ashore in this first boat, so stop worrying and get your things together."

Joseph F. looked from one apostle to the other, his eyes pleading that they listen. "But...this freight boat is ungainly, Elder Snow, and will be easily capsized by seas this high. If you insist on going ashore now, then at least allow me to go first and return for you in a better boat."

Elder Benson laughed. "What good would that do, Joseph? If the boat is going to capsize as you believe, then you might perish and we will never get a better boat."

"But at least the rest of you would be safe—"

"A noble gesture, Joseph, but quite unnecessary, I am sure. Now, get your things—"

Joseph F. squared his shoulders. "I am not going on that boat—not under present circumstances!"

Instantly all his traveling companions looked at him in surprise. Joseph F. did not mind the expressions on the faces of Alma and William, but it nearly broke his heart to see that the two apostles were more than unhappy with him. After all, he was very young and they were not, and there was no doubt that they held superior authority and were used to being obeyed—

"Joseph," Elder Snow stated quietly but firmly, "we will all be going to shore together—now!"

His heart racing, for he knew he was standing on very treacherous ground, Joseph thought of the strong impression he was having and stood firm. "I...can't do it, Brethren. I can't! The danger is too great!"

"Come, Joseph—"

"Very well," Joseph F. suddenly capitulated, "I will go with you on one condition. "If you, by the authority of the priesthood of God which you hold, tell me to get into that boat and attempt to land, I will do so, but unless you command me in the authority of the priesthood, I will not do so, because it is not safe to land in a small boat while this storm is raging."

For a moment the two apostles stared at the young man, saying nothing. Then they looked at each other; Elder Snow shrugged his shoulders, and Elder Benson nodded.

"We won't presume to do that, Joseph. You go ahead and stay here on the ship for the time being, and we shall go on. You will have to catch us, though; you understand that?"

Joseph F. nodded, his heart heavy with the near certainty of what was about to happen. "If you will not stay with me," he then pleaded, "will you at least refrain from boarding your luggage and other items?"

Again the two Brethren looked at each other, and this time they both shrugged—as if at the helpless spiritual state of this young upstart who would not listen to authority. "You will be responsible for them?" pressed Elder Snow.

"I will!"

"Very well. We will leave our things with you. But remember, Joseph, we must have them by tonight..."

As Joseph F. stood on the deck watching the freight boat carry his companions and leaders toward the thundering opening through the reef that March day in 1864, it is likely that he never in his life prayed more fervently in behalf of others. Yet the matter was out of his hands, and all he could do was observe from the unsteady deck of the anchored schooner, his heart almost literally in his throat as the heaving sea took charge.

Describing the amazing events that followed, William W. Cluff declared:

> The entrance to the harbor is a very narrow passage between coral reefs, and when the sea is rough, it is very dangerous, on account of the breakers. Where the vessel lay, the sea was not rough, but only presented the appearance of heavy swells rolling to the shore. As we approached the reef it was evident to me that the surf was running higher than we anticipated. I called the captain's attention to the fact. We were running quartering across the waves, and I suggested that we change our course so as to run at right angles with them. He replied that he did not think there was any danger, and our course was not changed. We went but a little further, when a heavy swell struck the boat and carried us before it about fifty yards. When the swell passed it left us in a trough between two huge waves. It was too late to retrieve our error, and we must run our chances. When the second swell struck the boat, it raised the stern so high that the steersman's oar was out of the water, and he lost control of the boat. It rode on the swell a short distance and swung around just as the wave began to break up. We were almost instantly capsized into the dashing, foaming sea.[1]

As Joseph F. watched helplessly from aboard ship, the disaster slowly played itself out. Gradually the passengers and sailors appeared on the sea's surface and gathered around the capsized

Illustration by Robert T. Barrett

boat, climbing onto it or clinging to the edges. Some rescued others; even the captain was rescued by two sailors, though a sack of several hundred silver dollars he gripped tightly in his hands came near to drowning him.

William Cluff continued: " 'Nothing yet had been seen of Brother Snow, although the natives had been swimming and diving in every direction in search of him. We were only about one-fourth of a mile from shore.' "2

At that point some rescuers arrived in a lifeboat, and pulling aboard all the struggling passengers but the captain, some of whom were very nearly drowned, they began to pull toward the captain. As a second lifeboat had put out from shore and was approaching the captain, William Cluff persuaded those manning the first boat to stay in the area and continue their search for the still-missing Lorenzo Snow. After a time one of the native divers, while edging around the boat, felt the top of Elder Snow's head with his bare foot. Retrieving the apparently lifeless body, which had already stiffened, he boosted it into the boat, where all could see that Elder Snow had drowned.

Nevertheless, his companions laid his body over their knees and prayed over him, using their faith and priesthood authority according to the impressions of the Holy Spirit. Meanwhile both the natives and the seamen who were observing declared that such efforts were of no use and that Elder Snow had obviously drowned. Still the brethren labored over their companion's body as the boat sped toward shore, endeavoring to work the water out of his lungs while he lay lifeless upon their knees. Once ashore he was carried to some empty barrels on the sandy beach, and being laid face down upon one, was rolled back and forth a great number of times, thus expelling a great deal more of the water he had swallowed. The brethren then resorted to placing their mouths, one at a time, over that of their companion, blowing air down his throat and sucking it back out again.

For over an hour they labored, and all the while, Joseph F. was watching intently from the heaving deck of the schooner. He could see that someone was in great distress, yet the distance was too great for him to discern the victim's identity. All he could do was wait—wait and continue with his seemingly unending prayers.

Finally the brethren discovered signs of life returning to their companion. After another few moments Lorenzo Snow regained consciousness enough to communicate, whereupon he was taken to the nearby home of a Portuguese man who kindly offered him a bed. There he remained for several days until his strength had returned, during which time the storm abated and Joseph F. was able to come ashore, with the luggage and other personal belongings of his bedraggled companions.

"After all was adjusted and Elder Snow had recovered, the brethren felt more kindly toward this headstrong young missionary whose experience had taught him the dangers of this particular place in the briny deep."3

President Snow declared that after this incident the Lord revealed to him that this young man, Joseph F. Smith, who had refused to get off the vessel that had carried them from San Francisco to Honolulu, and then to the harbor of Lahaina, and get in the whale-boat to go to shore, would some day be the Prophet of God on the earth.4

On the 2ND of April the group continued their journey, being ferried across the channel to the island of Lanai. On the morning of April 3RD they reached Palawai, where Walter Gibson had established the seat of his "kingdom." He received them very coldly, as did the native Saints who had been led to believe that the Brethren were impostors and were not to be trusted.

Lorenzo Snow

CA. *mid 1800's*

Church Archives, The Church of Jesus Christ of Latter-day Saints

229

Gibson, a worldwide adventurer, had come into the Church in Washington, D. C., under the influence of Dr. John Bernheisel, Utah Territory's delegate to Congress. In 1860 he had persuaded Brigham Young to send him on a mission to the islands of the sea and was soon deeply ensconced in the Sandwich Islands. There he:

> mixed LDS teachings with native traditions to win popular support and set himself up on Lanai as the supreme authority. All church property and livestock were registered in his name. Church services were conducted with extraordinary pomp and ceremony. The natives went to work when Gibson rang the bell and quit when he sounded it again. He claimed the right to ordain his own bishops, apostles, and temple priestesses, and sold church offices for personal gain.5
>
> [Gibson] had surrounded himself and his residence with such a holy sacredness in the minds of the natives that they only approached the place on their hands and knees. This was the old customary way in which the natives had been taught to pay their respects to their kings, and the custom had been revived by Mr. Gibson as a means of increasing his personal prestige and power on the islands.6

For the better part of two days Elders Snow and Benson met with Gibson, endeavoring to learn all they could of the Church's affairs and members, with but little success. The apostasy into which Gibson had led his flock was too deep, and neither he nor they would cooperate.

In the meantime, Joseph F. and the other two interpreters were taken on a horseback ride around the valley by Gibson's daughter, who intended to show them the wonderful work her father had done.

Walter Gibson

N.D.

Church Archives, The Church of Jesus Christ of Latter-day Saints

About one-half mile from Mr. Gibson's residence there was a great rock which rose several feet above the ground. Mr. Gibson had a chamber cut in this rock where he had deposited a copy of the Book of Mormon and a number of other things. This he called the cornerstone of a great temple which was to be built. He had set up a framework of poles in circular form around this rock, and these and the rock he had covered with brush. By his appeal to the superstitions of the natives, Mr. Gibson had made them feel that this spot was sacred, and if any person not authorized to do so touched it he would be struck dead, as Uzziah was when he attempted to steady the ark. The daughter, whose name was Talulua, seemed to have great faith in the teachings of her father, and she related to these brethren this story and declared that a hen flying upon this booth immediately fell down dead. She advised the brethren for their own safety not to approach this sacred rock lest sudden destruction come upon them. The two Elders Smith, ignoring her protest, immediately went inside of the covering and examined the rock and came out unharmed while Elder Cluff desecrated the tabooed stone by pulling away the brush covering, exposing the rock. These acts shattered the superstition of the natives who thus saw the stone exposed to rain and sun.[7]

On April 6th and 7th, conference sessions were held. In the first session Gibson spoke, endeavoring to excite the natives against the Brethren and to solidify his own position among them. Joseph F. was asked to speak next, and "when he arose the Spirit of the Lord rested upon him mightily."[8] According to Elder Snow, "It seemed impossible for any man to speak with greater power and demonstration of the Spirit."[9] That afternoon the two apostles spoke, and the conference was adjourned to the next day.

On the 7TH the missionary brethren took up the morning meeting, after which they announced a priesthood meeting for that evening, when the actions of Gibson would be considered. Both legitimately ordained brethren as well as those ordained by Gibson attended, and all listened to the complaints and charges proffered against Gibson.

"He arose and made a harangue repeating nearly all that he had said at the other meetings on the previous day. His reply was given in a bombastic manner and with a display of letters of appointment and recommendations from Brigham Young. To these... he had attached ribbons and seals... to give the document[s] the air of great importance and official significance in the eyes of the simple natives. Holding these papers up so that all could see them, and pointing to them in a dramatic way, he said with emphasis: 'Here is my authority, which I received direct from President Brigham Young. I don't hold myself accountable to these men.'"10

Elder Benson "replied to him and showed how he had departed from the Gospel in making merchandise of the offices of the Priesthood and in introducing pagan superstitions into the Church,"11 as well as many other things which were pertinent to the tragic situation. Still, when a vote was called, only one native elder stood with the Brethren. All the rest remained under the artful spell of Walter Gibson, who was quite naturally elated by the results.

Elder Snow then took the stand "and prophesied that Mr. Gibson would see the time when not one of the Saints would remain with him as a follower."12 Joseph F. Smith next arose and told the congregation that " 'among the scores of Elders who had labored on the islands not one had been so utterly wanting in the spirit and power of the Gospel as to charge the Saints anything for conferring on them the blessings of the Priesthood, until Walter

M. Gibson came, and had the presumption to claim that he had a right to ordain Apostles and High Priests for a price for money.' "13

Elder Benson reiterated these things, pointing out that Gibson's real intent was to build up a great temporal power in the Pacific Islands. He also informed the natives that Joseph F. would be left in charge of the mission when the apostles returned to Utah and that all those who wished to remain in good standing in the Church would need to follow his leadership.

The next day, April 8TH, the Brethren returned to Lahaina on the island of Maui. There they called a council and excommunicated Walter Murray Gibson from the Church and also devised plans on how Joseph F. and his two counselors, Alma L. Smith and William W. Cluff, should conduct the affairs of the mission.

It was eight days before Elders Snow and Benson departed for the mainland. During that time Joseph F. wrote Levira of his need to stay for a time with the Saints in the Islands but promised her that his stay would be brief and that he would soon be with her again.

Once the Brethren had departed with his letter to his wife, Joseph F. and his counselors went to work, visiting the numerous branches and endeavoring to instruct the members in the true doctrines of the Kingdom of God. Gibson also went to work, and with his cunning and natural ability sought to turn the natives against the Brethren. "From the moment of his excommunication, however, he lost ground rapidly among the people. His influence was broken, and many who had gathered at Lanai returned to their homes on the other islands. Daily the members came to Elder Smith and his companions confessing their sins and manifesting a repentant spirit, declaring that they had been deceived by the claims of Mr. Gibson. It was but a short time until all of his following deserted him and pledged their loyalty to the Elders and the Church, thus fulfilling the prophecy of Elder Lorenzo Snow at

William Cluff

CA. *1858*

the conference in Lanai."14

Besides laboring with the members of the Church, for the next six months Joseph F. visited through the Islands looking for a tract of land suitable for a Church headquarters and gathering place. He found tracts available on Kauai, Hawaii, and Oahu, and after serious consideration he made his recommendation to the Brethren that they consider the tract located at Laie, Oahu. This recommendation was later followed.

Joseph F. was also in regular communication with Levira. During the summer he had made arrangements for her to travel to San Francisco, where she stayed "with their Aunt Agnes, Don Carlos Smith's widow; her divorced daughter, Ina Coolbrith; and other relatives."15 In the fall of 1864 Joseph F. received his release and set sail for the mainland, arriving in San Francisco on November 5. There he and Levira spent a glorious month together, visiting with loved ones, sightseeing, attending concerts and other artistic events, celebrating Joseph F.'s twenty-sixth birthday, and doing their best to mend their strained relationship.

Anxious to return to Salt Lake City, however, they left San Francisco in late November. Unfortunately, the further they traveled, the more ill Levira grew. Though it is unlikely that they knew it at the time, she had finally conceived during their month of carefree relaxation together, and it was likely that which was contributing to her illness.

At Dutch Flats Levira felt that she could proceed no further; yet Joseph F. was obligated to report his labors to the Brethren in Salt Lake City. After much discussion they parted—she to return to San Francisco, where she later miscarried, and he to continue on to Salt Lake City, where he ended up boarding with his Aunt Mercy Rachel while he grieved the loss of their unborn child and awaited Levira's ultimate return. Sadly, "Levira remained under a physician's care for another year, complaining of headaches, nervousness, and depression. Ina wrote Joseph F., "It appears to me Levira is something of a hypochondriac.'" 16

In January of 1865, Brigham Young hired Joseph F. to work as a clerk in the Church Historian's Office, assisting Church Historian George A. Smith, who had always been like a father to him, and Assistant Church Historian Wilford Woodruff. Soon Joseph F. had also been elected to the first of what turned out to be seven consecutive terms in the Territorial House of Representatives, and so it seemed to him as if he was finally going to be allowed to stay home and live! Now, if only Levira were there to share that life with him—

APOSTLE AND FAMILY MAN

The upper room of the Church Historian's Office was hot and stuffy. Earlier, twenty-seven-year-old Joseph F. had opened the windows so all might enjoy the cool morning air, but now even the light breeze had died, and those in the room were obviously uncomfortable. For Joseph F., however, it was worse, for as secretary to the group he was feeling great tension to record all that transpired, including all that was said. Added to the tension was the constant motion of his hand and arm: writing as quickly as possible, dipping his quill pen feverishly into the ink bottle, and writing again. He was soaked with perspiration, and so far as he could tell, no relief was in sight.

It was Sunday, the first day of July, 1866, and he had been called the afternoon before to serve as secretary to the weekly council and prayer meeting held by Brigham Young. His usual daily work was conducted in the same building but one floor down, where (under the direction of his uncle, friend, and mentor, George A. Smith) he assisted in keeping the records of the Church. In fact the Historian's Office was also home to George A. and Bathsheba Bigler Smith, his wife, and so Joseph F. was always being thrown into contact with the whole family.

For a moment a slight smile crossed his face, for he could not help thinking of one particular family member, Julina Bigler Lambson, who was his Aunt Bathsheba's niece. Seventeen years old, she had moved in with her aunt and uncle in early April, though at first Joseph F. had hardly noticed her and had paid no outward attention to her whatsoever. After all, he was a married man; Levira was home from California and living with him again, and his life was mostly fulfilled.

But then had come a series of quiet, private meetings with Brigham Young. He had been called to enter into the law of celestial marriage, and everything had changed. Not only had the call been repeatedly issued, but more recently had come the recommendation that he consider the vivacious Julina as candidate for his plural wife.

Finally going to Levira almost in fear and trembling, Joseph F. had presented her with the facts of his calling as well as the identity of the proposed candidate. Levira had known Julina for years and a fond friendship had existed between them, but still Joseph F. had been surprised by his wife's immediate and even enthusiastic response. Most definitely she would support him in this new calling, Levira had informed him, and she was thrilled to add her name to that of President Young's in recommending Julina Lambson as Joseph F.'s plural wife.

So armed, but with even more fear and trembling, Joseph F. had approached the lovely candidate in mid-April, asking if she might be willing to spend a little time with him. To his further surprise Julina had been more than willing; their relationship had quickly progressed, Levira had continued her firm support, and in the Endowment House on May 5TH he and Julina had been sealed eternally, in the presence of his approving first wife, by President Heber C. Kimball.

Moreover, Joseph F. thought as he brushed a pesky fly away

from the paper, he was absolutely happy with Julina. She was a delight in every way, and constantly his heart was made to rejoice because of her.

Of course there was also a terrible sadness in his heart, for things were not going so well with Levira. Since returning from San Francisco she had found their two-room house confining and life in Utah dull. Moreover, they often seemed to be at each other's throats, usually over silly little things but occasionally over the same old issue of serving further missions. Of course Joseph F. had assured her time and again that, after three missions comprising almost the entire last ten years of his life, the Brethren were certain to leave him alone. Still, Levira wouldn't let the issue rest. He argued back sharply, and the arguments left him feeling consumed with guilt. Only, he could not seem to initiate any real changes in himself, and Levira seemed to have little disposition for it. Truly it was as painful an experience as he had ever been through—

With a start, Joseph F. realized that the Brethren were finishing the prayer circle. Somehow, even though his mind had been wandering, he had managed to record the prayer. Now, though, as the men prepared to return to their seats, Joseph F. readied himself for more intense writing. President Young had a habit of talking rapidly in his clipped, New England style, and he had little patience with clerks who could not keep up. Therefore, it was requisite that he pay better attention—

"Hold on," the prophet suddenly declared as he turned to face the group of apostles who had not yet even taken their seats. Every one of them, Joseph F. and his well-poised pen included, waited to see what might be wrong.

"Shall I do as I feel led?" Brigham Young continued as he stepped up behind his chair and took hold of it, his eyes meanwhile boring into Joseph F.'s. "I always feel well to do as the Spirit

constrains me. Brethren, it is in my mind to ordain Brother Joseph
F. Smith to the Apostleship, and to be one of my counselors."

Stunned, Joseph F. could not even react. Him? An apostle?
The very idea seemed preposterous! He was not old enough, he
had nowhere near enough experience, he— Well, there was also
the terrible trouble he was having with Levira. Surely that would
make him far too unworthy...

Each of the men in the room was now responding to
President Young's proposal, one at a time, and each was stating
that such proposal met with their hearty approval. George A.
Smith, John Taylor, Wilford Woodruff, George Q. Cannon—all
were speaking for him. For his own part, however, Joseph F.'s mind
was crying that such a call would mean that the entire balance of
his life would be a mission! How in the world would that affect
poor Levira—

"Joseph," Brigham said as the last of the Brethren concluded
his statement of approval, at the same time pointing to the floor in
front of him, "would you please kneel yourself about there?"

Numbly, almost in a daze, Joseph F. laid down his pen, arose,
stumbled forward, and knelt where he had been instructed.

"Brethren, if you will join me in laying hands upon this good
brother's head, I will be voice."

Quickly the men formed a circle. Joseph F.'s mind was still in
a whirl, but he thought it best to at least try and listen.

"Brother Joseph F. Smith," Brigham Young then prayed,
"we lay our hands upon your head in the name of Jesus Christ, and
by virtue of the Holy Priesthood we ordain you to be an apostle in
The Church of Jesus Christ of Latter-day Saints and to be a special
witness to the nations of the earth. We seal upon your head all the
authority, power, and keys of this holy Apostleship; and we ordain
you to be a counselor to the First Presidency of the Church and
Kingdom of God upon the earth. These blessings we seal upon you

in the name of Jesus Christ and by the authority of the Holy Priesthood. Amen."

The brethren in the circle chorused the "Amen," after which there was a general handshaking and expressions of good luck and good will all around.

"Joseph," President Young then declared, "inasmuch as you are still secretary to this council, you will need to record this action and blessing quickly, before it leaves your memory."

Wondering how he might ever forget such a profound moment, Joseph F. returned to his chair and picked up his pen, which he once again dipped into the bottle of ink.

"Now, Brethren," Brigham Young continued as Joseph began to write, "I do not wish in the recording of this blessing to lead anyone to suppose that this mode is the only way in which such an ordination can be performed. Moreover, I feel to admonish all of you, Joseph F. included, to keep the fact of this ordination strictly to yourselves, for it is not wisdom that it should be revealed publicly for the present time. Is that understood?"

Everyone in the room affirmed their assent, Joseph F. included. And then, still numb with the overwhelming enormity of what had just transpired, and trying at the same time to digest the fact that he must not speak of it with either Levira or Julina, the struggling son of Mary Fielding and Patriarch Hyrum Smith dipped his pen back into the ink and began, once again, to write.

On that July day in 1866, Joseph F. Smith, aged twenty-seven and without any prior interview of which there is record, was ordained an apostle of the Lord Jesus Christ and set apart as a counselor in the First Presidency of The Church of Jesus Christ of Latter-day Saints. Furthermore, he was placed under constraint not to speak of it to anyone.1 What a challenge, especially in light of circumstances then extant in his life!

Joseph F. Smith

CA. 1867–68

Levira had returned from San Francisco to Salt Lake City the previous fall, after almost a year of absence, and both she and Joseph F. had determined to make a new start. Unfortunately the circumstances that had contributed to the difficulties in the first place, including constant ailments on her part and constant missions on his, remained the same. Then, too, Levira had the glamorous city life of San Francisco to hold up in comparison to the rather dull life of Salt Lake City; besides which, the home Joseph F. had rented near the Historian's Office was anything but the stylish California homes to which she had grown accustomed.2 Discontent grew, and with it the distance between the struggling young couple.

Then Julina Lambson, a close friend of Levira's, entered the picture, having moved into the home of George A. and Bathsheba Smith on April 3, 1866. "Joseph F. 'did not lose any time,' Julina recalled. 'He had never paid any special attention to me, and I do not think that he had thought of getting another wife, but President Young advised him and he had told him a number of times, so he thought he should obey.' Julina's mother cautioned, 'Joseph has a wife whom he loves and he is not marrying you for love,' but Julina replied, 'Mother, I love him and if I am good, he will learn to love me. He is the only man I have ever seen that I could love as a husband.'"3

No doubt wondering if having her friend become her sister-wife might actually help strengthen her own marriage, Levira willingly agreed to allow Joseph F. to proceed. Joseph F. and Julina were married by Heber C. Kimball on May 5, with Levira's permission and in her presence. Of that, Joseph F. declared, "My first wife... was intimately acquainted from her childhood with the young lady who became my second wife, and it was with their full knowledge and consent that I entered into plural marriage, my first wife being present as a witness when I took my second wife,

Family Portraits.

Jos. F. Smith

Julina L. Smith

Sarah E. Smith

Edna L. Smith

C.R. Savage. The Smiths' Family Bible, Walken Collection

Top: Joseph Fielding Smith,
Julina Lambson Smith;
Bottom: Sarah Ellen Richards Smith,
and Edna Lambson Smith

and freely gave her consent thereto. Our associations as a family were pleasant and harmonious."4

Several weeks after his marriage to Julina, Joseph F. was invited to speak to a gathering of the Saints in the Tabernacle. Among those in attendance was Wilford Woodruff, who wrote: " 'The power of God was upon him, ...& he manifested the same spirit that was upon his Uncle Joseph Smith the Prophet & his Father Hyram (*sic*) Smith.' "5

It seems likely that Brigham Young was also in attendance and perhaps witnessed the same things as Elder Woodruff, for it was on the following Sunday, July 1, at the conclusion of the prayer circle held in the upper room of the Historian's Office, that he abruptly ordained Joseph F. to the Apostleship and called him as a counselor in his presidency.

It also turned out that Brigham Young's instructions to keep the ordination silent were very strictly observed. "A few days after his ordination as an Apostle and an assistant Counselor to President Brigham Young, President Heber C. Kimball, who was not present on that occasion, approached Elder Smith and said he was impressed that the time would come when he would be called to the Apostleship. Elder Smith said this was rather embarrassing to him, for he was not at liberty to inform President Kimball, who was a Counselor in the First Presidency, that such action had taken place."6

It would be more than a year before Joseph F.'s ordination would be made public, and in the meantime he continued his employment in the Historian's Office and quietly assisted President Young whenever he was asked. Besides his duties in the Historian's Office, Joseph F. "was also engaged in the ordinance work and recording in the Endowment House under the direction of Presidents Brigham Young, Heber C. Kimball, and the Apostles, who were trained in this labor under the Prophet Joseph Smith. He also served as a traveling missionary in various parts of the territory."7 In a marvelous way, his work as assistant historian provided Joseph F. with a true formal education. Until his mother's death, with the exception of a few months in Nauvoo, she had been his only teacher. The few months' education he received after Mary's death ended with his whipping of the schoolmaster and being expelled. "However, being of a studious mind, Joseph F. Smith never let an opportunity to gain knowledge escape him. The early records which he kept all bear strong evidence of this great desire, and it can truthfully be said, that in his later life he stood preeminently among his fellows for the extensive knowledge and wide understanding which he possessed. Especially was this true in relation to his knowledge of the principles of the Gospel and Church organization wherein he was the peer of any of his fellows; none surpassed him in the great fund of information and clear understanding of the revealed religion restored to his Uncle Joseph Smith."8

Late in the fall of 1866 Joseph F. accompanied Brigham Young on an assignment to the northern parts of Utah. Upon his return he discovered, to his great sadness, that Levira had left him and had returned to her mother. No amount of persuading would change her mind, and on June 10, 1867, "they filed a legal separation that ended in a bitter divorce. This was perhaps the most painful period of Joseph F.'s life, for [to him] family was second only to God... and he knew that his quick temper had played a part in the failure of his first marriage. 'My greatest difficulty has been to guard my temper—to keep cool in the moment of excitement or trial,' he later wrote his son Alvin. 'I have always been too quick to resent a wrong, too impatient, or hasty. I hope you will be very careful, my son, on these points. He who can govern himself is greater than he who ruleth a city.'"9

As Joseph F.'s divorce from Levira became more generally

known, the story began to circulate that Levira had left her husband over domestic conflicts brought about by the issue of plural marriage. Apparently some of these rumors, promoted by men who had become his enemies, were vicious enough that Joseph F. felt a need to respond to them. He said, "' It was not until long after [my] second marriage that my first wife was drawn from us, not on account of domestic troubles, but for other causes. In eight years of wedded life we had no children. She constantly complained of ill health and was as constantly under a doctor's care. She concluded to go to California for her health and before going procured a separation. This all occurred previous to 1868. Later Levira A. Smith returned to Utah and then went to St. Louis where she died' "10 on December 18, 1888.

For the young apostle who continued month after month keeping his ordination and calling to the First Presidency bottled inside him, the only relief from Levira's leaving came in the company and presence of Julina, who was growing large with their first child. How the anticipation of that baby's birth must have eased Joseph F.'s sorrow during the long, hot summer of 1867. Finally, on August 14, Julina gave birth to a tiny daughter whom the elated couple named Mercy Josephine. As it turned out, she would be "the first of Joseph F.'s forty-three children (in addition to five adopted children). 'Oh! How good and kind the Lord has been to me and mine in this regard!' he later wrote. 'It seems to me I could endure anything, if only I could feel that all was well with those I love... My children...are all the wealth I have, or cherish as of immortal worth.'"11

This intense love for his children began with Mercy Josephine and continued unabated throughout Joseph F.'s long life. On one occasion he said, "the richest of all my earthly joys is in my precious children. Thank God!"12 And near the end of his life, he fervently declared, "When I look around me, and see my boys and my girls whom the Lord has given to me—and I have succeeded, with his help, to make them tolerably comfortable, and at least respectable in the world—I have reached the treasure of my life, the whole substance that makes life worth living."13 Finally, his son Joseph Fielding declared, " 'His love for his wives and children was boundless in its magnitude and purity. The world did not know—could not possibly know—the depths of his love for them. The wicked and the depraved have ridiculed and maligned him; but the true condition of his family life and wonderful love for his family is beyond comprehension. O how he prayed his children would always be true.' "14

During the October General Conference of 1867, on October 8, Joseph F. was sustained as a member of the Council of the Twelve Apostles, succeeding Amasa M. Lyman. Shortly thereafter, on an assignment with Brigham Young and other brethren to Cache Valley, he met and became acquainted with Charles W. Nibley, "which acquaintance ripened into the most intimate friendship which continued during their entire lives."15 Of this meeting, Elder Nibley later wrote:

> The first time I ever remember seeing Joseph F. Smith was in the then little village of Wellsville, in the year 1867. He was twenty-eight years of age, and had recently been chosen one of the Twelve Apostles. President Brigham Young and company were making a tour of the northern settlements, and the new Apostle, Joseph F. Smith, was among the number. I heard him preach in the old meeting-house in Wellsville, and I remarked at the time what a fine specimen of young manhood he was—strong, powerful, with a beautiful voice, so full of sympathy and affection, so appealing in its tone, that he impressed me, although I was a youth of but eighteen. He was a handsome man.

Charles W. Nibley

N.D.

Church Archives, The Church of Jesus Christ of Latter-day Saints

At that time I was clerking in a little store owned by Father Ira Ames, one of the old Kirtland veterans of the Church. Apostle George A. Smith was one of that company and he was entertained at Brother Ames' home, where I also lived. I recall that at the dinner table, Father Ames asked George A. who of the Smiths this young man Joseph F. was.

George A. replied that he was Hyrum's son; his mother, Mary Fielding Smith.

Brother Ames remarked that he looked like a likely young fellow, and George A. replied in about these words:

"Yes, I think he will be all right. His father and mother left him when he was a child, and we have been looking after him to try to help him along. We first sent him to school, but it was not long before he licked the schoolmaster, and could not go to school. Then we sent him on a mission, and he did pretty well at that. I think he will make good as an Apostle."16

On the first of March, 1868, again at the suggestion of Brigham Young, Joseph F. took another plural wife. She was seventeen-year-old Sarah Ellen Richards, daughter of Willard Richards, former counselor to Brigham Young. Ultimately Sarah and Joseph F. would have eleven children.

Also in 1868, Brigham Young called Abraham O. Smoot "to go to Provo as 'President, Mayor, and Bishop,' with John Taylor as judge, and among others, Wilford Woodruff and Joseph F. Smith as city counselors."17 The brethren were given such "callings" because of a disorderly element in Provo who "delighted in their lawlessness,"18 including cattle rustling and other trespasses. President Young felt that it would be well to send a few faithful men to Provo to correct such wrongs and bring about a reformation.

The brethren, when they had resided in Provo long enough to qualify, became members of the City Council of Provo and through this body and by other means soon brought peace and tranquillity to the troubled community.

While residing in Utah County Joseph F. earned a living by laboring for wages of $2.00 a day in a cabinet shop, which at times was paid in produce. It was not much with which to support two households, and later in life he only half-joked that he may not have been worth even that.

In fact, Joseph F. never managed to accumulate a great deal of worldly goods, and there were many times when he and his family were in dire straits financially. One particular Christmas in his early married life he recalled by saying, "'I owed no man through all those days, and I had to work—I could not be idle.' He said that he and his family labored by 'tugging away with all our mights to keep body and soul together.' It was under those conditions that he went out just before Christmas with the intent of doing something special for his children. He said, 'I wanted something to please them, and to mark the Christmas day from all others—but not a cent to do it with! I walked up and down Main Street, looking into the shop windows... and then slunk out of sight of humanity and sat down and wept like a child, until my poured-out grief relieved my aching heart; and after awhile returned home, as empty as when I left, and played with my children, grateful and happy for them.'"19

It was because of such experiences, and the soul-satisfying consequences of them, that he was able later to declare:

It is very gratifying to parents to be able to respond to the desires of their children, but it is undoubtedly a cruelty to a child to give it everything it asks for. Children may wisely be denied things which even in themselves are harmless.

Our pleasures depend often more upon the qualities of our desires than upon the gratification. A child may be ladened with gifts which afford him little or no pleasure, simply because he has no desire for them. The education then of our desires is one of far-reaching importance to our happiness in life.20

In 1869 Joseph F. returned from Provo to Salt Lake City and again took up his work in the Historian's Office. He continued his service in the territorial legislature and was also elected to the Salt Lake City Council, where he served for several terms. "The effects of his influence in that body are seen today, as it was due to his persistent efforts that Liberty Park was secured and also Pioneer Park. The mayor and some influential members of the City Council were opposed to the securing of these tracts of land for parks as being unnecessary and the monetary outlay connected with them uncalled for. The earnest pleading of Joseph F. Smith won his fellow legislators to his view."21

On January 1, 1869, again following the counsel of President Brigham Young and his counselors, Joseph F. took a third plural wife. She was nineteen-year-old Edna Lambson, youngest sister of his wife Julina. Together Edna and Joseph F. would have ten children. Almost fourteen years later, on December 16, 1883, Joseph F. entered into plural marriage for the fourth time, marrying "twenty-five-year-old Alice Ann Kimball, daughter of Heber C. Kimball, and adopt[ing] her three children. They would have four more of their own. Finally, on January 13, 1884, he married eighteen-year-old Mary Taylor Schwartz, niece of John Taylor. They would have seven children."22

Defending his participation in plural marriage, which he was required to do on numerous occasions and under just as many different and even difficult circumstances, Joseph F. often waxed

Alice Ann Kimball (Smith)
Photo taken before she married
Joseph F. Smith in 1883

CA. 1880

Mary Taylor Schwartz Smith   CA. 1884

Nichols Collection

eloquent. For instance, on one occasion he said, " 'When I entered into celestial marriage with my first wife, ...I solemnly covenanted and agreed, and so did my wife, "to observe and keep" not a part but "all the laws, rites" and &c appertaining unto the new and ever-lasting covenant of matrimony. I understood and still do that the eternity of the marriage covenant includes a plurality of wives, that the marriage of one wife in the new and everlasting covenant is the beginning of the law to be kept in righteousness, and that plural marriage is another part of the same law in the same covenant.' "23

Nevertheless, having and raising children during the nineteenth and early twentieth centuries was fraught with difficulty, and quite often parents faced the trauma and grief that came with losing a child to death. Joseph F. and his wives were required to face this deep sorrow twelve times, and it never grew any easier. The first time, though, was particularly poignant, when on June 6, 1870, he and Julina lost their firstborn child, Mercy Josephine. Expressing his terrible sorrow, Joseph F. wrote:

O God only knows how much I loved my girl, and she the light and the joy of my heart. The morning before she died, after being up with her all night, for I watched her every night, I said to her, 'My little pet did not sleep all night.' She shook her head and replied, 'I'll sleep today, papa.' Oh! how those little words shot through my heart. I knew, though I would not believe, it was another voice, that it meant the sleep of death and she did sleep. And, Oh, the light of my heart went out. The image of heaven graven in my soul was almost departed... Thou wert a heavenly gift directly to my heart of hearts.24

As many times as Joseph F. experienced the death of a child, up to and including the death on January 23, 1918, of his son Hyrum M., who was a member of the Council of the Twelve Apostles, it never ceased being a devastating blow. Joseph F. loved each of his children with a nearly pure and perfect love, and each loss was absolutely soul wrenching.

Nevertheless, he knew with a perfect assurance that, through the atonement of Jesus Christ, each of his dear departed ones would be fine, and he would one day hold them in his lonely arms again. The Lord made certain the oft-grieving father had this knowledge, for at the death of his daughter Ruth, on March 17, 1898, he was given the following glorious revelation: "O my soul! I see my own sweet mother's arms extended welcoming to her embrace the ransomed glorious spirit of my own sweet babe! O my God! For this glorious vision, I thank Thee! And there too are gathered to my Father's mansion all my darling lovely ones; not in infantile helplessness, but in all the power and glory and majesty of sanctified spirits! Full of intelligence, of joy and grace, and truth."25

Joseph F. knew, and with the knowing, rejoiced over his beloved family through all the days of his life.

13

WORDS OF A WITNESS

For a long moment the room in the Shaw Hotel was silent. Though several men sat around or upon the bed, none of them moved, none of them spoke. They all waited, the humid Missouri air leaving the two who were not used to it perspiring uncomfortably. The others, it seemed, didn't notice it. It was Saturday afternoon, September 7, 1878, and though other places were more commodious and less burdened by the heat, they had retired to this room for its relative privacy. Still, if they could hold a conversation uninterrupted, Elder Joseph F. Smith felt, then any personal discomfort would be well worth the price.

He and his companion, Elder Orson Pratt, who was now Church Historian, had left Salt Lake City on September 3RD for Ogden, where they had taken berths on a sleeper car for Omaha. They were on a mission to the East to gather historical material and information relative to the early days of the Church. Two days later, in Omaha, they had transferred to the Kansas City, St. Joseph, and Council Bluffs Line, arriving in Kansas City early in the morning of September 6TH.

It never ceased to amaze him, Joseph F. had thought as he had climbed off the train earlier, how in little more than three days he had crossed the same country it had taken his mother and her large family, himself included, more than two years to traverse. Truly this was a day of miracles!

In Kansas City they had, for thirty cents each, purchased tickets to Independence, where they had visited the site that the Prophet Joseph had dedicated as the place for the temple in the central stake of Zion. They had also visited with Dr. William E. McLellin, an apostle in the early days of the Church, finding him very tall, quite gray, and remarkably well preserved. Despite the darkness of his mind regarding the Restoration he had once been a part of, he had been friendly and had showed the two the site where the printing office had been demolished by the mob, as well as many other places of interest. To Joseph F.'s surprise, it turned out that Dr. McLellin had been baptized there in Jackson County by his own father, Hyrum Smith, back in 1831.

From Independence they had taken the train to Richmond with the intent of meeting with David Whitmer, one of the Three Witnesses to the Book of Mormon. They had spent a restful night at the Shaw Hotel, the best place in town, and now they were with the venerable old Witness himself, hoping to learn a little more about the early days of the Restoration of the Lord's gospel. With them in the room were James R. B. Vancleave, a Chicago reporter; John C. Whitmer, Jacob Whitmer's son; George Schweich, David Whitmer's grandson; Philander Page, son of Hiram Page; and a Mr. W. W. Warner. Still, all eyes were upon old Father Whitmer, for it was he who had seen—

"Well," the old man suddenly chuckled, "I am wonderfully pleased to see you, Orson. But you have grown so fat and stout that I should never have known you. In my mind you should still be a slender, bashful, timid boy."

"Sometimes I think of myself that way," Orson Pratt replied easily. "But then my rheumatism strikes, and I am reminded that I know better."

"I understand completely. I can scarcely imagine that I have passed my three-score-and-ten and am now seventy and three years old. Well," he then declared, abruptly changing the subject, "what do you think of our big blow?"

David Whitmer was speaking of the tornado that had ripped through Richmond not very long before, doing terrible damage. Joseph F. and Elder Pratt had given themselves a walking tour first thing that morning and had been amazed by the destruction. The debris of wrecked houses, fences, sidewalks, and trees strewing the face of the ground bore mute evidence of the storm's power and fury. Scarcely a tree had been left standing, much less a shed or fence. The bark had even been stripped from the few trees still standing, while those uprooted had been twisted, twirled, and hurled to bits. Yet there were other, stranger events: a giant old oak that had been uprooted and carefully let down two hundred yards away while its neighbors had remained untouched; a woman knocked down by an immense beam blown from a house had been saved by a child who had easily lifted one end of it to rescue the woman; or the water and mud being sucked up from a nearby lake clean down to the bedrock, destroying thousands of fish and leaving a dry pathway from shore to shore. It had occurred to Joseph F., on hearing the account, that a similar means might have been used by the Lord in parting the Red Sea for Israel or the Jordan for Elijah to pass over dry shod.

So, yes, it had indeed been quite a blow.

"This gold ring," George Schweich declared as he held up his hand, "was sucked right off my finger and was later found in the ruins of a house some one hundred feet distant. The wind also took some money off my bureau and strewed it, coin by coin, in a line leading almost directly to where my ring was found."

"Yes, and our mechanic shop," David Whitmer added, "which

was built over the spot where stood the jail in which your brother Parley and others were incarcerated in 1838 and '39 was utterly destroyed!"

"So, the old jail is gone?"

"Yes, Orson, these many years. And now my shop is destroyed in its place, as was my barn and my home—all save the room in which the record was kept."

"You are referring to the manuscript copy of the Book of Mormon?"

"That is correct. It is in Oliver's handwriting, and Oliver gave it to me to keep."

"Would you consider parting with it?" Joseph F. asked quietly.

David Whitmer shook his head. "No, Brother Smith, I would not! Oliver charged me to keep it, and Joseph said my father's house should keep the records. I consider these things sacred and would not barter them for money."

"We would not offer you money in the light of bartering for the manuscript," Joseph F. stated, "but we would like to see it preserved in some manner where it would be safe from casualties and from the caprice of men, in some institution that will not die as a man does."

"That is all right," David Whitmer responded. "While camping around here in a tent and all my effects exposed to the weather following our big blow, everything in the trunk where the manuscript was kept became mouldy, but that was preserved, not even being discolored."

"Do you think," pressed Philander Page, son of Hiram Page, one of the Eight Witnesses, "that the Almighty cannot take care of his own?"

It was a fairly stinging rebuke, and in consequence Joseph F. grew silent. He knew absolutely of the Lord's goodness and abilities to bless and preserve his righteous children, but he could see that

Joseph F. Smith

Church Archives, The Church of Jesus Christ of Latter-day Saints

CA. *1874*

these people placed even greater reverence on what they considered a sacred relic. After further questioning by Elder Pratt, it became obvious that they were not only imbued with the idea and faith that the manuscript was under the immediate protection of the Almighty, safe from all possible contingencies, but they also held to the belief that it was a source of protection to the place or house in which it might be kept—with the possessor having legitimate right to that same divine protection.

In short, they would not part with it for love nor money. Joseph F., therefore, obtained the next best thing: the promise that he and Elder Pratt could at least see the manuscript before their departure.

"Very well, David," Orson Pratt stated after this had been agreed upon, "let us, then, change subjects. Can you tell the date of the restoration of the Apostleship by Peter, James, and John?"

Abruptly the atmosphere in the room lost its hostility, and once again all eyes were upon the aging witness, David Whitmer—

Until 1874 Joseph F., though serving as an apostle, continued his employment in the Historian's Office and his labors in the Endowment House, as well as his associations with his loving wives and growing children. He was also farming a homestead he had taken up, endeavoring to make a living from it. In the October Conference of 1873, however, he was called to leave everything and preside over the European Mission. Of this experience he said:

I was called on a mission after I had served four years on a homestead and it was only necessary for me to remain one more year to prove up and get my title to the land; but President Young said he wanted me to go to Europe on a mission, to take charge of the mission there. I did not say to him, "Brother Brigham, I cannot go; I have got a

homestead on my hands, and if I go I will forfeit it." I said
to Brother Brigham, "All right, President Young; whenever
you want me to go I will go; I am on hand to obey the call
of my file leader." And I went. I lost the homestead, and yet
I never complained about it; I never charged Brother
Brigham with having robbed me because of this. I felt that
I was engaged in a bigger work than securing 160 acres of
land. I was sent to declare the message of salvation to the
nations of the earth... and I did not stop to consider myself
and my little personal rights and privileges; I went as I was
called, and God sustained and blessed me in it.1

Early in 1874 he once again took leave of those he loved so dearly
and traveled to England, where he took up the reins of his presidency. Shortly after his arrival he addressed his fellow laborers,
declaring:

As bearers and sowers of the precious seed of eternal life,
let our lives correspond with our professions, our words be
consonant with the truth we bear, and our acts agreeable to
the revealed will of God; for without these fruits do follow
in some degree our professions of faith, we, as Elders or
Saints, are only obstacles to the progress of the work,
stumbling-blocks in the way of the practically-minded
observer, and are not only not enhancing the prospects of
salvation of others, but are jeopardizing our own.2

As people throughout the Church were beginning to discover,
Joseph F.'s strong exhortations perfectly matched the demands he
placed upon himself. "Never did he ask of anyone the performance
of any duty which he considered too difficult for himself. He was
known as an earnest and forceful speaker and an able defender of

the faith. No duty needing attention ever escaped his careful [scrutiny], and he endeared himself to the members of the Church and won their hearts in all of the missions which it was his privilege to visit. These friendships thus formed, as well as those formed on his previous missions, remained and became stronger even to the end of life."[3]

People also learned much from watching the way Joseph F. approached his labors, both personal and public. "Always clean and neat, [he] was extremely methodical, and nothing annoyed him more than disorder. He noted the date of receipt of every letter before carefully filing it away. Every piece of clothing, document or article—even something as common as a nail—had its proper place. According to Bishop Charles W. Nibley, even in the dark he could go to a cupboard, closet, or drawer and put his hand unerringly on the item he wanted, for he knew exactly where to find it. 'He was the most methodical in all his work of any person I ever knew.'... A related habit was his frugality. His youth had taught him to make the most of meager resources, a habit that served him well as the father of a large family and also as"[4] one who had been called to preside over large areas of the Church.

On the other hand, "despite a life marked by tribulation, persecution, and heavy responsibilities, he was cheerful and light-hearted. He had a marked sense of humor, greatly relished a good story or joke (but never tolerated the slightest shade of vulgarity), and encouraged his wives and children to share humorous jokes and stories. As a result, his home was filled with laughter...

" 'At the core of his personality and talents was a deep spirituality that gave color and life to all he did. And that spirituality was never more evident than when he bore testimony of the reality and divinity of God and of the saving effect of the principles of the gospel.' "[5]

Joseph F.'s responsibilities as president of the European

Mission were many and varied. "Conditions in the mission were trying. The Saints were poor, and few paid tithing. Joseph F. had only a couple dozen missionaries to cover all of England, and he rarely received counsel from Brigham Young."6 In addition to touring the several missions on the Continent and holding conferences in all the districts of the British Isles, he was editor-in-chief of the *Millennial Star* and supervised all emigration to Utah. "For instance, he saw 150 off on the steamship Wyoming on October 14, 1874... Elder Smith reported this was the sixth immigration company to leave Liverpool in 1874, totaling '1996 souls.'"7

Joseph F. was also responsible for the spiritual well-being of the missionaries, constantly building them up and encouraging them, and occasionally administering discipline when circumstances demanded it. After sending an elder home because of serious moral transgression, he reflected "gratefully on the important role of his own chaste ideals, [writing] eloquently: 'O! how I thank my God for his protecting, watchful care which has been over me thus far through life; Preserving me from the deadly sins of the world, and many thousand times from my own weaknesses and proneness to err: Snatching me several times in my life from the brink of moral ruin, which to me would have been more intolerable than lingering death. That man who can...stand erect in honest pride of truth, morally and sexually pure from his youth up, is in the world unlooked for, and would be disbelieved. But such an one who is considered a moral anomaly alone can feel how glorious a thing it is, to look back upon a clean, unspotted record of the past.'"8

Often during his tenure as mission president, Joseph F.'s thoughts were drawn to his home and family. Well he knew that his wives and little children were struggling along on meager help. Yet he also knew that they were "living in peace as a happy family, and assisting each other in their daily cares, in the spirit of true love and sisterhood. This condition was astonishing to the world, but of common occurrence among the families of the Latter-day Saints, where love of truth and the spirit of true virtue prevailed to the exclusion of the selfishness and immorality so common among families in the world."9

Still, there were days of terrible homesickness. On his birthday in 1874 he wrote:

The day was cold, bleak and dreary, a fit and proper anniversary of the dark and trying day of my birth; When my father [Hyrum] and his brother [Joseph] were confined in a dungeon for the gospel's sake and the saints were being driven from their homes in Missouri by a merciless mob. The brightest sunshine of my soul has never thoroughly dispelled the darkening shadows cast upon it by the lowering gloom of that period.

Yet the merciful hand of God and his kindliest providences have ever been extended visibly toward me, even from my childhood, and my days grow better and better thru humility and the pursuit of wisdom and happiness in the kingdom of God; The objects of my life becoming more apparent as time advances and experience grows. Those objects being the proclamation of the gospel, or the establishment of the kingdom of God on the earth; The salvation of souls, and most important of which to me— that of myself and family.10

"'I had peculiar feelings,' he wrote after receiving a letter and pictures from home, 'went into my room and wept and prayed and wept again and felt relieved.'"11 In a letter written to Julina in 1874, he wrote:

It is now bed time; I have been studying all day but just as I was about to lay aside my books, I came upon a synopsis of a discourse by the Prophet Joseph Smith in which I read the following words: "The Lord takes many away even in infancy that they may escape the envy of man and the sorrows and evils of this present world; they were too pure, too lovely, to live on earth; therefore, if rightly considered, instead of mourning we have reason to rejoice as they are delivered from evil, and we shall soon have them again."

Of course my thoughts at once turned upon my little angel babies, my "Dodo," (Josephine) and Ella, and as usual, ran high, deeply moving me with affectionate reminiscences; my fondest recollections and hopes of my precious "first-born" rushed in upon my mind until almost in a moment I had three happy years again lived through.

O how happy, from the low front room of her natal place into the new house! The quiet evenings; the new cradle, its rosy, beauteous innocent treasure calmly sleeping; its rapid development to prattling lovely engaging attractiveness each moment twining itself more closely to the heart until an angel she stood, the brightest, purest heavenly light that ever shown upon my dreary path.

The glory of my home, the joy of my heart!

Then, alas; but it cannot be told; no power can tell the history of this grief. O, how those prophetical little words—"I'll sleep today, papa," rang through the empty caverns of my soul at the terrible thought forced upon it by them, of parting from her—losing my treasure! Losing her!

Just then the postman rapped and I received the enclosed copy of "Dodo's" photograph for which I have waited for three months. I could no longer contain my feelings, and gave way for relief in mingled feelings of joy and sorrow! Sorrow? No! Lose her? My priceless treasure, jewel! whose angel form lighted the darkness of the world to me; whose image is enshrined in the very center of my heart, radiating to my soul! Lose my first born, my "Dodo?" No! No! She is mine the gift of God! Too pure, too lovely to live on earth and has gone with her little sister back to their glorious home with God! Lose them, my two darling babies? Ah! Not while those bright stars of innocence, purity and love, shine for me, to guide my erring footsteps back to their bright home!

O I will come, my "Dodo," for thou art still the soul of joy and happiness to me. The rosy dawning of my brightest day that gave me hope and filled my soul with strength and made me what I am in God! In thee I loved my Father more and sought Him nearer to give Him gratitude for thee! I only ask for time to watch with care the full development of all my precious little gifts for they are one and all more dear than temporal life or liberty. I love them no less because I loved thee more, and it is for them and their mothers under God, I live, or shrink from coming now.12

Again from his journal, Joseph F. added: "'I live in the pure unsullied love of my darling children. My wives can trust me. I would not abuse their love and confidence for all I have or am... O! My father preserve me in thy holy keeping from the power of temptation I could not resist, and forgive my past foolish inclinations and desires and be thou my master, my head, by thy spirit control me ever.'"13

In the fall of 1875 Joseph F. received word of the death of George A. Smith—one of the early converts to the Church and "the youngest man ever sustained as an Apostle in this dispensation, being 22 years of age. He was called to be first counselor to President Brigham Young, Oct. 6, 1868. He was well known for his remarkable memory and his thorough understanding of Gospel principles and the history of the Church. He was greatly loved by the Prophet Joseph Smith and was looked upon by the Smiths in Utah as their counselor and leader."14

This news was a severe blow to Joseph F., who had looked upon George A. Smith as his closest friend and advisor among the General Authorities of the Church. He grieved for weeks, "unable even to write his regular editorial for the *Millennial Star*. 'I cannot tell with what terrible weight this melancholy intelligence fell upon my soul,' he wrote. 'My whole being seems oppressed with a sense of loneliness... O! how I loved him! How I honor his memory!'"15

Shortly thereafter Joseph F. was released and allowed to return home. "Though he had been gone less than two years, conditions in Utah had changed dramatically. Utah's economy had not recovered from the depression of 1873, and United Orders were being established throughout the territory. Joseph F. was appointed to preside over the Saints in Davis County and was elected president of the Davis County Cooperative Company, which consisted of several small cooperatives, including a tannery, shoe shop, cattle, horse and sheep herds, and other projects. In addition, he worked in the Endowment House, served on the Salt Lake City Council, and supervised the calling of families to settle Arizona."16 This was his work for the next year and a half.

The April conference of 1877 was held in St. George in conjunction with the dedication of the St. George Temple—the first temple to be completed since Nauvoo. On the second day of that conference, Joseph F. was once again called to " 'take charge of the European Mission, with headquarters in Liverpool.' Elders Alma

L. Smith, a former missionary companion in Hawaii, and Charles W. Nibley, were appointed to accompany him."17

Reaching Liverpool on May 27, this time Joseph F. "had with him his wife Sarah and her son Joseph Richards, about four years old."18 He "found the... [m]ission 'flat as a pancake, broke entirely.' There was no money from the Perpetual Emigrating Fund to help the Saints emigrate, and tithing had dropped to half of the 1875 level. Despite his lumbago and eyestrain, [Joseph F.] maintained a steady, demanding pace to inspire proselyting among the missionaries and faithful living among the Saints."19

It was the intention of President Brigham Young that Joseph F. should remain in Europe for several years, hence the reason for him taking with him his wife and son, but shortly after the arrival in August of Elder Orson Pratt "to consult with British pheneticists and shorthand experts to develop a new system of spelling and to publish the standard works, primers, and grammars"20 word was received of the death of President Brigham Young, who had passed away August 29, 1877. Both apostles returned immediately to Salt Lake City and entered with their brethren of the Quorum of the Twelve into directing the affairs of the Church. This interim period without a First Presidency was to continue for the next three years.

It was during this period, in September of 1878, that Joseph F. was asked to go east on a mission in company with Elder Orson Pratt, who had been appointed Church Historian following the death of George A. Smith. They were to visit Church historic sites and to interview former Church leaders with an eye to filling in more of the details of early Church history. One of these interviews, detailed at the beginning of this chapter, was with David Whitmer.

[David Whitmer], one of the Three Witnesses to the Book of Mormon, was born Jan. 7, 1805, at a small trading

Joseph F. Smith (center)
with European missionaries
(from the left): John H. Smith,
E.G. Freeman, Milton H. Hardy
and Francis M. Lyman.

CA. 1875

Church Archives, The Church of Jesus Christ of Latter-day Saints

post, near Harrisburg, Pennsylvania. While yet an infant his father, who served his country through the revolutionary war, removed with his family to western New York and settled on a farm in Ontario county, near Watkin's Glen— at a point midway between the northern extremities of Cayuga and Seneca lakes, two miles from Waterloo, seven from Geneva, and twenty-five from Palmyra—where David lived until the year 1831. The father, who was a hard-working, God-fearing man, was a strict Presbyterian and brought his children up with rigid sectarian discipline. Besides a daughter who married Oliver Cowdery, there were five sons— Peter, Jacob, John, David and Christian— who helped their father on his farm until they had arrived at the age of manhood.21

Because David Whitmer's testimony of the Book of Mormon is so germane to the history and factuality of The Church of Jesus Christ of Latter-day Saints, we will quote verbatim from the existing records. Brother Whitmer granted the visiting apostles two major interviews. Joseph F. and Orson Pratt each made a separate record, perhaps more than once, and so the following integrates certain of the various details together.

   " 'On Saturday morning, Sept. 7 (1878), we met Mr. David Whitmer (at Richmond, Ray county, Mo.), the last remaining one of the Three Witnesses of the Book of Mormon. He is a good-sized man, 73 years of age last January, and well preserved. He is close shaven, his hair perfectly white, and rather thin; he has a large head and a very pleasant, manly countenance that one would readily perceive to be an index to a conscientious, honest heart... After a few moments' conversation he excused himself, saying he would return again to see us. This meeting was in the barroom of the hotel. When he called again he was in company with Col. Childs, a

THE THREE WITNESSES.

THE HILL CUMORAH

David Whitmer,
Oliver Cowdery
and Martin Harris

Late nineteenth century print

Church Archives, The Church of Jesus Christ of Latter-day Saints

middle aged man, and a resident of the place. By invitation we accompanied them to Mr. Whitmer's office, where we were introduced to Mr. David J. Whitmer (eldest son of David), Mr. George Schweich (grandson of the old gentleman), Mr. John C. Whitmer (son of Jacob Whitmer), Col. James W. Black, of Richmond, and several others."22

Another interview later in the day was conducted in the visiting apostles' hotel room. David Whitmer brought with him "James R. B. Vancleave, a fine looking, intelligent, young newspaper man, of Chicago. George Schweich, John C. Whitmer, W. W. Warner and another person whose name [the brethren] did not learn."23 There David Whitmer apologized for not inviting the brethren to his home, after which the interview continued.

Elder Orson Pratt: Do you remember what time you saw the plates?

David Whitmer: It was in June, 1829, the latter part of the month, and the Eight Witnesses saw them, I think, the next day or the day after (i.e. one or two days after). Joseph showed them the plates himself, but the angel showed us (the Three Witnesses) the plates, as I suppose to fulfill the words of the book itself. Martin Harris was not with us at this time; he obtained a view of them afterwards (the same day). Joseph, Oliver and myself were together when I saw them. We not only saw the plates of the Book of Mormon, but also the brass plates, the plates of the Book of Ether, the plates containing the records of the wickedness and secret combinations of the people of the world down to the time of their being engraved, and many other plates. The fact is, it was just as though Joseph, Oliver and I were sitting just here on a log, when we were overshadowed by a light. It was not like the light of the sun, nor like that of a

Orson Pratt

CA. *about 1879*

Church Archives, The Church of Jesus Christ of Latter-day Saints

fire, but more glorious and beautiful. It extended away round us, I cannot tell how far, but in the midst of this light about as far off as he sits (pointing to John C. Whitmer, sitting a few feet from him), there appeared, as it were, a table with many records or plates upon it, besides the plates of the Book of Mormon, also the sword of Laban, the directors [i.e., the ball with spindles which Lehi had], and the interpreters. I saw them just as plain as I see this bed (striking the bed beside him with his hand), and I heard the voice of the Lord, as distinctly as I ever heard anything in my life, declaring that the records of the plates of the Book of Mormon were translated by the gift and power of God.

Elder Orson Pratt: Did you see the angel this time?

David Whitmer: Yes, he stood before us. Our testimony as recorded in the Book of Mormon is strictly and absolutely true, just as it is there written. Before I knew Joseph, I had heard about him and the plates from persons who declared they knew he had them, and swore they would get them from him and that he had promised them an interest in them when he should get them. The fact is he could not, for they were not to be made merchandise of, nor to be a matter of profit to anyone—they were strictly for sacred purposes. When Oliver Cowdery went to Pennsylvania, he promised to write me what he should learn about these matters, which he did. He wrote me that Joseph had told him his (Oliver's) secret thoughts, and all he had meditated about going to see him, which no man on earth knew, as he supposed, but himself, and so he stopped to write for Joseph. Soon after this, Joseph sent for me (Whitmer) to come to Harmony to get him and Oliver and bring them to my father's house.

I did not know what to do, I was pressed with my work. I had some twenty acres to plow, so I concluded I would finish plowing and then go. I got up one morning to go to work as usual, and on going to the field, found between five and seven acres of my ground had been plowed during the night. I don't know who did it; but it was done just as I would have done it myself, and the plow was left standing in the furrow. This enabled me to start sooner. When I arrived at Harmony, Joseph and Oliver were coming toward me, and met me some distance from the house. Oliver told me that Joseph had informed him when I started from home, where I had stopped the first night, how I read the sign at the tavern, where I stopped the next night, etc., and that I would be there that day before dinner, and this was why they had come out to meet me; all of which was exactly as Joseph had told Oliver, at which I was greatly astonished.

When I was returning to Fayette, with Joseph and Oliver, all of us riding in the wagon, Oliver and I on an old-fashioned wooden spring seat and Joseph behind us — when traveling along in a clear open place, a very pleasant, nice-looking old man suddenly appeared by the side of our wagon and saluted us with, "good morning, it is very warm," at the same time wiping his face or forehead with his hand. We returned the salutation, and, by a sign from Joseph, I invited him to ride if he was going our way. But he said very pleasantly, "No, I am going to Cumorah." This name was something new to me, I did not know what Cumorah meant. We all gazed at him and at each other, and as I looked around inquiringly of Joseph, the old man instantly disappeared, so that I did not see him again.

Joseph F. Smith: Did you notice his appearance?

David Whitmer: I should think I did. He was, I should
think, about five feet eight or nine inches tall and heavy
set, about such a man as James Vancleave there, but heavier;
his face was as large; he was dressed in a suit of brown
woolen clothes, his hair and beard were white, like Brother
Pratt's, but his beard was not so heavy. I also remember
that he had on his back a sort of knapsack with something
in, shaped like a book. It was the messenger who had the
plates, who had taken them from Joseph just prior to our
starting from Harmony.

Soon after our arrival home, I saw something which led
me to the belief that the plates were placed or concealed in
my father's barn. I frankly asked Joseph if my supposition
was right, and he told me it was. Some time after this, my
mother was going to milk the cows, when she was met out
near the yard by the same old man (judging by her description
of him), who said to her: "You have been very faithful and
diligent in your labors, but you are tired because of the
increase in your toil; it is proper, therefore, that you should
receive a witness that your faith may be strengthened."
Thereupon he showed her the plates. My father and mother
had a large family of their own, the addition to it, therefore, of Joseph, his wife Emma and Oliver very greatly
increased the toil and anxiety of my mother. And although
she had never complained she had sometimes felt that her
labor was too much, or at least she was perhaps beginning
to feel so. This circumstance, however, completely
removed all such feelings and nerved her up for her
increased responsibilities.

I, as well as all of my father's family, Smith's wife,
Oliver Cowdery and Martin Harris, were present during
the translation. The translation was by Smith, and the

manner as follows: He had two small stones of a chocolate color, nearly egg shape, and perfectly smooth, but not transparent, called interpreters, which were given him with the plates. He did not use the plates in the translation, but would hold the interpreters to his eyes and cover his face with a hat, excluding all light, and before his eyes would appear what seemed to be parchment, on which would appear the characters of the plates in a line at the top, and immediately below would appear the translation, in English, which Smith would read to his scribe, who wrote it down exactly as it fell from his lips. The scribe would then read the sentence written, and if any mistake had been made, the characters would remain visible to Smith until corrected, when they faded from sight to be replaced by another line. The translation at my father's occupied about one month, that is from June 1 to July 1, 1829.24

Orson Pratt: Have you any idea when the [sealed portion of the] records will be brought forth?

David Whitmer: When we see things in the Spirit and by the power of God they seem to be right here present. The signs of the times indicate the near approach of the coming forth of the other plates, but when it will be, I cannot tell. The Three Nephites are at work among the lost tribes and elsewhere. John the Revelator is at work, and I believe the time will come suddenly, before we are prepared for it.

Orson Pratt: Have you in your possession the original manuscript of the Book of Mormon?

David Whitmer: I have; [the pages] are in Oliver Cowdery's handwriting. He placed them in my care at his death, and charged me to preserve them as long as I lived;

they are safe and well preserved.

Joseph F. Smith: What will be done with them at your death?

David Whitmer: I will leave them to my nephew, David Whitmer, son of my brother Jacob, and my name-sake.

Orson Pratt: Would you not part with them to a purchaser?

David Whitmer: No, Oliver charged me to keep them, and Joseph said my father's house should keep the records. I consider these things sacred, and would not part with nor barter them for money.

Joseph F. Smith: We would not offer you money in the light of bartering for the manuscript, but we would like to see them preserved in some manner where they would be safe from casualties and from the caprices of men, in some institution that will not die as man does.

David Whitmer: That is all right. While camping around here in a tent, all my effects exposed to the weather, everything in the trunk where the manuscripts were kept became mouldy, etc., but they were preserved, not even being discolored. (We supposed his camping in a tent, etc., had reference to his circumstances after the cyclone, in June last.) The room in which the manuscripts were kept, was the only part of the house which was not demolished, and even the ceiling of that room was but little impaired. "Do you think," said Phil. Page, a son of Hiram Page, one of the Eight Witnesses, "that the Almighty cannot take care of His own?!"

Next day (Sunday, Sept. 8TH) Mr. Whitmer invited us to his house, where, in the presence of David Whitmer, Esq. (son of Jacob), Philander Page, James R. B. Vancleave, David J. Whitmer (son of David the Witness), George

Schweich (grandson of David), Colonel Childs and others, David Whitmer brought out the manuscripts of the Book of Mormon. We examined them closely and those who knew the handwriting pronounced the whole of them, excepting comparatively a few pages, to be in the handwriting of Oliver Cowdery. It was thought that these few pages were in the handwriting of Emma Smith and John and Christian Whitmer. We found that the names of the eleven Witnesses were, however, subscribed in the handwriting of Oliver Cowdery. When the question was asked Mr. Whitmer if he and the other witnesses did or did not sign the testimonies themselves, Mr. Whitmer replied that each signed his own name.

Then where are the original signatures?

David Whitmer: I don't know, I suppose Oliver copied them, but this I know is an exact copy... Joseph F. Smith suggested that perhaps there were two copies of the manuscripts, but Mr. Whitmer replied that, according to the best of his knowledge, there never was but the one copy.25

Herein, of course, he is evidently uninformed. Elder Orson Pratt again felt closely after the subject of procuring the manuscript, but we found that nothing would move him on this point. The whole Whitmer family are deeply impressed with the sacredness of this relic. And so thoroughly imbued are they with the idea and faith that it is under the immediate protection of the Almighty, that in their estimation, not only are the manuscripts themselves safe from all possible contingencies, but that they are a source of protection to the place or house in which they may be kept, and, it may be to those who have possession of them.26

David Whitmer lived another ten years following the visit of Elders Smith and Pratt, several times publicly repeating, and even having his testimony published. Following his interview with David Whitmer, Joseph F. wrote:

> I always knew that David Whitmer's testimony was true, since I received the witness myself, but now I know that David Whitmer is as conscious of the truth of that testimony as he is of his own existence. No man can hear him tell his experience in these matters but he can see and sense that he is conscientiously telling the truth of his own knowledge... David remarked, "Many things have been revealed which were designed only for the Church, and which the world cannot comprehend, but the Book of Mormon and those testimonies were to go to all the world." I repeated, "Yes, and we have sent it to the Danes, the Swedes, the Spanish, the Italians, the French, the Germans, and to the islands of the sea, in fulfillment of that great design. So we have not been idle, and it is also translated into the language of the East Indians." In parting, he said to Brother Pratt, "I may never meet you again, in the flesh, so farewell."[27]

17

EXILED FOR THE TRUTH

"Joseph?" Julina's voice was filled with concern. "Joseph, what is it? What is wrong?"

Looking away from his brother-in-law Albert W. Davis and toward his wife, Joseph F. could not hide the sorrow that was filling his heart or the tears that were already stinging his eyes. Neither, for that matter, could Albert, who had brought him the news.

This business of being in exile was hard—perhaps as hard as anything he had ever been called upon to bear. For though he was in hiding from literally hundreds of federal marshals and their spies who were seeking to arrest and imprison him for practicing plural marriage; and though he had been driven from one hiding camp to another in the mountains before finally being sent by President Taylor to the islands of the sea, bringing with him for safekeeping the records of the Endowment House in Salt Lake City; it was not the agents of the government that troubled him. Those Joseph F. had truly been exiled from were his dear wives and adorable children.

For a moment he allowed himself to think of his patient, courageous wives—Sarah, Edna, Alice Ann, Mary, and of course dear Julina, who had been urged by President Taylor to accompany him to Oahu more than a year before. She had brought along her sweet Julina Clarissa, still less than two years old and affectionately nicknamed "Baby," but had been forced to leave behind in the care of her sister-wives her daughters Mamie and Donnie and her sons Joseph Fielding, David Asael, and George Carlos. The separation was a terrible test of any mother's heart, and Joseph F. knew her "pets" were constantly on Julina's mind. So, too, was her anxiety over how soon they might be able to return home to the valleys of the mountains.

However, back home the "Raid" against polygamists had not let up, even a little, but was being pressed by government agents and officers with ever greater ferocity. As a "much-married" member of the Church's First Presidency, Joseph F. and his wives were highly visible targets. The previous February one Sam Gilson and three other deputy marshals had made a raid on his houses, finding his Aunt Melissa Smith and Albert J. Davis at home and subpoenaing them to appear before the grand jury. Albert had refused to give his name and so was subpoenaed as "John Doe," and neither he nor Aunt Melissa had appeared.

For Joseph F., however, the worst aspect of that raid was that five of his children had also been at home: three of Julina's and one each of Sarah's and Edna's. The deputies had also interrogated them, but all had refused to give the deputies their names, telling them it was "none of their business." In spite of his present grief, Joseph F. smiled a little at the spunk his wee ones had displayed. Of course there had been many raids since that one, and well and long would his wives and children remember the abuse and threats they had been forced to hear.

He did not fear prison, not at all! Many of the Lord's servants had suffered prison through the years and the ages; yes, and worse than prison—his own dear father and uncle included! With the

Apostle Paul, he was willing to suffer all things for the Lord's sake and to "glory in tribulations also: knowing that tribulation worketh patience; And patience, experience; and experience, hope: And hope maketh not ashamed; because the love of God is shed abroad in our hearts by the Holy Ghost which is given unto us."

Nevertheless, these were frightening times for Joseph F. and his families. It was them he worried about, not himself. Often he felt compelled to turn his dear ones over to the Lord, which he had done again and again, pleading with all the fervor of his being for their safety and protection. Unfortunately, that didn't stop the worry and the fear —

"Please, Joseph." Julina was coming toward them now, her hand at her throat and her face stricken with fear. "Why are you both looking so sad? What terrible news has Albert brought us?"

It was nearing dark on the Church plantation in Laie, where he and Julina were staying as "Mr. and Mrs. Speight." A soft breeze had picked up, coming out of the west, and the luxuriant tropical growth was swaying with it. A quarter of a mile away the ocean waves were beating their steady tattoo on the volcanic shore, and even from this distance their muted thunder was audible. Everything seemed so peaceful and serene, Joseph F. was thinking. But how could that be, when elsewhere there was such great tragedy, such terrible sorrow—

"Your children are all right, Julina."

It was Albert Davis who had spoken, and now Julina drew to a halt, obviously thinking that he meant all of Joseph F.'s children and not just her own. "Then, is it one of your children, Albert? Has one of them died?"

"No."

"Is... Is it Mother?"

"It is not your mother, my dearest," Joseph F. said softly as he took his wife into his arms, his own tears of sorrow and grief streaking his cheeks. "It is our little Robin; he has passed away!"

"O dear God, no!" Julina's voice was strained, almost strangled. "Not Robert! Not my sweet Edna's little darling! O, Joseph, how can we bear this loss? He is one of the nicest children our family has had! And now to lose him with us so very far away? O! how can poor Edna bear it?"

And with a terrible shudder as with acute physical pain, Julina finally burst into tears, which at last mingled freely with those of her husband.

Three months after Joseph F. and Orson Pratt returned from their eastern tour, "the Church was thrown into confusion. This resulted from the Reynolds decision on January 6, 1879, in which the Supreme Court held that the 1862 antibigamy act [signed into law by Abraham Lincoln] was constitutional. This eliminated the legal basis on which the Church had ignored the 1862 act."[1] Worse, with this act now declared constitutional, there was a growing wave of sentiment across the country to prosecute Mormons and do away with their religion altogether.

Despite all this, the year 1880 "was the jubilee year of the Church. Special exercises were held during the April General Conference. The Church forgave one-half of the indebtedness held by the Perpetual Emigrating Fund Company, against individual members of the Church who had been helped by this fund to come to Utah... but on account of their restricted finances, [they] were forgiven. This sum amounted to $802,000.00; one thousand cows and five thousand sheep were also distributed among the needy, and in other ways the people were blessed by forgiveness of debts in accordance with the ancient law given to Israel. This spirit of jubilee was carried through the entire year, with special program and exercises on Pioneer day, July 24th."[2]

Yet terrible trouble was looming on the horizon, both for

Joseph F. and for the Church. "At this celebration in July, President John Taylor uttered a [prophecy] in which he said: 'There are events in the future, and not very far ahead, that will require all our faith, all our energy, all our confidence, all our trust in God, to enable us to withstand the influences that will be brought to bear against us... We cannot trust in our intelligence; we cannot trust in our wealth; we cannot trust to any surrounding circumstances with which we are enveloped; we must trust alone in the living God to guide us, to direct us, to teach us and instruct us. And there never was a time when we needed to be more humble and more prayerful; there never was a time when we needed more fidelity, self-denial, and adherence to the principles of truth, than we do this day.'"3

Joseph F. was ushered closer to the forefront of the Church's trials when, on October 10, 1880, President John Taylor organized the First Presidency, calling as his counselors George Q. Cannon and Joseph F. Smith. Forty-one years of age, Joseph F. was vigorous, firm and outspoken; styled by some the "fighting apostle," though in reality his heart was tender and soft. The Lord was working with him, giving him experiences and placing him in circumstances which would best prepare him for that which was to come.

Already there were premonitions regarding Joseph F.'s future role in the Church. In February, 1881, Joseph F. accompanied Wilford Woodruff to a stake conference in Weber County, several miles north of Salt Lake City. "Wilford Woodruff noted in his journal, reflecting events of the morning service: 'Statistics of the Stake read. Then Joseph F. Smith spoke in much power for one hour and 35 M(inutes).'

"In the afternoon session, Wilford Woodruff addressed the Saints: 'Bore testimony to the work of God and what Joseph F. Smith had said and... his remarks... (and declared) Joseph F. Smith was One of the first Presidency and would be Preside(n)t of the Church of

LDS Church First Presidency
(from left): George Q. Cannon,
John Taylor and Joseph F. Smith

CA. 1880

Church Archives, The Church of Jesus Christ of Latter-day Saints

Jesus Christ of Latter-day Saints in his DAY."₄ On another occasion

> President Woodruff was...relating to a group of children
> some incidents in the life of the Prophet Joseph Smith. He
> turned to Elder Joseph F. Smith and asked him to arise to
> his feet. Elder Smith complied. "Look at him, children,"
> Wilford Woodruff said, "for he resembles the Prophet
> Joseph more than any other man living. He will become
> the President of The Church of Jesus Christ of Latter-day
> Saints. I want everyone of you to remember what I have
> told you this morning.₅

Meanwhile, the storm predicted by President Taylor continued to
gather across the land in dark clouds of prejudice and hatred,
readying itself to burst forth in full fury upon the heads of the
Latter-day Saints. And as had been the case in both Missouri and
Illinois, once again the persecution was being led by "Christian"
ministers who had been made bitter, usually over LDS doctrines as
well as missionaries who were robbing them of their flocks. In Salt
Lake City and elsewhere they railed against the Mormons, filling
the *Tribune* and other papers with anti-Mormon sentiment, attacking especially the doctrine of plurality of wives.

For instance, on November 26, 1880, the Reverend DeWitt
Talmage proclaimed against the Mormons in the *Brooklyn
Tabernacle* in New York. " 'I tell you that Mormonism will never be
destroyed until it is destroyed by the guns of the United States
government. It would not be war. I hate war. It would be national
police duty executing the law against polygamy... If the Mormons
submit to the law all right. In not, then send out troops of the
United States government and let them make the Mormon
Tabernacle their headquarters, and with cannon of the biggest
bore thunder into them the seventh commandment.' "₆

Political sentiment towards the Mormons had also changed politically. Whereas Abraham Lincoln had signed into law but refused to prosecute the Antibigamy Law of 1862, with the 1879 Supreme Court decision, one U.S. President after another began railing against the Mormons. "President Rutherford B. Hayes, who had been entertained by the Gentile faction in Utah in September 1880, made some strong recommendations on the Mormon question when he addressed Congress in December. 'Polygamy will not be abolished if the enforcement of the law depends on those who practice and uphold the crime. It can only be suppressed by taking away the political power of the sect which encourages and sustains it... I recommend that the right to vote, hold office and sit on juries in the Territory of Utah be confined to those who neither practice nor uphold polygamy.' President James A. Garfield, who succeeded Hayes in 1881, urged similar congressional action on Utah affairs, as did Chester A. Arthur when he assumed presidency [near the end of 1881], with the result that Congress was flooded with hundreds of petitions relating to the Mormon question, and a number of bills and amendments dealing with polygamy were introduced. The only one which materialized into law was the Edmunds bill, introduced... [by] Senator George F. Edmunds, Republican senator from Vermont."[7]

In explaining his position, Senator Edmunds warned that " 'the problem must now or in the near future be solved and the irrepressible conflict between polygamous Mormonism and the social and political systems of the people of the rest of the United States must have a decided issue.' "[8] To that end, Edmunds introduced his bill in the Senate on January 24, 1882.

In reality the Edmunds Law was an amendment to the Antibigamy Law of 1862, serving to strengthen and give the law real teeth. "It not only declared polygamy a felony, with penalty on conviction of not more than five years imprisonment and/or a

$500 fine, but also defined polygamous living, which it termed unlawful cohabitation, as a misdemeanor punishable by six months imprisonment and/or a $300 fine. The law disfranchised polygamists and declared them ineligible for public office. Polygamists, whether in practice or merely in belief, were disqualified for jury service. All registration and elective offices in Utah Territory were declared vacant and a board of five members was to be appointed by the president to assume temporarily all duties pertaining to elections."9

While the bill met with strong opposition in both houses, with many arguing that the government had no authority to take away the rights of any of its citizens even if they were Mormon, nevertheless it was pushed through Congress and signed into law on March 22, 1882.

President John Taylor, in the April 1882 General Conference, reacted forcefully by saying:

> We have no fault to find with our government, we deem it the best in the world, but we have reason to deplore its maladministration...
>
> We shall abide all constitutional law, as we always have done; but while we are God-fearing and law-abiding and respect all honorable men and officers, we are no craven serfs, and have not learned to lick the feet of oppressors, nor to bow in base submission to unreasoning clamor. We will contend inch by inch, legally and constitutionally, for our rights as American citizens and plant ourselves firmly on the sacred guarantees of the constitution.10

Perhaps the most difficult aspect of the Edmunds Law for the Mormons to accept was the fact that it had been "very carefully worded to exclude any 'Gentile' who cohabited with any female other than his legal wife, from its penalties. It was well known that many of the very officers who were the most bitter against the Latter-day Saints during this crusade were guilty of the grossest immoralities, but since their practices were in accord with the practices of the monogamous world, and their cohabitations were with women whom they did not recognize as their wives, they were exempt from prosecution and punishment by the provisions of the law but were thereby apparently better qualified to prosecute the 'Mormon' polygamists who openly acknowledged their plural wives and cared religiously for them and their children."[11]

Thinking that a more liberalized state constitution, which included using "Utah" instead of "Deseret" as the name of the state, might pacify the national government into granting statehood and thus relief from the control of carpetbagging officers, President Taylor urged the territorial legislature to hold another constitutional convention. Joseph F., who had served on the city council of Salt Lake City and in the territorial legislature, was appointed by that body to preside over the convention. A new constitution was immediately drafted and submitted to Congress, yet it did no good; the Utah Commission (over elections) was already speeding its work by declaring elected offices to be vacant, administering a "test-oath" regarding polygamy which had to be signed before voter registration, impaneling grand juries composed wholly of non-Mormons who had passed the test-oath, and assisting federal officers in pressing charges against all who could be arrested and charged with polygamy. The years of crusading, tyranny, and oppression that followed were known by the Gentiles nationwide as "The Crusade." The Mormons, however, called it "The Raid."

Paid spies—men of base character—were employed to gather evidence. Some of the men who sat to judge the 'morals' of the Latter-day Saints were themselves recreant to every law of decency. This crusade and campaign of evil spread throughout the United States and even into other countries and resulted in the murder of missionaries in the Southern States.12

At first convinced that they could win at the law because of the legal correctness of their course, as well as their constitutional guarantees as U.S. citizens, Joseph F. and the other members of the First Presidency and the Church could now see that the courts were now interpreting the law directly against them. One after another, General Authorities and other leading brethren lost at trial and were sent to prison or driven into exile.

"Starting with the conviction and sentencing of Rudger Clawson to four years imprisonment and $800 fine the 'crusade' moved ahead until the 1887 report of the Utah Commission to the Secretary of the Interior listed 541 indictments since 1882 and 289 convictions for unlawful cohabitation plus another 16 for polygamy. Before the crusade had run its course nearly 1000 Mormons had been imprisoned. The campaign at its worst became a reign of terror including a system of espionage and invasion of homes without regard to the sacred rights of privacy. Women were imprisoned for refusal to testify or answer indelicate questions. Among the most wanted by the 'crusaders' were the church officials including President John Taylor with his counselors George Q. Cannon and Joseph F. Smith. In search of these the U.S. Marshal and his numerous deputies periodically raided the Guardo House..., the Temple Block, the Church offices, Tithing Yards, Historian's Office and private homes suspected of harboring them. Spying and follow-up raids spread terror into every Mormon village in the Territory."13

In March 1887 Congress passed a supplemental act known as

the Edmunds-Tucker Law, which "disincorporated the Church, confiscated its property and placed the affairs of the Church in the hands of a receiver, who was unfriendly, of course, to the Church."14 Meanwhile the courts kept reinterpreting the law. Many of the brethren who had made arrangements to live with only one of their wives found that "simply to acknowledge marital responsibility to more than one woman was sufficient to bring heavy penalties and imprisonment. The vindictive spirit in which the law was enforced often wiped out distinctions between prosecution and persecution. This spirit reached an extremity in the doctrine of 'segregation' introduced by Judge Zane in September of 1855. It permitted dividing of the time of the continuance of the offense of unlawful cohabitation so that an indictment could be found for each period [a day, an hour, and so forth]. The doctrine would permit prison sentences to become accumulative and fines to become exhorbitant."15

Convinced that their relationships with their families were "a divinely given command from God, and knowing the immoral practices of their persecutors, it was only natural that [Mormon leaders and others] should rise up in righteous indignation."16 Joseph F., who had gone into hiding, or "underground," both through lengthy visits by rail and wagon to outlying stakes as well as by staying at secluded camps in the nearby mountains—camps with names such as Solitude Gloria and Serene Plentiful—penned the following from one of them:

Uncle Elias Smith and Aunt Susan E. Smith were sub-poened (sic) this morning. I am said to be in great demand! I often feel wrathy and perhaps never more so than now, but I will not express my wrath, for it would be inadequate to the occasion. I rely upon the promise that God has made—"Vengeance is mine and I will repay!" Retribution will come upon the heads of this whole nation, and especially on the immediate enemies of the Latter-day Saints. I cannot conceive of anything more contemptible or more execrable than the present and continued attempts of the Federal Officials to blast the peace and break up the sacred relations of husbands and wives, parents and children! What business is it of theirs if I and my family are happy in the relation of plural marriage? Have I wronged any one? Have I or my family interfered with the rights of others? Is anybody injured? According to their own theory no one is injured except it may be those who practice plural marriage themselves. Then why not let those who are injured complain and seek liberation and redress? The law favors this theory and the courts are open and anxious to sustain the law and liberate the so-called victims of polygamy. I am satisfied that God's punishment will be just, so I will wait.17

In December 1884, President Taylor sent word to Joseph F. that he was to remain concealed while arrangements were being made to send him out of the country on a mission, perhaps to Hawaii. Bishop Albert W. Davis, Joseph F.'s brother-in-law, volunteered to go on this mission with him. The week before Christmas, after having his teeth pulled and a plate made, Joseph F. gave his family blessings, except for Julina and her baby, who were to go with him, and bid them good-bye. Then he set out for Pocatello where he could use the railroad without being recognized.

"This sad story is aptly told in his son's biography, written by Joseph F.'s grandson, Joseph Fielding Smith, Jr., and John J. Steward:

It was just a week before Christmas, December 18, 1884,

but instead of it being a time of pleasant anticipation and excitement, as it should be for a youngster, it was for eight-year-old Joseph Fielding Smith a dreaded, lonely day.

He along with his several brothers and sisters sat quietly in the big parlor of the Smith home while his father gave each of them in turn a blessing. His four 'aunties'—his father's other wives—each received a departing blessing too. But not his mother, nor his baby sister Julina, ten months old, for they were going with Papa this time, on a long journey, far away, for a very long time.18

In Idaho deep snows forced their train to stop, and since it could be weeks before it might run again, the Smith party was forced to turn back to Utah. Traveling south incognito, he received word from President Taylor that he was to take another mission to the southern settlements. While awaiting this departure at a place he called Camp Proximity, he wrote some interesting counsel to his nephew, Albert J. Davis:

> I want you to listen to my counsel and I will guarantee you prosperity and honor, and yet I will tell you nothing new, nor attempt originality altho' I will quote no man.
> 1. Love and trust in God, the Creator of all things, with all your heart.
> 2. Love and honor your parents and do all you can to make them happy.
> 3. Be very kind to your brothers and sisters.
> 4. Respect your neighbors.
> 5. Be generous and forgiving even to your enemies.
> 6. Be liberal to the poor.
> 7. Be considerate of the aged and the infirm.
> 8. Never affect to be what you are not, or to do what you

cannot. Be real and act natural.

9. Make no promises you cannot keep, and when you make a promise keep it.

10. Weigh your thoughts, think before you speak, say only the truth, speak not without meaning, and your words will be as good as your bond.

11. Avoid quarrels and shun quarrelsome people; be a peacemaker.

12. Live within your means.

13. Drink no intoxicating liquors, never gamble or bet, nor risk anything to chance.

14. Never swear, truth will stand by itself; never attempt to bolster it by an oath. One who swears needs a witness who does not prove his veracity.

Observe these few things with all else of good you can learn and you will be loved of God and honored of men. Your affectionate uncle.19

In January of 1885 Joseph F. and the others of the First Presidency, as well as a large number of other brethren, left Salt Lake City in a private rail car to visit the southern settlements. However, in Ogden President Cannon left them and returned to Salt Lake City. Traveling to Denver and then south through New Mexico and Arizona, the remaining brethren went far south into Mexico, calling on Governor Luis E. Torres at Hermosillo, who received them very kindly. Back in Arizona they continued on into California, holding meetings with the Saints as they traveled. In San Francisco they called on Governor Leland Stanford and had a pleasant interview. They also received word from President Cannon that a messenger was on his way with important information.

Upon the messenger's arrival the brethren learned that a plan had been concocted at home to arrest the First Presidency and others of the leading brethren and "wring out of them much coveted information or commit them for contempt. Warrants had been issued for this purpose. "For some little while President Taylor was undecided what course to take. Finally he decided that the company should return home notwithstanding the threatened dangers which awaited them... As President Taylor meditated over the situation he turned to President Joseph F. Smith and said that he should go on a mission to the Sandwich Islands, as they were then called, or wherever he pleased for the time being. He felt it was unwise for President Smith to return. The reason being not only the nature of President Smith's family, but since he had been in charge of certain phases of the work and had much to do with the records of the Church, it would be well for him to remain away and have charge of certain records which, through the bitterness of the enemies of the Church they would endeavor to obtain or confiscate. This matter was put to a vote and the brethren present sustained President Taylor's decision."[20]

Joseph F. declared, " 'I at once made preparation to leave the train, and part with the pleasant company that I have been privileged to journey with for the past 3 weeks. The train halted at Sacramento 30 minutes for supper. I dined with six others of the brethren at the station dining room and took a room at the Silver Palace Hotel, and at 7:30 p.m. I shook hands with and bid good bye to President Taylor and all the brethren of the party. They wending their way homeward and I to seek a tropical clime.' "[21]

Though he had been "on the underground" since the first of September, 1884, seeing various members of his family only occasionally, and then secretly, Joseph F. could not go home. Instead he was "to continue in exile until the storm of hate, indefinite and bitter, should eventually pass."[22]

In San Francisco he telegraphed for Julina and her baby to join him and also sent other telegrams to make arrangements for her travel, signing them "J. Field." In Oakland he called on his cousin, "'Ina Coolbrith,' daughter of his uncle Don Carlos Smith, who was born in Nauvoo, but having been led away by apostate relatives after the death of her father, she was raised out of the Church and made to despise the 'Mormons.' Being ashamed of her name she took her mother's maiden name of Coolbrith, and the name of 'Ina.' This cousin was a very talented woman, and gained great prominence in the literary world, eventually being honored as the Poet Laureate of California. She received President Smith very coldly, but kindly."23

Sailing on the steamship *Mariposa*, Joseph F., Julina, and their infant daughter, now traveling as Mr. and Mrs. Speight and child, arrived in Honolulu on February 9, 1885, and continued on to the Laie Plantation that night. There they began what would become nearly two years of separation from their family in Utah. And there they were residing when word came, a little more than a year later, of the death of Julina's younger sister's little boy Robert, affectionately called Robin.24

In her journal two weeks later, Julina wrote:

Jos has fretted so much and felt so very bad over the loss of his little Robert one of the nicest children we had. At first I thought it was no comfort to him my being here with little Ina, but I can see now that if he had been here alone, it would have been harder. It seems that he can not stand it to be alone.

This last week I have been doing the work in the kitchen. Have been obliged to be out of my room most of the time, and it has made me feel terrible to go in and see his [Joseph F.'s] eyes red and swollen with crying, but Ina has been with him much of the time.25

Joseph F.'s heart was wrung at this death, for "now he was in a foreign land where he could be of little help and comfort to the bereaved mother and the members of his family who were home. In the midst of his sorrow he penned the following:

"'I started a letter to Edna in which I quoted the following verses from a hymn by Henry W. Naisbitt:

> Rest for the weary soul,
> Rest for the aching head,
> Rest on the hill-side, rest,
> With our sweet angelic dead."

"He [Joseph F.] then added the following, his own composition:

> But O, the strife's not o're;
> Nor is the battle won;
> The warfare rages still;
> Our race of life's not run.
> Welcome that rest shall be
> If, when the trial is o're,
> We meet with those now gone,
> To part from them no more.
>
> Let the oppressed be freed,
> Then may the "weary rest."
> Safe where the Angels guard;
> Safe on their "mother's breast."
> Now the trial is hard,
> For, O, our darling's fled!
> In humble faith brought low,
> We bow our aching head.

But soon our peace shall come;
Soon shall our woes be past;
Peaceful our rest shall be—
Our "hill-side home" at last.26

Despite the grief and misery brought on by his exile, Joseph F. was kept busy, presiding over the Church's affairs in the Islands, hiking in the canyons looking for fruit, climbing on horseback the volcano Hale A Ka La (a ride which nearly confined Julina, who was pregnant), and writing numerous letters and entries in his journal. He was also able to strike one mighty blow against the enemies of the Church.

Shortly after the organization of the Church, opposition to its growth began appearing in print, as newspaper articles, periodicals, and books. Generically termed "anti-Mormon literature," most of these early works were based either on misinformation and innuendo or outright lies and false accusations. Once in print, these lies seemed to take on the aura of truth, so that the Church found it virtually impossible to surmount them. One of the most damaging of these lies, one that went on year after year, was that the author of the Book of Mormon had not been Joseph Smith, but Solomon Spaulding. He, supposedly, had written a manuscript from which Joseph Smith, Sidney Rigdon, or someone else in power had plagiarized the Book of Mormon.

While in hiding in Hawaii, Joseph F. learned that "Mr. L. L. Rice, then living in Honolulu, had in his possession the Spaulding romance, or 'Spaulding Story,' which Mr. D. P. Hurlburt and Mr. E. D. Howe, with the help of others as wicked as themselves, maliciously and wickedly made do such wonderful service in the world of falsehood against the Book of Mormon. The title page of this miserable pack of lies which laid the foundation for the attacks on the Book of Mormon and the Church of Jesus Christ of Latter-day

Saints from 1834, when it was first published, until the discovery of the Spaulding manuscript, is as follows:

Mormonism Unveiled
or
A faithful account of the singular imposition and
DELUSION
From its rise to the present time
With sketches of the characters of its
Propagators,
And a full detail of the manner in which the famous
GOLDEN BIBLE
WAS BROUGHT FORTH BEFORE THE WORLD
to which are added
Inquiries into the probability that the historical part
of the said Bible was written by one
SOLOMON SPAULDING
more than twenty years ago, and by him intended to have
been published as a romance.

———

By E. D. Howe

———

Painesville:
Printed and published by the Author

1834

"Of all the lying attacks ever made upon the Book of Mormon and the Church, this stands at the peak as the most stupendous. It formed the basis of most of the attacks during all the years from 1834 to the time of the discovery of the manuscript in the possession of Mr. Rice. It was never intended by Mr. E. D. Howe and those associated with him that it should ever be found, but Providence ruled that it should not be destroyed and that eventually it should be revealed to the world, thus exposing these hypocrites who prepared the story of 'Mormonism Unveiled,' and their despicable methods of fighting the work of the Lord."27

After several meetings with Mr. Rice, during which Joseph F. both saw and handled the old manuscript, and after he had broken down many of the elderly man's prejudices against the Church, he obtained the manuscript on loan and forwarded it to Salt Lake City. There it was copied and printed, after which it was returned and delivered to Mr. Rice according to Joseph F.'s agreement.

Meanwhile, others were also reading the manuscript and ascertaining the truth. A *Deseret News* article, under the heading "The Spaulding Manuscript Story Completely Exploded," reads in part:

> Before us is the April number of Frank Leslie's *Illustrated Sunday Magazine*. It contains a *fac simile* of the religious department page of the *New York Observer* of February 5th, 1885, on which appears this interesting statement:
>
> Solomon Spaulding and The Book of Mormon
>
> "The theory of the origin of the Book of Mormon in the traditional manuscript of Solomon Spaulding will probably have to be relinquished. That manuscript is doubtless now in the possession of Mr. L. L. Rice, of Honolulu, Hawaiian Islands, formerly an anti-slavery editor in Ohio, and for many years State printer of Columbus...
>
> "There seems no reason to doubt that this is the long

lost story. Mr. Rice, myself and others, compared it with
the Book of Mormon and could detect no resemblance
between the two, in general or detail. There seems to be no
name or incident, common to the two. The solemn style of
the Book of Mormon, in imitation of the English
Scriptures, does not appear in the manuscript. The only
resemblance is in the fact that both profess to set forth the
history of the lost tribes. Some other explanation of the
origin of the Book of Mormon must be found, if any
explanation is required.

James H. Fairchild."28

With Joseph F. "on the underground" in the Islands, and with
Presidents Taylor and Cannon also in hiding, the affairs of the
Church were in a precarious situation. In as great a disarray were
the families of the Church's polygamous members. "The family of
President Smith much of the time while he was away was scattered;
his homes were constantly raided by some of the vilest men that
ever drew mortal breath. Inmates and attendants were grossly
insulted, and defenseless children intimidated. Nothing was considered
sacred from the morbid gaze and indecent acts of men who had
been given power to search and seize, and who frequently did both
without warrant of law. Bedrooms were forcibly entered while the
inmates were in peaceful slumber. Women were insulted, not
having the privilege of properly clothing themselves, and in that
condition forced to stand before these fiends and answer their
indecent and vulgar questions."29

In anguish, Joseph F. wrote, " 'These are momentous times!
My heart feels sick of the world and the awful corruptions and
abominations that revel it, not only not checked, but upheld and
encouraged by the powers that be. O Lord, have mercy on the
upright and speedily adjudge and award the wicked according to

their works...' "

Later he said, " 'I have never wronged any man, nor committed crime, nor was ever charged with crime, [but now] I am called upon to desert and renounce my family, abandon my wives, brand them and my children with infamy, and acknowledge myself a craven and a traitor to God and my own flesh and blood, or be condemned as a felon and doomed to bonds, fines and imprisonment.' "30

Joseph F. took seriously ill in November, 1886, and remained so for several weeks, growing more thin and weighing less than he had ever done in his adult life. Patiently Julina nursed him back to health, after which, in March 1887, she took her two small children and returned with them to Utah and the remainder of her family.

Upon their departure, Joseph F. wrote in his journal, "The steamer cut loose at 12 p.m. and at exactly 12:15 she commenced her course out of the harbor; and I took the last look at the receding forms of my loved and loving ones until God in his mercy shall permit us to meet again. When the ship passed the line of sight, I hastened [to a better vantage point]...to look again at the speeding steamer Australia with her precious sacred treasures until lost behind Diamond Head. When once alone, my soul burst forth in tears and I wept their fountains dry and felt all the pangs and grief of parting with my heart's best treasures on earth."31

Perhaps Joseph F. knew that Julina and her little ones were sailing toward difficulties that would be anything but pleasant. Not only were the wives and children missing their "Papa," but without his presence, their economic situation had become bleak. Soon after Julina's arrival in Salt Lake City, Edna wrote: " 'We are living at our poorest now. No butter, no meat, but imported bacon, and we women folks cannot eat that... Some of us are almost starved... The most of Ina's talk is about Papa... She said, '...When he comes back I'll hold him just as tight as tight, so he cannot leave us anymore.' Oh! My Papa I can only think of you in that lonesome room all alone. The silent tears have wet my pillow at night, when I have been thinking of you, my sorrow seems greater than my joy. For when oh when will we ever meet again?' "[32]

Such grief and loneliness is only understandable when the deep love of this unusual family is considered. " 'To the astonishment of the unbelieving world, [Joseph F.'s] wives loved each other dearly. In times of sickness they tenderly waited upon and nursed each other. When death invaded one of the homes and a child was taken, all wept and mourned with sincere grief... The children recognized each other as brothers and sisters, full-fledged not as half, as they would be considered in the world. They defended each other and stood by each other no matter which branch of the family was theirs...

" 'Joseph F. ...loved his wives and children with a holy love that is seldom seen, never surpassed. Like Job of old, he prayed for them night and day and asked the Lord to keep them pure and undefiled in the path of righteousness...

He loved his children as eternal children of his Heavenly Father and diligently taught them his own great faith and scriptural knowledge. His son, Joseph Fielding Smith, recalled: "My father was the most tender-hearted man I ever knew... Among my fondest memories are the hours I have spent by his side discussing principles of the gospel and receiving instruction as only he could give it. In this way the foundation for my own knowledge was laid in truth." ' "[33]

Three months after Julina's departure, Joseph F. received word that President Taylor was seriously ill, and on July 1, 1887, he also sailed from Honolulu toward the mainland. Traveling directly to the home of Thomas F. Rouche in Kaysville, Utah, where President Taylor was in hiding, Joseph F. and President Cannon entered President Taylor's room together. It was July 18TH, the first time since 1884 that they had been together, and the three spent some time alone. Thereafter the two counselors labored at or near President Taylor's bedside each day until the 25TH, when he quietly passed away.

With President Taylor's death the First Presidency was dissolved, and Joseph F. returned to the ranks of the Quorum of the Twelve Apostles, presided over by Wilford Woodruff. Meanwhile, the fires of persecution still raged, and Joseph F. was forced to continue living in seclusion.

A COUNSELOR'S CALLING

"Well, Brethren." Wilford Woodruff looked first at one of his counselors, and then at the other. "So far as I can tell, we have examined this issue from every conceivable angle and looked at every imaginable contingency. Thank you for being forthright with me. I value your opinions more than you can know. President Cannon, may I hear your final recommendation?"

George Q. Cannon, President Woodruff's first counselor, sat with his back to the large bay window, facing into the sitting room where he, President Woodruff, Joseph F., and the clerk had gathered daily for the past two weeks in presidency meeting. Out the window behind Elder Cannon spread the garishly decorated, gabled roofs of the aristocratic dwellings on Nob Hill, home to San Francisco's financially elite. Beyond them and off a little distance to the north and east were the bay and harbor, sparkling blue in the warm September sun.

As he sat gazing past Elder Cannon and out the window, Joseph F. thought of the oft-told story of how, following the initial surge of the gold rush in 1851, more than 800 ships had floated at anchor in that harbor, deserted by their crews who had joined the mad search for gold. It had been one of those abandoned ships that had nearly spelled disaster for himself and the other missionaries endeavoring to get to the Sandwich Islands back in 1854. Now Joseph F. smiled at the memory and found himself wondering once again at the marvelous changes that had come upon the city in the years since then.

For two weeks he and the others of the First Presidency had been in residence there on Nob Hill, preferring to rent private quarters rather than to stay in one of the more opulent hotels that now graced the city. They had come there on President Woodruff's recommendation, he knew, for two reasons: first, to visit with politicians, railroad and newspaper officials, and leaders of the Republican Party concerning the Church's chances of legally continuing plural marriage; and second, because in thoroughly cosmopolitan San Francisco they would be unrecognized and therefore free to move about at will and discuss these same troubling issues without fear of arrest and/or imprisonment.

They had spent nearly every moment since their arrival in earnest, deep discussion. Yes, they had gotten about the city, enjoying the beautifully mild fall weather as they rode the famed cable cars, took hacks when necessary, or walked as occasion permitted. They had visited Chinatown and the old Spanish Mission; though they avoided the Barbary Coast and its gaudy wickedness, they had been to the shipping wharfs and the Presidio; and they had dined at some truly amazing restaurants. Billed as the Athens, Paris, and New York of the West, San Francisco, while never quite losing the wildness of its frontier days, had indeed matured into one of the world's more wicked cities. As Rudyard Kipling had recently observed, "San Francisco is a mad city, inhabited for the most part by perfectly insane people..."

With those sentiments, Joseph F. perfectly agreed. It was not a city with which he desired a more thorough acquaintance. And so they had held most of their discussions either in the solitude of the newly built Golden Gate Park, looking out over the vast Pacific, or in their rooms on Nob Hill, where they could labor together in fasting and prayer. It had been an exhausting though spiritual two weeks, but it was drawing to a close, and Joseph F. knew that he and the others must now come to a firm and uncompromising decision.

George Q. Cannon took a deep breath. "My sense, President, is that we have no choice but to bring it to an end."

"Thank you, President Cannon." President Woodruff turned in his chair and regarded the younger of his two counselors. "President Smith, you know something of the martyrs of this Church, perhaps more than anyone of the Brethren save President Taylor and your brother, Patriarch John Smith. You know the doctrines, the principles for which Joseph, Hyrum, Parley, David Patten, and others have given their lives, and thus far, you have essentially given your life for the same. With that as background, I should like to hear your final recommendation."

"Thank you, President." Joseph F. regarded the prophet. "Like yourself and President Cannon, I entered into the law of Patriarchal Marriage at the urging of President Brigham Young, and as with all other acts of obedience, my life has been richly blessed because of it. Without exception my wives are noble daughters of God, pure and holy in their hearts and filled with a burning desire to do righteousness all the days of their lives. To the best of my knowledge, my children are the same. With the furthest reaches of the imagination, I cannot fathom how a man might be more blessed than to have eternal claim to such a family as has been given to me. Neither can I imagine how pitifully empty my life would surely be without them.

"As far as this crusade against us goes, I would rather choose to stand, with them, alone—persecuted, proscribed, outlawed—to wait until God in his anger should break the nation with his avenging stroke!"

Joseph F. took a deep breath. "That being said, President, and knowing that my recommendation will perhaps deprive millions of people, mostly yet unborn, of the same glorious blessings that I presently enjoy, I am nevertheless inclined to add my voice to that of President Cannon. Because we have been commanded since the days of the Prophet Joseph Smith to be obedient to the laws of the land, and because the laws against Patriarchal Marriage, as well as against us as a people, have been judged legally sound by the highest court of the land, I am forced to recommend that the practice of plural marriage be halted."

"Thank you, Joseph," President Woodruff stated quietly. For a moment then, he, too, stared out the window. "You are right, though," he finally said as he looked back at his second counselor. "If the action is taken that you and President Cannon are recommending, a very great number will be deprived of the particular blessings available only through the righteous practice of plural marriage. Nevertheless, my faith in the Lord is fixed, and I know he will continue in some manner we do not yet understand to provide for the spiritual salvation of his people.

"Unfortunately, I know just as surely that if we don't take the action you have each recommended, we as a people will be stopped in our tracks, and in a generation or so there will be none left to receive any sort of blessings, spiritual or otherwise. In broken and contrite spirit I have sought the will of the Lord, and the Holy Spirit has revealed that it is necessary for the Church to relinquish the practice of that principle for which the Brethren have been willing to lay down their lives."

Again President Woodruff took a deep breath. "Therefore, I have arrived at a point in the history of my life as the President of The Church of Jesus Christ of Latter-day Saints where I am under the necessity of acting for the temporal salvation of the Church. The Lord has shown me by vision and revelation exactly what will take place if we do not stop this practice. Therefore, the God of Heaven has commanded me to end it; and it is all clear to me."

"But, how will we get the Saints to follow such a course?"

President Woodruff smiled sadly. "First, the Lord has told me to issue a proclamation, or manifesto, suspending the practice of plural marriage. He then told me to ask the Latter-day Saints a question, and he has also told me that if they would listen to what I said to them and answer the question put to them, by the Spirit and power of God, they would all answer alike, and they would all believe alike in regard to this matter. The question is this: Which is the wisest course for the Latter-day Saints to pursue—to continue to attempt to practice plural marriage, with the laws of the nation against it and the opposition of sixty million people, and at the cost of the confiscation and loss of all the temples, and the stopping of all ordinances therein, both for the living and the dead, and the imprisonment of the First Presidency and the Twelve and the heads of families in the Church, and the confiscation of personal property of the people (all of which of themselves would stop the practice), or after doing and suffering what we have through our adherence to this principle to cease the practice and submit to the law, and through doing so leave the prophets, apostles, and fathers at home, so that they can instruct the people and attend to the duties of the Church, and also leave the temples in the hands of the Saints, so that they can attend to the ordinances of the gospel, both for the living and the dead?"

"If that question is put to them, President, I believe they will see that there is no other course but to cease the practice."

"The Lord promised me they would."

"Nevertheless, I fear there will be those who will doubt that the Lord is in it."

President Woodruff nodded. "I am certain you are right. There will be some good men in this Church, including some of the leaders, who will be tried and will feel as though President Woodruff has lost the Spirit and is about to apostatize. Now, I want you and them to know that he has not lost the Spirit, nor is he about to apostatize. The Lord is with him and with this people. As I said a moment or so ago, he has told me exactly what to do—and what the result would be if we did not do it.

"But I wish to say this, Brethren, and I pray you will hear me. I should have let all the temples go out of our hands; I should have gone to prison myself just as President Cannon has done, and let every other man go there, had not the God of heaven commanded me otherwise. We are to stop the practice immediately and save the people!

"Now, allow me to read the manifesto I have prepared to present to the Saints—"

As the Council of the Twelve Apostles took up the task of governing and regulating the Church following the death of President John Taylor, they did so under almost impossible circumstances. The Edmunds-Tucker Law "had disincorporated the Church and confiscated all of its property in excess of $50,000; women's suffrage had been abolished in the territory; and no one could vote, serve on a jury, or hold public office without taking an oath in support of antipolygamy laws. The Church faced financial ruin and its members complete disfranchisement."[1]

The Church fought this and the other anti-polygamy laws at every turn, arguing in the courts that they were unconstitutional and took away the freedoms of religion guaranteed U.S. citizens. Gradually these cases came together and moved upward toward the Supreme Court of the United States, and in February, 1888, Wilford Woodruff " 'proposed that Joseph F. Smith go to Washington, to help manage the financial part of the business there...'" He was "also fully authorized to act as [the Church's] agent in political matters."2

After blessing his wives and children and visiting his Aunt Mercy Rachel Thompson, Joseph F. and Charles W. Penrose left on the train for Washington. After meeting John T Cain, L. John Nuttall, and others there, Joseph F. entered immediately into the work of setting the Church's financial affairs in order. At the time, John W. Young, son of Brigham Young and Assistant to the Twelve Apostles, was living in New York and Washington, supposedly representing the Church but lavishly spending money which he did not have. When he made a claim against the Church for $25,000, Joseph F. and the others felt that it was more for personal reasons than to help the Church. " 'When I desired to know for what purpose [he wanted the money],' " Joseph F. wrote, " 'he got mad and vowed he would never ask the Church for another dollar. It was quite evident he needs money... I assured him that I could only order the payment of money for legitimate expenses. He railed against the brethren for not sustaining him, for slighting him and ignoring him, and much of that sort of thing, to which I paid but little attention. Brother Penrose did some sharp talking to him, and I threw oil upon the troubled waters.' "3

Laboring under the name of Jason Mack, the name of his mother's eldest brother, Joseph F. and the others did their best to prevent further unfavorable legislation and to break down prejudices on the part of senators and others against Utah and the Mormon people. "They met the President of the United States, who treated them kindly, but showed no great disposition to help them at that particular time. His counsel was that if the 'Mormon' people would do away with their doctrines in prophets and revelation and their practice of plural marriage, and become like other men, all their difficulties would vanish into thin air. The brethren agreed that if they did as he suggested the result would be as he predicted; but to follow such counsel was to destroy the Church and bring to naught the work which the Lord planted in the earth never again to be taken away or destroyed."4

Though much prejudice was overcome, by and large the brethren had little success in changing the government's course of action towards the Saints. Far too many in the seats of power "knew too much to ever be correctly informed... Writing of one senator, whom the brethren interviewed, President Smith said they 'found him a prejudiced, senseless, soulless old duffer, who, while admitting facts, utterly ignored their force and purpose.'"5 There were simply too many like him for the brethren to overcome.

Called home in June of 1888, Joseph F. labored for the remainder of the year with his brethren of the Council of the Twelve, keeping out of sight but doing much work in directing the affairs of the Church. From January to March of 1889 he was again in Washington, continuing his duties and labors of the year before—and experiencing the same results. In early April, after Joseph F. had returned home, President Wilford Woodruff, who was then President of the Quorum of the Twelve, stated that he felt it was the will of the Lord that they reorganize the First Presidency. After some discussion the Brethren agreed and sustained him as President of the Church. He then called as his counselors George Q. Cannon, who had finally been freed from prison, and Joseph F. Smith.

"When the First Presidency was reorganized at the April 1889 general conference, Joseph F. Smith was sustained as Second Counselor to President Wilford Woodruff. 'I would rather have taken a mission to Vandeman's land [Van Dieman's Land—pronounced as Joseph F. spelled it—was then the name for Tasmania] as an elder,' he confided to his diary, 'than to be called to the responsibilities of a counselor in the First Presidency if my own choice was to be consulted.' He had no illusions about the work, nor aspirations to high office. [Yet he] accepted the call willingly,

Church Archives, The Church of Jesus Christ of Latter-day Saints

Joseph F. Smith and Utah Lobbyists: CA. *1888*
(back row from left) George F. Gibbs,
L. John Nuttall and Charles W. Penrose;
(front row from left) John T. Caine,
Margaret Nightingale Caine,
Joseph F. Smith, Emily S. Richards
and Franklin S. Richards

LDS Church First Presidency: *6 April 1893*
George Q. Cannon,
Wilford Woodruff
and Joseph F. Smith

determined to serve devotedly."6

"In the early days of the administration of President Woodruff, the crusade against the Church continued. In Idaho it became extremely bitter, one of the officials who afterwards for years and years was honored by that state [Fred Dubois] boasting that he could and had organized a grand jury that would convict the Savior Himself, although his expression in so stating it was of such a vulgar nature that his exact words cannot be used. The members of the Church in that state, were disfranchised and denied their constitutional rights... [Yet church authorities] fought and contended for what they sincerely felt to be their constitutional privileges and the protection which that basic law afforded them."7

Late in the fall the new First Presidency issued a proclamation calling for a day of fasting throughout the Church. The Saints had been directed to "set apart December 23, 1899 — the anniversary of the birth of the Prophet Joseph Smith—as a general fast-day throughout the entire Church." Joseph wrote that prayers included petitions asking that all who conspire in any manner to injure or destroy the work of God or take from the people their rights and liberties might be defeated...

"[Asking] for the Lord to come to our help and deliver us from the many snares spread around us for our overthrow and destruction, to make our path plain before us, and to lead us to escape the pits dug at our feet...

"[And asking] that the Lord will pour out in great power His Holy Spirit and the gifts thereof upon his servants that they may be filled with the qualifications and power necessary to enable them to magnify their offices acceptably to Him, and to fill the hearts of the Saints with comfort and peace, and witness unto them that he has not forgotten and does not neglect Zion. And to pray for such other things as the Saints saw and felt that we needed."8

The answers to the Saints' fasting and prayers came fairly rapidly, and probably not as they had hoped. Though not publicly announced, "after a series of defeats at the polls, a decision by the Supreme Court upholding Idaho's test oath, and the threat of even more stringent federal legislation, the First Presidency, on June 30, 1890, formulated a new policy regarding plural marriage. 'The times have changed,' Joseph F. wrote to Charles W. Nibley. 'The conditions are not propitious and the decrees of the 'Powers that be' are against the move [for Nibley to take another wife]. I do not care so much for the outside powers as I do those within, although common prudence would suggest that deference should be paid to both. The decree now is that there shall be no p----l m-------s in the United States, and that there shall be none anywhere else unless one or both of the parties remove beyond the jurisdiction of this government to make their home. This comes to within one of being absolute prohibition. How long this condition of things may last no man knoweth, but for the present it is the 'law.' " 9

Despite the fact that this policy was not made public, there had been almost constant discussion among the Latter-day Saints regarding the discontinuance of plural or celestial marriage. Yet most members of the Church understood that this could come only through revelation. Some thought this might happen, some didn't; but with the U.S. Government's determination to enforce ever stricter laws, the pressures on the Church were becoming unbearable.

In September 1890 President Wilford Woodruff and his two counselors, George Q. Cannon and Joseph F, Smith, went to San Francisco for two weeks to "confer with politicians, railroad and newspaper officials and leaders of the Republican Party."10 They also spent a great deal of time alone, "discussing and praying about this sensitive matter. On September 25 President Woodruff was inspired to take the historic action. Known from then until now as the Manifesto, this revelation was approved at the general conference in October,"[11] and advised the Saints "to refrain from contracting any marriage forbidden by the law of the land."

The discussions regarding this document may have occurred in California or in Utah—it probably doesn't matter. Regardless, they reflected not only sincere logic and reasoning but also the clear hand of the Lord in giving revelation to the prophet. It was during a stake conference in Logan, Utah, on November 1st, 1891, that President Wilford Woodruff read from his diary entry of September 25, 1890, the remarks used to create the discussion between he and his two counselors at the beginning of this chapter. " 'I have had some revelations of late, and very important ones to me,' " President Woodruff stated, " 'and I will tell you what the Lord has said to me. Let me bring your minds to what is termed the manifesto...' "[12]

At a meeting with the Council of the Twelve and a few others held prior to General Conference, President Woodruff asked President Cannon to open the discussion. He did so, after which "several voiced the questions uppermost in the minds of all present: Did the Manifesto mean the cessation of plural marriage? Would they be required to separate from their families—to cease living with them? According to Frank Cannon [son of George Q. and a man at odds with the Church], the President replied that it did. He said that the Mormon representatives in Washington saw no other way out, and 'that it was the will of the Lord; that we must submit.'

"Cannon [, in a rather fanciful account,] describes what followed:

> I saw their faces flush and then slowly pale again—and the storm broke. One after another they rose and protested, hoarsely, in the voice of tears, that they were willing to suffer "persecution unto death" rather than to violate the

covenants which they had made "in holy places" with women who had trusted them...

Joseph F. Smith was one of the last to speak. With a face like wax, his hands outstretched, in an intensity of passion that seemed as if it must sweep the assembly, he declared that he had covenanted at the alter of God's house, in the presence of his Father, to cherish the wives and children whom the Lord had given him... He would rather choose to stand, with them, alone—persecuted—proscribed—outlawed—to wait until God in His anger should break the nation with His avenging stroke. But—

He dropped his arms. He seemed to shrink in his commanding stature like a man stricken with a paralysis of despair...

"I have never disobeyed a revelation from God," he said. "I cannot—dare not—now."

He announced—with his head up, though his body swayed—that he would accept and abide by the revelation.13

The Manifesto was read to the membership of the Church on October 6, 1890, after which Lorenzo Snow called for a sustaining vote. It was given as requested.

Though it did not bring immediate relief, over time the Manifesto achieved the desired effect. Even as bitterness continued to rage in the hearts of many, "prosecution of polygamists was relaxed, and the way was opened for the return of Church property and Utah's statehood in 1894 and 1896. Joseph F. appealed to President Harrison for amnesty in August 1891, and it was granted the next month. In October [1891, he] was able to attend a general conference of the Church for the first time in seven years. 'The house was full to the gallery,' he wrote. 'I spoke briefly, for I was so overcome by my feelings that I could scarcely restrain them... I

shook hands with my friends until my hand and arm felt lame...
This is a memorable day for me, and no words at my command can
express my gratitude to God.' At last Joseph F. Smith was free to
associate with the Saints and resume a [little more] normal life
with his family, which now numbered five wives and twenty-six
children."14

Nevertheless, three weeks later as the Presidency testified
before the master in chancery "to obtain a return of Church
property [, they] were required to state that the Manifesto was
intended to apply universally, not just in the United States, and
that it included a prohibition on cohabitation in existing plural
marriages as well."15 In other words, the brethren in the Church
who had entered into plural marriage, including Joseph F., could
never again live with those wives and children. In compliance,
Joseph F. began sleeping at his office, but each evening went "about
among his homes... when he had worked from early morning until
late at night, [going] from home to home to plant the loving kiss of
a father upon his children and his wives in recognition of the great
love he bore them."16 Later this restriction was eased, but for a
time the Saints who had entered into plural marriage continued to
endure great stress within their families.

Still, from 1890 until the death of President Woodruff, the
members of the First Presidency were able to go about their affairs,
and to transact Church business, without fear or hindrance. This
business included temple work. On April 6, 1892, the capstone of
the Salt Lake Temple was laid, and the building was dedicated one
year later. Joseph F.'s "life and ministry were closely tied to temple
work. His personal experiences began in Nauvoo in the winter of
1845–46 when his mother and her sister, Mercy R. Thompson,
'were much engaged in the work going on in the temple.' President
Smith said later, 'It was there that my father's children were sealed
to their parents.' He was present at the laying of the cornerstone of

the Salt Lake Temple in 1853 and at the dedication of the temple in 1893.

"In anticipation of the dedication, he said: 'For forty years the hopes, desires, and anticipations of the entire Church have been centered upon the completion of this edifice... Now that the great building is at last finished and ready to be used for divine purposes, need we say that we draw near an event whose consummation is to us as a people momentous in the highest degree?' He [Joseph F.] served as president of the Salt Lake Temple from 1898 to 1911, nine of those years while he was President of the Church."17

Meanwhile, the issue of polygamy wouldn't seem to go away. "As far as the general membership of the Church was concerned, plural marriage had ended, though exceptions were granted [for marriages outside the continental USA] until President Smith ended the practice in 1904."18 What most Saints didn't realize, however, was that eliminating plural marriage was never really the focus of the nation's governing forces. Rather, they were opposed to the Church's political clout—to the Mormons' tendency to follow the Prophet in temporal as well as spiritual issues. Rather than following along national party lines, the Church had established a People's Party to which most of the Saints belonged, and governing leaders in Washington saw this as completely un-American. More to the point, they saw it as a threat to their own political lives. Through attacking polygamy, therefore, they felt that they could stop this practice and preserve themselves and their political futures. According to Idaho's anti-Mormon senator, Fred Dubois:

> Those of us who understand the situation were not nearly so much opposed to polygamy as we were to the political domination of the Church... We made use of polygamy in consequence as our great weapon of offense and to gain

recruits to our standard. There was a universal detestation of polygamy, and inasmuch as the Mormons openly defended it we were given a very effective weapon with which to attack.19

In the early 1890's the First Presidency determined to disband the People's Party and to encourage the Saints to affiliate with either of the two national political parties. Only in this way, they could see, would Utah ever be granted statehood. Because most Church members would gravitate toward the Democratic Party with its conservative leanings, Joseph F. was assigned to campaign for the Republicans—not an easy task. In fact, in 1892, following a sound defeat of Republican candidates at the polls the previous fall, Joseph F. wrote and published "Another Plain Talk: Reasons Why the People of Utah Should Be Republicans." His efforts must have been effective, for by 1896, when Utah was granted statehood, the two parties in Utah were fairly equal.

Though these were busy times for Joseph F., he was never so busy that he couldn't spend time with his families. In March of 1898 he suffered another tragedy when his daughter Ruth, only a little more than four years old, passed away in his arms. With her mother, Edna, and the rest of his growing family, he grieved terribly the loss of this child. But the words he wrote at the time are indicative of the larger love that the Lord had granted him.

> At last I took her in my arms and walked the floor with her and helplessly, powerless to aid my darling, dying child, I watched her feeble breath depart to come no more in time, and her glorious intelligence, her bright angelic spirit took her flight to God from whence she came. It was then about 20 minutes to 8 p.m. With her was swept away all our fond hope and love and joy of earth. Oh! how I loved that child!

Church Archives, The Church of Jesus Christ of Latter-day Saints

LDS First Presidency and Council of the Twelve. At center: President Lorenzo Snow and counselors George Q. Cannon and Joseph F. Smith

CA. 1898

She was intelligent beyond her years; bright, loving, choice and joyous! But she is gone to join the beauteous and glorious spirits of her brothers and sisters, who have gone before! Sara Ella, M. Josephine, Alfred, Heber, Rhoda, Albert, Robert and John. O my soul! I see my own sweet mother's arms extended welcoming to her embrace the ransomed glorious spirit of my own sweet babe! O my God! For this glorious vision, I thank Thee! And there too are gathered to my Father's mansion all my darling lovely ones; not in infantile helplessness, but in all the power and glory and majesty of sanctified spirits! Full of intelligence, of joy and grace, and truth. My darling little petling in her own bright home with those of her brothers and sisters who had preceded her. How blessed, how happy is she! How sorrowful are we![20]

On September 2, 1898, President Wilford Woodruff passed away. Prior to his death, he had declared that " 'it was not the will of the Lord that in the future there should be a lengthy period elapse between the death of the president and the re-organization of the First Presidency.' "[21] Accordingly, eleven days later Lorenzo Snow was sustained by the Brethren of the Twelve as President of the Church. He chose for his counselors George Q. Cannon and Joseph F. Smith.

"One of the grave problems which confronted the Church at the time of this organization was the financial distress which had been brought upon it during the persecutions, when the property of the Church was escheated, and all that could be liquidated was confiscated by unscrupulous officials. The Church was mercilessly robbed and plundered and forced into the inconsistent position of paying exorbitant rentals for the use of its own property."[22] The Panic of 1893 had also contributed to the Church's distress, for literally every property had become devalued when (and if) it was finally returned.

To relieve this burden, and to gain immediate operating capital, President Snow determined to issue bonds—two series, "A" and "B," for $500 each; the first series to be redeemed in 1903 and the second in 1906. Senator Frank Cannon asked for the right to sell these bonds in Washington—for a healthy commission. President Snow at first agreed, but Joseph F. "strenuously objected, taking the ground that there was no reason to fear that these bonds could not be sold at home and that too without paying any man a commission. 'I opposed it,' said President Smith, 'and voted against it. I was opposed to giving a commission at all, and thought the bonds should be sold at home'... The result was that the first issue was readily disposed of locally, and when the second issue was ready for the market it met with a like response... The blocking of the scheme of this individual, who hoped to become the agent of the Church in disposing of the bonds, brought down upon the head of President Joseph F. Smith the wrath of [Frank Cannon], who in later times joined forces with the enemies of the Church in a campaign of bitterness and hate which in some respects surpassed any expression of bitterness ever before manifested against the Church."23 But more on this later.

Under President Snow's direction the Church refocused on the law of tithing. He also taught that a person should " 'never marry unless the Spirit of God bears witness that you are getting a companion for all eternity as well as for time. It is better not to marry at all, than to do so contrary to this principle.' "24 This doctrine struck particularly at Joseph F.'s heart. To it he added his own sweet testimony when he wrote to one of his daughters:

She (mother) is better than gold or rubies. Oh! who can compare with or what is so precious and priceless as a loving mother! How God has blessed me with pure and loving wives and my children with darling, precious mamas! To be untrue to them in word or thought or deed, would be a crime of awful magnitude, either in myself or in my children. I would not for all this world wilfully [*sic*] wrong one of them, nor cease to love them—for they love me—and mine! And truer wives have never lived, nor more loving mothers, nor better women, according to their knowledge. Not only would they die for me but they live for me and my happiness, and they have been not only faithful to me but to my children and to God! Oh! how I have been, am and will be, blessed in them in time and in eternity! How happy I am! And what joy I feel when they are well, comfortable and happy. Next to the love of God, my Savior, is my love for my wives and children, and next to them I love myself, and more for their sakes than for my own; and I would love my neighbor as myself, if I were as good as I should be. God help me to fulfill the whole law!25

In addition to his preaching and journal and letter writing, Joseph F. was also kept busy in other ways. In 1899 he made a visit to Hawaii in company with his wife Sarah, who had been seriously ill. In 1900 he visited the settlements in Canada, as well as twice visiting those in Arizona and Mexico. Perhaps more than any other activity, however, Joseph F. continued to treasure the precious times when he could be in the homes of his wives and children. No longer did he have to flee and hide, no longer was he filled with anxiety because he could not be with his little ones personally. In every way, and at every possible moment, he was with them, singing, laughing, comforting, teaching. According to his friend Charles W. Nibley, Joseph F.'s "love for little children was unbounded. During [a trip] through the southern settlements to

St. George...when the troops of little children were paraded before him, it was beautiful to see how he adored these little ones. It was my duty to try and get the company started, to make time to the next settlement where the crowds would be waiting for us, but it was a difficult task to pull him away from the little children. He wanted to shake hands with and talk to every one of them...

"I have visited at his home when one of his children was down sick. I have seen him come home from work at night tired, as he naturally would be, and yet he could walk the floor for hours with that little one in his arms...loving it, encouraging it in every way with such tenderness and such a soul of pity and love."26

Edith, a daughter, recalled that the family " 'would kneel down always in the morning or in the evening and have our family prayer. Many times I actually thought that the Lord was right in the house because of the way Father would talk to him and express his feelings. He was talking to his Heavenly Father, and we felt it keenly. Often as a little girl I wanted to open my eyes during the prayer to see which direction the Lord was in because Father was talking to him and we knew it.' "27

"Marjorie Virginia Smith, born December 7, 1906, was the first of two children to be adopted by Joseph F. and Julina. She recalls his kindness and tender love. 'I'll always remember when one of the children I was playing with one day told me I did not belong to my family because I was adopted. I felt like there was something horribly wrong with me and I ran home crying.' Emily, her sister eighteen years older, 'caught me as I came in the door. She said, 'What in the world is wrong?' I asked what it meant to be adopted. I felt there must be some terrible curse on me. Father happened to be in his office, so Emily took me right in.

"'Papa picked me right up and put me on his lap and said that he and Mama could have no more babies and that I was sent to them. He explained it to me in such a way that I felt very much loved and wanted. Papa said that when a child is sealed, even though adopted, that child is as much a part of that family as if she had been born to them. That has always been a great comfort to me.'"[28]

On April 12, 1901, President George Q. Cannon passed away in Monterey, California. From then until the October General Conference, Joseph F. served as President Snow's only counselor. On October 6, Joseph F. was sustained as First Counselor to President Lorenzo Snow, and Rudger Clawson was sustained as his Second Counselor. Unfortunately, this presidency would be more than brief, and in fact the two counselors were never even set apart. Immediately following the conference President Snow grew ill, and on October 10, 1901, he passed quietly away. With his passing, Joseph F. became the senior apostle on the earth.

CA. 1889–90

Joseph F. Smith's photo taken by C.R.
Savage. Joseph F. wrote a humorous poem
about this picture (which appears on this
book's dust jacket):

In 'underground days', as the saying goes
The great C.R. Savage kindly proposed
To take my photograph in modern pose.
I gladly consented the Savage to meet
And sit for my picture expecting a treat;
To my disapointment, as you may suppose
Instead of my features he photoed my nose!
True my whiskers came in for a liberal stare,
In the picture before you, as you will declare,
But then you'll agree with my wail of despair
T'was a Savage act on the part of C.R.
To photograph only my nose and my hair!

19

"PRESIDENT PAPA"

"Is Papa going to be a prophet?" The questioner was seven-year-old Edith Smith.

"He already is a prophet," thirteen-year-old Franklin replied with some disdain. "All the Brethren are prophets!"

It was Thursday, October 17, 1901, and word had been carried to the five Smith families that their "Papa," Joseph F., wanted to hold a general meeting with all of them. They were mostly gathered now, and quietly waiting, though four-year-old Martha and her sister Agnes, three, were doing their usual running around giggling and screaming. Besides Joseph F.'s five wives, there were thirty-six of his children in attendance, eighteen of them thirteen years and under; several grandchildren; and seven sons or daughters-in-law. It was quite a group, especially considering that an additional ten of Joseph F.'s children had already passed on to the eternal world.

"Let me explain this, Edith," thirteen-year-old Emma declared. "The First Presidency and Quorum of the Twelve Apostles are all prophets..."

"Yeah, and seers and revelations, too," Calvin, who was eleven, interjected.

"Not revelations," Franklin laughed. "Revelators."

"That's right," Emma agreed. "And since Papa is a member of the First Presidency—"

"I thought he was an apostle!" Edith whined, screwing up her face as if she was about to cry.

"He is!" ten-year-old Rachel declared. "All the First Presidency are Apostles."

"Uh-uh," five-year-old Jesse argued. "They're first presidencies, 'cause Mama says so!"

Alice Ann, Jesse's mother, looked around and shrugged helplessly while the remainder of the adults tried not to laugh at the small boy's humorous innocence.

"All right, all of you," twenty-nine-year-old Hyrum Mack said as he balanced one of his own children on his knee, "listen carefully, and I'll explain what Papa is."

"Just 'cause you're an adult, Hyrum, doesn't mean you know everything!"

"You're right, Jesse; it doesn't. But I think I know this. When a man is ordained to be an apostle, he is also given the keys to be a prophet, seer, and revelator."

"Keys?"

"Yes, like house keys that you keep in your pocket. Only, the keys apostles receive are spiritual keys, or keys to spiritual power. And since only one man on the earth can use those keys at any given time, and since that man is to be the senior apostle and President of the Church, those keys are held in abeyance by all the other apostles."

"What's 'abeyance' mean?"

"It means they can't use them."

"How come?"

"Well, uh..." Hyrum struggled for an explanation, "because Heavenly Father sort of stitches their pockets shut, so they can't take them out."

"Wow!" Jesse's eyes were large. "Does He ever unstitch them?"

Hyrum smiled. "Only if one day they become the senior apostle. Then the Lord unstitches their pockets, and they can use their keys."

"Well, what about the rest of the First Presidencies, like Papa has been? Are their pockets unstitched?"

Hyrum and several others chuckled. "Samuel, as counselors in the First Presidency, they assist the President, who is also the prophet, seer, and revelator. The counselors are still apostles, and their own keys remain stitched up tight until—and if—they become the senior apostle."

"Hyrum is right, children, and I want you to remember what he has told you. Only the Lord can unstitch a man's pockets so that he may use his priesthood keys."

"Papa!" several exclaimed as they scurried toward sixty-two-year-old Joseph F. "When did you come?"

"A few moments ago, Jeanetta." Joseph F. hugged the smaller children and then shrugged out of his coat. "I even heard the arguing, which disappointed me very much."

"We're sorry, Papa."

"I know you are, Rachel. But remember this, all of you. Contention is always of the devil, and when you participate in it, you invite his spirit to rule your life."

Smiling, Joseph F. then went from one to another as he passed around the room, hugging and kissing each of his family members no matter how old they had become. At last he took the large chair that had been held in readiness for him.

"Very well," he said kindly as he looked from one eager face to another, "let me add a little to what Hyrum has already told you. I'm certain I look old to you, but I wish you to remember that the senior apostle is not senior because of his age, but rather because of the order in which he was ordained. For instance, I became a member of the Quorum of the Twelve at age twenty-seven. Later, several brethren who were older than me were brought into the Twelve; nevertheless, I was senior to them, for I had been ordained prior to them."

"Are there any who are older than you now, Papa?"

"Yes, Emily, there are several. John R. Winder, for instance, is nearly fifteen years older than I. Brigham Young, Jr. is older, so are George Teasdale and Marriner W. Merrill. Nevertheless, because I was ordained before any of them, I am now the most senior of the living apostles."

"Does that mean that you are going to be President of the Church?"

"Yes, Emily, as Senior Apostle, that burden now falls upon my shoulders."

"You mean it's automatic?" Calvin questioned. "That doesn't seem very fair, Papa! I mean, just because a fellow has been an apostle the longest doesn't necessarily mean he's the most qualified!"

"Calvin, you're talking about Papa!"

Calvin, suddenly realizing what he had said, turned quite red. "I... I'm sorry, Papa. I didn't mean—"

Joseph F. smiled. "Your concern is quite valid. But allow me to remind you of two things. First, being the senior apostle means that I have been in the Quorum of the Twelve the longest and have had the most experience. In other words, the Lord has had the longest time to endeavor to beat out of me all of my bad habits. Remember me telling you that as a young man I was often filled with anger and regularly lost my temper? Well, over the years I have been allowed to experience enough hard times and difficult ordeals to winnow most of that anger completely away. Now I can hardly remember the last time I lost my temper."

"I've never seen you lose it," Julina said softly.

"And I hope you never will," Joseph F. smiled at his wife.

Joseph F. Smith, President of the
Church of Jesus Christ of Latter-
day Saints with counselors John R.
Winder and Anthon H. Lund

CA. 1902

"The second issue I wish all of you to remember, is that this is the Lord's church and not the church of President somebody-or-other, who is only a man. There never was a time since the organization of The Church of Jesus Christ of Latter-day Saints when a man led it—not for one moment. It was not so in the days of Joseph; it was not so in the days of Brigham Young; it has not been so since; it never will be so. The direction of this work among the people of the world will never be left to men. It is God's work. Jesus Christ, God's Son, presides in this church. It is named after him, and it is he who chooses who will become President."

"But you just said that the senior apostle—"

"Just a moment, Zina, and I believe you will understand. The Lord has a unique way of choosing which man is to preside over his earthly church. It cannot be argued about, neither can it be doubted. And never, ever, can there be a power struggle over the position. But how does the Lord accomplish such a great miracle, you may ask? Simply by taking in death those who, for one reason or another, are not to become the senior apostle and therefore President.

"For instance, George Q. Cannon was senior to me in the Quorum, having been ordained some time before me. For years we labored together, and he was as fine a man as I have ever known. In fact, he was the only man I have ever known who could consistently outwork me. Had he outlived President Snow, he would now be the senior apostle, and we would be sustaining him as President. For whatever reasons, however, it was not to be. Though I wish with all my heart that it were otherwise, the Lord took President Cannon in death this past April, leaving me as the most senior of the apostles after President Snow."

"And now you will become President?"

Joseph F. smiled a little sadly. "To tell you the truth, Wesley, that is why I sent word asking all of you to gather together. This morning in our regular meeting in the upper room of the Temple, we as a Quorum, myself presiding as senior apostle and president of the Quorum, reorganized the First Presidency. I was chosen and set apart as President. Your Uncle John Smith, who is patriarch to the Church, acted as voice. I chose as my counselors John R. Winder and Anthon H. Lund, who were also set apart. An announcement to this effect is already being published in the *Deseret News*."

"Goodness, Papa! You're the President? Of the whole Church?"

"I am now, Alice."

"Wow! You hold a lot of power!"

"Not really, Willard. You see, the Lord never did intend that one man should have all power, and for that reason he has placed in his church, presidents, apostles, high priests, seventies, elders, and the various offices of the lesser priesthood, all of which are essential in their order and place according to the authority bestowed on them. The Lord never did anything that was not essential or that was superfluous. There is a use for every branch of the priesthood that he has established in his church, and I have a deep and abiding respect for the power of those offices. If at any time my brethren of the apostles shall see in me a disposition to depart from this principle, I expect them to come to me, as my brethren, and remind me of him whom I have been called to serve."

"But you're still the prophet, seer, and revelation?"

Joseph F. chuckled as he reached for his small son. "That's correct, Calvin. As President of the Church, I am also the prophet, seer, and revelator, and as the Lord explains, the only man on earth who holds and is authorized to exercise all priesthood keys."

"Did Heavenly Father reach down and unstitch your pockets?"

As everyone laughed, Joseph F. smiled. "In a way, he did, Jesse, at the exact moment when President Snow died and I became senior apostle."

"Goodness! Did you see him?"

"Papa, do we have to call you President now?"

Again there was laughter. "No, Calvin," Joseph F. smiled as the laughter again subsided. "In fact, I will feel very badly if any of you ever call me anything but Papa!"

While the above meeting with all of Joseph F.'s family gathered together may or may not have happened, certainly all of them had to deal with the reality that their husband and father was now President of the Church. That day's edition of the *Deseret News* contained the following:

> To the Officers and Members of the Church of Jesus Christ of Latter-day Saints:
>
> This certifies that at the regular meeting of the Council of the Apostles, held in the Salt Lake Temple, this 17th day of October, 1901, at which the following Apostles were present: Joseph F. Smith, Brigham Young, John Henry Smith, George Teasdale, John W. Taylor, Marriner W. Merrill, Anthon H. Lund, Matthias F. Cowley, Abraham O. Woodruff, Rudger Clawson and Reed Smoot; also Patriarch John Smith; the following business was unanimously transacted:
>
> Joseph F. Smith was chosen and set apart as President of the Church of Jesus Christ of Latter-day Saints; and John R. Winder was sustained and set apart as First, and Anthon H. Lund was sustained and set apart as Second Counselor in the First Presidency of the Church.
>
> President Smith was then sustained as Trustee-in-trust for the Church of Jesus Christ of Latter-day Saints.
>
> President Joseph F. Smith was also sustained as President of the Salt Lake Temple with John R. Winder as his assistant.

Elder Brigham Young was sustained and set apart as President of the Quorum of the Twelve Apostles.

And it was decided to hold a special general conference of the Church for the purpose of voting upon the several actions; said conference to be held in Salt Lake City on Sunday the 10TH day of November next.

George F. Gibbs, Secretary

To the Officers and Members of the Church of Jesus Christ of Latter-day Saints:

Dear Brethren and Sisters:—Agreeable with the decision of the Council of Apostles at their regular meeting, Thursday, October 17, we hereby call a general conference of the Church of Jesus Christ of Latter-day Saints to be held in the Tabernacle, Salt Lake City, on Sunday, the 10TH of November, next, at 10 o'clock a.m., for the purpose of voting upon the Church authorities.

Joseph F. Smith,
John R. Winder,
Anthon H. Lund,
First Presidency.1

At the next regularly scheduled meeting of the First Presidency and the apostles, one week later, "the Apostles submitted the name of Hyrum M. Smith to fill the vacancy in that Council, and this nomination was unanimously accepted."2 Hyrum, the twenty-nine-year-old son of Joseph F.'s fourth wife, Edna Lambson, was a dutiful and righteous young man who was worthy in every way of the calling. Still, it must have thrilled Joseph F. thoroughly to see his son, at nearly the same age, embark on the same grand journey of service and spiritual growth that he had been called to pursue so many years before.

Near the time when Joseph F. was set apart as President of the Church, "he stood five feet eleven inches tall, weighed [on average] 185–195 pounds, wore a full beard and glasses. He was kind, humorous, loyal, charitable (despite attacks on his character by the national press), and was always clean and orderly in his personal habits. He was known as 'a preacher of righteousness.'"3

Without delay the *Improvement Era* provided readers with its own description of the Church's new President:

"'President Joseph F. Smith has an imposing physical appearance. He has completed his sixty-third year; he is tall, erect, well-knit and symmetrical in build. He has a prominent nose and features. When speaking, he throws his full, clear, brown eyes wide open on the listener who may readily perceive from their penetrating glimpse the wonderful mental power of the tall forehead above. His large head is crowned with an abundant growth of hair, in his early years dark, but now, like his full beard, tinged with a liberal sprinkling of gray. In conversation, one is forcibly impressed with the sudden changes in appearance of his countenance, under the different influences of his mind; now intensely pleasant, with an enthusiastic and childlike interest in immediate subjects and surroundings: now absent, the mobility of his features set in that earnest, almost stern, majesty of expression so characteristic of his portraits—so indicative of the severity of the conditions and environments of his early life.'"4

At the special conference of the Church held on November 10TH, 1901, President Smith "sounded the theme of his presidency: 'We have been looked upon as interlopers, as fanatics, as believers in a false religion; we have been regarded with contempt, and treated despicably; we have been driven from our homes, maligned and spoken evil of every where, until the people of the world have come to believe that we are the off-scourings of the earth and scarcely fit to live... The Lord designs to change this condition of things, and to make us known to the world in our true light—as true worshippers of God...and that our mission in this world is to do good, to put down iniquity in the hearts of the people, and to establish in the minds of our children, above all other things, a love for God and His word...making them firm believers in the word of the Lord, in the restored Gospel and Priesthood, and in the establishment of Zion, no more to be thrown down nor given to another people.'"5

It quickly became apparent to the Saints that Joseph F. had lost neither his humility nor his zeal. He declared, "'I cut no figure personally in this work, and I am nothing except in the humble effort to do my duty as the Lord gives me the ability to do it.'"6 Nevertheless, he felt very strongly "that his two-fold mission was to convince the world that the principles taught by the Church were the true gospel of Jesus Christ, and to pass on to the next generation a testimony that the faith received of their fathers remained in fact the kingdom of God on earth."7

To that end, President Smith constantly bore witness to the divinely appointed mission of the Prophet Joseph Smith, as well as to the divinity of the Lord Jesus Christ who had sent him. On various occasions he explained:

> I was instructed to believe in the divinity of the mission of Jesus Christ... I was taught it from my father, from the Prophet Joseph Smith, through my mother...and all my boyhood days and all my years in the world I have clung to that belief.8

> As a child I knew the Prophet Joseph Smith. As a child I have listened to him preach the gospel that God had committed to his charge and care. As a child I was familiar in his home, in his household, as I was familiar under my own

ᴬ

father's roof. I have retained the witness of the Spirit that I was imbued with, as a child, and that I received from my sainted mother, the firm belief that Joseph Smith was a prophet of God; that he was inspired as no other man in his generation, or for centuries before, had been inspired; that he had been chosen of God to lay the foundations of God's Kingdom.9

O, [the Prophet Joseph] was full of joy; he was full of gladness; he was full of love... And while he could play with children and amuse himself at simple, innocent games among men, he also communed with the Father and the Son and spoke with angels, and they visited him, and conferred blessings and gifts and keys of power upon him.10

As a child I was impressed, deeply, with the thought, and firmly with the belief, in my soul that the revelations that had been given to and through Joseph the Prophet... were the word of God, as were the words of the ancient disciples when they bore record of the Father and the Son. That impression made upon me in my childhood has followed me through all the vicissitudes of more than sixty years of actual and practical experience in the mission field, throughout the nations of the world, and at home in the midst of the authorized servants of God.11

I bear my testimony to you and to the world, that Joseph Smith was raised up by the power of God to lay the foundations of this great latter-day work, to reveal the fullness of the gospel to the world in this dispensation, to restore the Priesthood of God to the world, by which men may act in the name of the Father, and of the Son, and of the Holy

Ghost, and it will be accepted of God; it will be by his authority. I bear my testimony to it; I know that it is true.12

Yet Joseph F. also wanted the Saints to understand that his testimony, like those of most in his hearing, was not based on the sorts of marvelous and dramatic experiences the Prophet Joseph enjoyed. "'When I as a boy first started out in the ministry,'" he explained, "'I would frequently go out and ask the Lord to show me some marvelous thing, in order that I might receive a testimony. But the Lord withheld marvels from me, and showed me the truth, line upon line, precept upon precept, here a little and there a little, until he made me to know the truth from the crown of my head to the soles of my feet, and until doubt and fear had been absolutely purged from me. He did not have to send an angel from the heavens to do this, nor did he have to speak with the trump of an archangel. By the whisperings of the still small voice of the Spirit of the living God, he gave to me the testimony I possess. And by this principle and power he will give to all the children of men a knowledge of the truth that will stay with them, and it will make them to know the truth, as God knows it, and to do the will of the Father as Christ does it.'"13

"'I have received the witness of the Spirit of God in my own heart, which exceeds all other evidences, for it bears record to me, to my very soul, of the existence of my Redeemer, Jesus Christ. I know that he lives, and that in the last day he shall stand upon the earth, that he shall come to the people who shall be prepared for him.'"14

And so Joseph F. themed his tenure as prophet, seer and revelator.

In 1905 the opportunity came for him to lead the Church in honoring the Prophet Joseph Smith. Early in the spring he sent "Junius F. Wells to Sharon, Windsor County, Vermont, to pinpoint the site of the Joseph Smith Sr. farm and to buy the land as agent for the Church. On 21 May, the first of four pieces of land of the Mack homestead in Sharon township were purchased. Soon thereafter, a decision was made to erect a monument and memorial cottage at the site on the one hundredth anniversary of the Prophet's birth."15 The shaft for the monument was to be a solid piece of granite cut to a length of 38½ feet, a foot for each year of Joseph Smith's life, and then polished just as the Lord had polished his prophet.

Early on the morning of Saturday, December 23RD, 1905, the one hundredth birthday of Joseph Smith, President Joseph F. Smith, who had traveled to Vermont by train, called the throng to order. After singing, prayer, and some brief remarks by President Smith and Elder Wells, President Smith offered the dedicatory prayer.

The cottage and monument erected in memory of Joseph Smith's birth and mission were the first such structures put up by the Church. Likewise, the Church's purchase of the Mack farm and homesite was a historic first. But no doubt because of Joseph F.'s very real connection with the early days of the Church, he was filled with a desire to preserve for the Saints as much of that early history as he could—including the exact locations where transcendent events from early Church history had occurred. These events, as well as the people who participated in them, were very real to him, and it was his desire that they be just as real to every other Latter-day Saint.

On their way home from Vermont, for instance, Joseph F. and his party stopped in Palmyra, New York, where they visited at the home near the Sacred Grove that had originally been built by Alvin for his parents. Within six months Joseph F. had directed that the home become the property of The Church of Jesus Christ of Latter-day Saints. On that same trip the Smith party also visited the Sacred Grove, climbed the Hill Cumorah, and a day or so later, visited at the temple in Kirtland, Ohio.

"This visit to Vermont, the purchase of the old Mack farm and the erection of the Joseph Smith Memorial Monument, met with such remarkable success in allaying prejudice and the making of friends, that it became the stimulant for the purchase in later years of the Hill Cumorah, the...Sacred Grove, and yet later the Whitmer farm, where the Church was organized and other sites of historical interest in the east, and the erection of the magnificent monument on top of the Hill Cumorah."16

On another front, despite the fact that Wilford Woodruff had issued the Manifesto in 1890, or that the Church had complied with the law so that Utah could be granted statehood in 1896, the problem of plural marriage seemed an ongoing issue that certain anti-Mormons would not let rest. In 1898 Elder B. H. Roberts was elected to Congress, despite the fact that all in Utah knew of his plural family and that he had been granted amnesty by U.S. President Benjamin Harrison. Moreover, his election had come about largely because of the "gentile" vote. Nevertheless, after his election the campaign of the anti-Mormons grew increasingly intense, demanding not only that Elder Roberts not be seated but insisting also that the Church had broken its pledge with the government and that, therefore, all its members should be permanently disfranchised. The *Salt Lake Tribune* joined in the cry, and in December the Salt Lake Ministerial Alliance published "an address 'most earnestly' calling upon the people of the United States to join them in a protest against the seating of Congressman-elect Roberts of Utah. They declared that the 'Mormon' Church...had broken its pledge with the government"17 by orchestrating the election of one of its own leaders.

In a telegram to the *New York World*, President Snow responded to this falsehood, though it did little good. After a bitter battle during which President Smith declared that Elder Roberts "made a magnificent fight before a bigoted and narrow-minded body and that his argument was unanswerable,"18 Congress refused to seat Elder Roberts.

That victory, unfortunately, gave the anti-Mormon agitators in Utah and elsewhere hope that they could be successful in disfranchising all members of the Church who held official positions or had been through the temple. Their next battleground was the seating of Elder Reed Smoot, an apostle who was elected to the Senate in January of 1903. Though Elder Smoot had never been a polygamist and had even publicly opposed it, those antagonistic to the Church felt that as a member of a ruling body that continued to promulgate plural marriage, which they wanted the world to think the Church was still doing, he could be denied his seat. (When all was said and done, Reed Smoot was seated and served in the Senate for the next thirty years).

Nineteen members of the Salt Lake Ministerial Alliance filed a formal protest, the *Salt Lake Tribune* hyped it daily, and by the time a Senate committee appointed to consider the protest commenced hearings on January 16, 1904, the Senate had received thousands of protests against the Mormons from all across the United States. The Smoot hearings continued until June of 1906, the high point of the hearings being the appearance of President Joseph F. Smith.

President Smith said that when he came before the committee as the first witness in this trial, March 2, 1904, and looked about him he was not slow to discover that he was in the house of his enemies. As he looked into the faces of the members of the Senate committee, he felt, as well as saw, a spirit of antagonism and bitterness expressed in the countenances of most, if not all, of those who were there to investigate him...

As the trial progressed day after day he felt that the sentiment on the part of some of the members of the committee was changing and they began to show him and others more friendly consideration... President Smith also declared that he faced this august body at first with some little feeling of timidity but he had not been before them long before he was possessed of a spirit of calmness and for some of these men he could not help feeling, although he did not show it, a spirit of extreme contempt, especially so for Fred T. Dubois, whose character was well known to him. Some of the members of the committee with the men who were responsible for the charges and their attorney, hoped and expected that when President Joseph F. Smith came before the committee he would endeavor to hide the true facts in relation to his own life and would be a very unwilling witness... To their utter astonishment, and it may well be said, with some feeling of disappointment, he took no such course but answered all their questions frankly, openly and honestly to the convincing of some, if not all of the members of the committee, that he was not the character they had been informed that he was and that the Church was not the kind of an organization which it had been published to the world to be.19

Church Patriarch Hyrum G. Smith, Joseph F.'s nephew, reported:

[W]hen Prest. Joseph F. Smith was taken as a witness before the United States Senate that people in the gallery, many of them influential persons and officers of the government with their friends, actually hissed at him when he was brought in before them as a witness; but before the close of that great case, these very persons, sought an opportunity to pay respect to him.20

"On the central question... President Smith denied any knowledge of new plural marriages. He did, however, acknowledge that his continued marital relations with plural wives were in technical violation of the law and Church rules."21 Even after that frank admission, "some of the members of the Senate expressed themselves as feeling that had he and others, who had entered into plural marriage honestly as a religious obligation before the proclamation of President Benjamin Harrison, abandoned their plural families they would have proved themselves to be less than honorable men."22

Despite such sentiments, trouble abroad for Joseph F. was soon to be compounded by troubles at home. The anti-Mormon American Party (organized by ex-Senator Thomas Kearns, a bitter enemy of Joseph F. and the Church who also owned the *Salt Lake Tribune*) gained control of Salt Lake City from 1905 to 1911. "In the early summer of 1905, Frederick M. Smith, eldest son of Joseph Smith of the 'Reorganized' Church, came to Salt Lake City under contract with the Thomas Kearns interests, to assist in the fight against the Church. Mr. Frederick M. Smith was given to believe that the Church of Jesus Christ of Latter-day Saints was in the throes of dissolution and by making a vigorous campaign—assisted by the enemies of the Church in Salt Lake City—he would shortly thereafter be able to pick up many of the broken fragments. He joined with these enemies of the Church in the hue and cry against the Church... Articles...which he signed... were published in the anti-'Mormon'... paper along with other falsehoods constantly hashed up by an apostate editor."23

Who was the editor doing all the hashing? Former Senator Frank J. Cannon, son of President George Q. Cannon, had been hired by Thomas Kearns as editor of the *Salt Lake Tribune*. "[F]rustrated by the lack of support for his own political ambitions, [Frank J.] mounted a scathing attack on President Smith, calling him 'a liar,' 'a sorcerer,' and 'a maker of evil.' President Smith, he proclaimed, 'will not need to wait to be cast down to hell in the next world, for he will get some of the condemnation here.'"24 For several years Cannon waged his war of persecution, using negative cartoons and equally negative editorials about Joseph F. and the Mormons to make the Church President's life as uncomfortable as possible.

"President Smith felt betrayed by one who knew the truth. 'Furious Judas' was his nickname for Frank J., but he made no response to [his] outrageous charges except to say, as in 1906, 'I do not care for and don't want to pay any heed to the ridiculous nonsense, the foolish twaddle, and the impious slurs that are being cast on me and my people, by wicked hearts and perverted minds. Let God deal with them as seemeth Him good.'"25

President Smith's daughter Edith recalled a time when she was " 'in about the fifth grade, [when] the news media was really persecuting my father. Some of the people at school had in their possession false reports and lies about Father. I went home from school furious one day. As soon as Father came in that evening I said to him, "Papa, why don't you do something? You're not doing one thing, and these mean men are taking advantage of you, printing all these lies, and you don't do one thing about it!'

" 'Father looked at me with his sweet smile and said, "Baby, don't get upset. They are not hurting me one bit; they are only hurting themselves. Don't you know, Baby, that when someone tells a lie, they are only hurting themselves more than anyone else?" That was a lesson I have never forgotten.' "26

Yet this was not an easy trial for Joseph F. to endure. His very nature revolted at all the lies and slander, and his natural inclinations were to strike back, just as he had done in his youth. One day he was "walking with his friend John Henry Smith down Main Street, and along came the editor of the *Salt Lake Tribune*... For years [the *Tribune*] had been attacking along two main themes; [that Joseph F. and all Church leadership under him were] a dynasty of authoritarian control, and that the Mormon Church did not believe in the separation of Church and State.

"Well, along came the editor of that paper, and John Henry Smith reached out and shook hands with him. Joseph F. smiled, but did not shake hands. Then, as they walked further, he said, 'I declare, John Henry, you'd shake hands with the devil himself!'"27

To the Saints assembled in General Conference during that time, he declared: "I confess it is hard for me to love my enemies—the enemies of the Church of Jesus Christ of Latter-day Saints—as I love my friends. It is a hard task for me to do. I confess I do not fully do it; it is hard for me; and yet, at times, the Spirit of the Lord will touch and soften my soul so much that I can readily say: I leave judgement in the hands of the Lord."28

More than perhaps any other living man, Joseph F. knew and understood the doctrines of Christ, and at least as well as most, he applied those doctrines in his own life. "I ask mercy for my enemies," he declared in another public address, "those who lie about me and slander me, and who speak all manner of evil against me falsely. In return, I beseech God my heavenly Father to have mercy upon them; for those who do it, not knowing what they are doing, are only misguided, and those who are doing it with their eyes open certainly need, most of all, the mercy, compassion and pity of God. May God pity them. May he have mercy upon them. I would not harm a hair of their heads, for all I am worth in the world. I would not throw a block in their way to prosperity. No; and I beseech my brethren that they keep hands off the enemies of our people and those who are paving their own road to destruction and will not repent, who are sinning with their eyes open, who know that they are transgressing the laws of God and vilifying and lying against the servants of the Lord. Have mercy upon them. Do not touch them; for that is just what they would like. Let them alone. Let them go."29

And so he did, putting all his energies into the affairs of the Church, directing it with inspiration and wisdom acquired from nearly a lifetime of sacrifice and service. First, to put to rest as well as he was able, the continued harangue against the Church with regards to plural marriage, Joseph F. presented to the General Conference in April 1904 the following Official Statement, which he read personally:

> Inasmuch as there are numerous reports in circulation that plural marriages have been entered into contrary to the official declaration of President Wilford Woodruff, of September 24, 1890, commonly called the Manifesto, which was issued by President Woodruff and adopted by the Church at its general conference, October 6, 1890, which forbade any marriages violative of the law of the land; I, Joseph F. Smith, President of the Church of Jesus Christ of Latter-day Saints, hereby affirm and declare that no such marriages have been solemnized with the sanction, consent or knowledge of the Church of Jesus Christ of Latter-day Saints, and
>
> I hereby announce that all such marriages are prohibited, and if any officer or member of the Church shall assume to solemnize or enter into any such marriage he will be deemed in transgression against the Church and will be liable to be dealt with, according to the rules and regulations thereof, and excommunicated therefrom.30

Joseph F. then continued, "They charge us with being dishonest and untrue to our word. They charge the Church with having violated a 'compact,' and all this sort of nonsense. I want to see today whether the Latter-day Saints representing the Church in this solemn assembly will not seal these charges as false by their vote."31

Not only was the vote unanimous in the affirmative, but within two years Apostles John W. Taylor and Matthias F. Cowley had resigned from the Council because they were out of harmony with President Smith's Official Statement. Both were officially sanctioned, though in later years Elder Cowley placed himself back in full harmony with the Church.

Another of Joseph F.'s major efforts as President was to pay off the Salt Lake Temple Bonds that had been issued under President Lorenzo Snow and to free the Church from debt. "Finally, in 1906, the debt was completely paid off. That day, President Joseph F. left his office adjoining the Beehive House, eagerly looking for his wife Julina. However, he met his daughter, Rachel. She recalled the occasion:

"'One day when we were living in the Beehive house, I came home from school and entered the door and walked into the little hall. My father had been in the kitchen and met me in the little hall. And he said, "Liddy, do you know where mother is? I've looked all over for her, and I've got some news I want to tell her." And I said, "No, sir." He said, "Do you think she is upstairs?" He said, "I've been every place." And I said, "I don't know...." He said, "Well, I wanted her to be the first one to hear this good news."... And the thing you don't know—and...he gave a little smile. He said, "I'll tell you, and I wanted mother to know." And he said, "The Church is at last out of debt," and he showed me his bonds.'"

"A few days later, she noted: 'He came in and he handed me a [canceled] bond, which I have today. And he said, "Seeing you were the first one to hear, I'm going to give you one of these [canceled] bonds.""'32

To the Saints in general, he declared:

> I want to say another thing to you, and I do so by way of
> congratulation, and that is that we have, by the blessing of
> the Lord and the faithfulness of the Saints in paying their
> tithing, been able to pay off our bonded indebtedness.
> Today the Church of Jesus Christ of Latter-day Saints owes
> not a dollar that it cannot pay at once. At last we are in a
> position that we can pay as we go. We do not have to bor-
> row any more, and we won't have to if the Latter-day Saints
> continue to live their religion and observe this law of
> tithing. It is the law of revenue to the Church.33

President Smith then began to prophesy—a dynamic prophecy that
took more than three quarters of a century before it came to pass.
He continued:

> Furthermore, I want to say to you we may not be able to
> reach it right away, but we expect to see the day when we
> will not have to ask you for one dollar of donation for any
> purpose, except that which you volunteer to give of your
> own accord, because we will have tithes sufficient in the
> storehouse of the Lord to pay everything that is needful for
> the advancement of the kingdom of God... That is the true
> policy, the true purpose of the Lord in the management of
> the affairs of His Church.34

In 1906 Joseph F. and his wife Edna, with several other of the
Brethren, toured the missions of Europe and Great Britain,
becoming the first Church President to do so. On his way home he
was persuaded to visit, for the first and only time in his life, the
Carthage Jail, where his father and uncle had been martyred and

which the Church had purchased in 1903. Of this difficult occasion, it is said:

> Charles W. Nibley prevail[ed] on Joseph F. Smith to go to Carthage. They walk[ed] up the steps. I don't know who was in charge, but as they turn[ed] right into the room, where all the bullets came—actually balls—the first thing the person [in charge] said was, pointing to the floor, "That stain is the blood of Hyrum Smith."
>
> Preston Nibley, who was there, told me that Joseph F. Smith walked over and sat down on the bed, put his hands over his face, and convulsively wept, until [Brother Nibley] could see the water coming through his fingers. [President Smith] then said, "Charlie, take me out of here!"
>
> They got in the little horse [drawn] buggy and rode the twenty-odd miles back to Nauvoo. Not one word was spoken.
>
> Brother Nibley then had business to take care of, and Joseph F. Smith took Preston, a student from the University of Chicago, all over the city. He pointed out the sites: "That's where the Relief Society was organized; that's where the Prophet stood when he preached the King Follett Discourse; this is where Edward Hunter lived when the Prophet was in hiding"; etc. Preston, who had taken Church History all for granted, said, "That was the day I knew I had to go home and start being serious about Church History."35

On one of his lengthy and tedious journeys by rail across the country, an event occurred that illustrated not only Joseph F.'s spirituality but his ability to hear and then obey the Spirit's still, small voice. According to Elder John Wells:

As the train was moving across the plains of Wyoming, President Smith stood at the back of the car taking a rest from a long, tedious day's journey. Any...who have traveled day after day in a railway train know what relief it is to stand up or move around for awhile... While standing at the back of the train he heard a voice telling him to go into the car, and he did so. Later he was walking up and down the corridor and was told by the same Voice to sit down. He did so. A few moments later the engine ran off the track and tilted the train on an angle which scared us all. Had President Smith been at the back of the train or walking in the corridor he might have been very seriously injured, but the Lord had regard for him and he was prompted by a Voice which he understood so well, and he acted accordingly. President Smith has always been susceptible to the influence of the Spirit of the Lord. He knew its promptings, and what they meant. As he heard the Still Small Voice directing him and inspiring him, he knew that Voice and knew it well.36

During his presidency, Joseph F. brought about remarkable and long-lasting advancements in Church status, government, policy, and doctrine. Besides finally relieving the Church of the burden of debt, he witnessed "the final resolution of tension between the Church and the federal government. During his administration the hostilities ended, and Latter-day Saints were accepted as loyal, law-abiding citizens."37

He dedicated the ground and began construction of the first temple to be built on foreign soil—in Cardston, Alberta, Canada. He also dedicated the ground for a temple in Laie, Hawaii. Under his administration the Church Office Building (now the Administration Building) was built, as was the Hotel Utah, next

Joseph F. Smith   26 May 1903

door. "He gave Church members a better appreciation of early Church history, acquired historical sites, and began building visitors centers. He clarified important doctrines, ...issued an official statement on the origin of humankind (1909), inaugurated the home evening program in 1915, created a committee that reformed and systemized priesthood work, instituted specific ages for Aaronic Priesthood ordinations (1908), and launched the seminary program in 1912...

[He opened] an information center... on Temple Square,...and *The Children's Friend* magazine began publication as part of the Primary program...

"He was the first President to be born to LDS parents, to drive an automobile, to be photographed in motion pictures, to occupy the Church Office Building (1917), and to visit Europe. He was the only President to be orphaned (age 13)."38

And yet, with all of this, President Joseph F. was first and foremost a father and husband, and his greatest joys were in his family. Though two of his sons were ordained to the Apostleship—Hyrum Mack Smith in 1901 and Joseph Fielding Smith in 1910—there was not one whom he did not love dearly and feel great admiration for. When World War I broke out, "several of President Smith's sons were drawn into the service of the United States in various departments, but only one of them saw actual service overseas, that was Calvin S., who was chaplain of the 91ST Division. He was in the thick of the fighting for a long period and in many engagements; was wounded several times, but his life was spared."39 One can only imagine the agony of President Joseph F. and his family during the tenure of Calvin's service.

To his wives and children, who gathered, first, on June 27, 1918, the anniversary of the martyrdom of Joseph and Hyrum Smith; and then again on November 10, 1918, to honor him on the anniversary of his being sustained as President of the Church, Joseph F. said:

...[w]hen I look around me and see my boys and girls, whom the Lord has given to me, and I have succeeded, with His help, to make them tolerably comfortable, and at least respectable in the world, I have reached the treasure of my life, the whole substance that makes life worth living. I have a family I am proud of, every individual member of it I love...40

I am blessed today with thirty-five children living, all of whom, so far as I know, have a standing in the Church of Jesus Christ of Latter-day Saints, and I believe their hearts are in the work of the Lord... I have today over eighty-six grandchildren, some of whom have reached nearly the stage of manhood and womanhood, and those who have reached the years of accountability are members of the Church in good standing...

I love them. I know them all. I never meet them but what I kiss them, just as I do my own children. I don't care how dirty their faces are, if I can only have the privilege of meeting with my grandchildren and kissing them and letting them know that I love them just as I love my own children. Then I shall be satisfied...41

When I can realize as I do that the Lord gave me five of the best mothers, the best wives, and best companions that any man in this world ever had, true as life itself, and that I have had the joy and pleasure of the blessings and the satisfaction, with the exception of the one dearly loved Aunt Sarah (here he wept, and said: "It is just as good for me to cry if I want to as it is for anyone.") of having them with me until now...

I feel very grateful."42

And so President Joseph F. continued forward, working quietly but constantly despite his advancing years, and seeking always the Spirit of the Lord.

20

A Preacher of Righteousness

The afternoon of November 18, 1918, was cold and blustery, and as sixty-two-year-old Heber Jeddy Grant closed the front door of the Beehive House behind him, the warmth that enveloped him was most welcome. He had not come far, only from the Church Office Building a few dozen yards away, yet that had been sufficient to remind him that winter was almost upon them and that he ought to start dressing more warmly.

"Good afternoon, Brother Grant."

"Good afternoon, David," Elder Grant replied as he stepped into the small office and removed his hat. "How is your father doing?"

First Counselor to Presiding Bishop Charles W. Nibley, David Asael Smith looked troubled. "Not well, I am afraid. Not well at all. Even since you were here this morning, he has weakened noticeably. I...I fear the end is near."

"Oh, dear. I hope it is not as bad as that!" For a moment Elder Grant struggled for words, trying to find a way to express his deep fears and concerns. As President of the Council of the Twelve Apostles, he knew that he was next in line should eighty-year-old President Joseph F. Smith pass away. Yet he felt so terribly ill-prepared for such a tragic eventuality, so utterly inadequate—

"I want you to know, David," he finally said, "that for years, one of the most sincere and earnest prayers of my heart has been that President Smith should live to celebrate the one hundredth anniversary of the birth of the Church. I prayed for this some months ago at the close of a temple fast meeting, and the Lord so abundantly blessed me that I felt my prayer would be answered, and I sat down weeping for joy."

"I hope that is what the Lord was confirming to you," David responded sadly.

"So do I, David. So do I. Should I visit your father, do you think?"

"Oh, yes! In fact, he has been asking for you."

Surprised, Elder Grant made his way into the room where Joseph F. Smith, sixth President of The Church of Jesus Christ of Latter-day Saints, lay suffering. To Elder Grant he looked very frail, his eyes sunken and hollow, his skin pallid, not at all like the man of vigor and vitality with whom he had labored the past thirty-six years as Joseph F. served in the First Presidency, either as a counselor or the prophet.

Truly, Elder Grant thought as he gazed down at the President, no man who ever lived, with whom he had been associated, had been so beloved by him as Joseph F. Smith. And no man could have possibly inspired more love and confidence than had this aged son of Hyrum Smith, the Patriarch. Yet now he lay very near to death's door, and as suddenly as that, Heber J. Grant knew that President Smith would soon be gone.

Joseph F. opened his eyes and looked up.

"Good afternoon, President," Elder Grant said softly, his voice trembling with countless conflicting emotions.

Without responding, the President reached out and took Elder Grant's hand firmly in his own. Then, pressing it with a

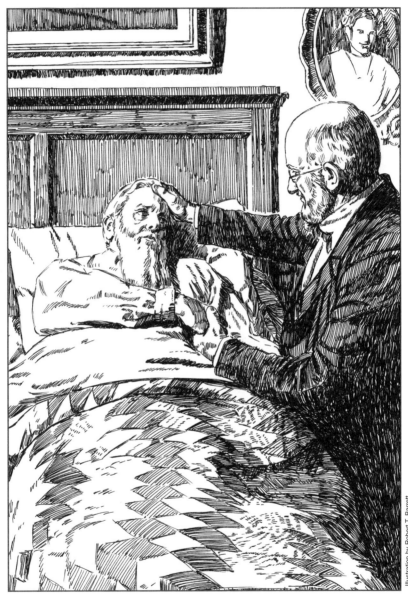

power and strength that was far from what one would expect from a dying man, Joseph F. began blessing Elder Grant with power and through the Spirit of the living God. With love in his eyes and the strong pressure of his hand, nearly every word he spoke thrilled Elder Grant's very being, so that in an instant, tears of gratitude to God and love for his mouthpiece upon the earth filled his heart. His blessing was all Elder Grant could have asked for—all that he could have expected had President Smith been his own dear father.

Still, it seemed neither right nor possible that President Smith was dying and that he, Heber J. Grant, should thereafter be called to preside over the Church. He knew himself far too well, was far too aware of his numerous weaknesses and foibles—

"The Lord bless you, my boy," President Smith then said as his hand continued to exert pressure on the hand of Elder Grant, just as if he were reading the younger apostle's mind, "the Lord bless you. You have a great responsibility. Always remember this is the Lord's work and not man's. The Lord is greater than any man. He knows whom he wants to lead his Church and never makes any mistakes. The Lord bless you."

More than any other thing during his years of service in the Church, President Joseph F. was known and loved as a gospel scholar and preacher of righteousness. He thought of himself that way, stating once, earlier in his life, that "the merciful hand of God and his kindliest providences have ever been extended visibly toward me, even from my childhood, and my days grow better and better thru humility and the pursuit of wisdom and happiness in the kingdom of God; The objects of my life becoming more apparent as time advances and experience grows. Those objects being the proclamation of the gospel, or the establishment of the kingdom of God on the earth; The salvation of souls, and most important of which to me—that of myself and family."[1]

Presiding Bishop Charles W. Nibley added, " 'As a preacher of righteousness, who could compare with him?... He was the greatest that I ever heard—strong, powerful, clear, appealing. It was marvelous how the words of living light and fire flowed from him. He was a born preacher, and yet he did not set himself up to be such. He never thought highly of his own good qualities. Rather, he was simple, plain and unaffected to the last degree; and yet, there was a dignity with it all which enabled anyone and everyone to say: "He is a man among men!" I ask, as a preacher, leader, teacher, husband, father, citizen and man, who among our mighty ones can be likened to him?' "2

Bishop Nibley's assessment rings as true as do the preachings of Joseph F. Smith. As though he were living in this age of hedonistic consumption, he declared:

> [T]here is no other way—no other course we can take in the world, in relation to our temporal welfare and health, better than that which the Lord God has pointed out to us [Doctrine and Covenants 89, commonly known as the Word of Wisdom]. Why can we not realize this? Why will we not come to a perfect understanding of it? Why will we not deny ourselves that which our craven appetites desire? Why can we not observe more closely the will of the Lord as made known to us in this revelation?... No man can violate the laws of God with reference to health and temporal salvation, and enjoy those blessings [of both temporal and spiritual health and strength] in the same degree that he would do if he would obey the commands of God. Don't you believe that? Can not Latter-day Saints accept the truth in their hearts? Can there be any room for argument..? I say to you, my brethren and sisters, that God knows better than we do what is and will be for our best

good, and when the Lord speaks to us, as He has spoken to us in this revelation...we should give it attention.₃

Another theme sounded by President Joseph F. that rings with even greater clarity today was directed toward the women of the Church as well as their husbands and daughters. He proclaimed:

> Never... at least within the period of my life—and I have lived in the world nearly seventy-five years—never, I say... have I seen such obscene, uncleanly, impure, and sugges-tive fashions of women's dress as I see today. Some of them are abominable. I lift my voice against these audacious practices and these infamous fashions, and I pray that you who have daughters in Zion will save them, if you can, from following these obscene fashions, that if followed, will destroy the last   vestige of true womanly modesty, and reduce them to the level of the courtesans [prostitutes] on the streets of Paris, from whence these debasing fashions come. They are the lowest and most degraded specimens of womankind, who have yielded their bodies to crime and their souls to death, if not to perdition, and are devoid of modesty and the sense of shame. We cannot afford to let our women follow such as these or to adopt the cursed fashions they set.₄

One wonders how President Smith would react now if he took a walk down Main Street in Salt Lake City or visited one of the schools, dances, or perhaps even rock concerts where Latter-day Saint youth gather. In a related vein, he taught:

> There are at least three dangers that threaten the Church within, and the authorities need to awaken to the fact that

the people should be warned unceasingly against them. As I see these, they are flattery of prominent men in the world, false educational ideas, and sexual impurity.

But the third subject mentioned—personal purity, is perhaps of greater importance than either of the other two. We believe in one standard of morality for men and women. If purity of life is neglected, all other dangers set in upon us like the rivers of waters when the flood gates are opened.5

Sexual union is lawful in wedlock, and if participated in with right intent is honorable and sanctifying. But without the bonds of marriage, sexual indulgence is a debasing sin, abominable in the sight of Deity.6

Like many bodily diseases, sexual crime drags with itself a train of other ills. As the physical effects of drunkenness entail the deterioration of tissue, and disturbance of vital functions, and so render the body receptive to any distemper to which it may be exposed, and at the same time lower the powers of resistance even to fatal deficiency, so does unchastity expose the soul to divers spiritual maladies, and rob it of both resistance and recuperative ability. The adulterous generation of Christ's day were deaf to the voice of truth, and through their diseased state of mind and heart, sought after signs and preferred empty fable to the message of salvation.

We accept without reservation or qualification the affirmation of Deity, through an ancient Nephite prophet: "For I, the Lord God, delight in the chastity of women. And whoredoms are an abomination before me; thus saith the Lord of hosts." (Jacob 2:28.)

We hold that sexual sin is second only to the shedding of innocent blood in the category of personal crimes; and that the adulterer shall have no part in the exaltation of the blessed.

We proclaim as the word of the Lord:

"Thou shalt not commit adultery." And:

"He that looketh on a woman to lust after her, or if any shall commit adultery in their hearts, they shall not have the Spirit, but shall deny the faith..."

[W]e are of the opinion there are more grades or degrees of sin associated with the improper relationship of the sexes than of any other wrongdoing of which we have knowledge. [But t]hey all involve a grave offense—the sin against chastity, but in numerous instances this sin is intensified by the breaking of sacred covenants, to which is sometimes added deceit, intimidation or actual violence.[7]

Giving the difference between knowledge and intelligence an inspired and thought-provoking spin, he explained:

There is a difference between knowledge and pure intelligence. Satan possesses knowledge, far more than we have, but he has no intelligence or he would render obedience to the principles of truth and right. I know men who have knowledge who understand the principles of the gospel, perhaps as well as you do, who are brilliant, but who lack the essential qualification of pure intelligence. They will not accept and render obedience thereto. Pure intelligence comprises not only knowledge, but also the power to properly apply that knowledge.[8]

True repentance was another of President Joseph F.'s favorite themes and was a doctrine that he felt was too little understood among the Latter-day Saints. In that context, he declared:

True repentance is not only sorrow for sins and humble penitence and contrition before God, but it involves the necessity of turning away from [our sins,] a discontinuance of all evil practices and deeds, a thorough reformation of life, a vital change from evil to good, from vice to virtue, from darkness to light. Not only so, but to make restitution, so far as it is possible, for all the wrongs we have done, to pay our debts, and restore to God and man their rights — that which is due them from us. This is true repentance, and the exercise of the will and all the powers of body and mind is demanded to complete this glorious work of repentance; then God will accept it.9

President Joseph F. Smith, "who had witnessed the mob violence of Nauvoo, often spoke of the importance of the rule of law in a civilized society. He...urged the Saints to be law-abiding and loyal citizens wherever they lived and to be faithful in their allegiance to their governments. On one occasion when a government official expressed contempt for the United States Constitution, President Smith countered: 'Latter-day Saints cannot tolerate such a spirit as this. It is anarchy. It means destruction. It is the spirit of mobocracy, and the Lord knows we have suffered enough from mobocracy, and we do not want any more of it... We cannot afford to yield to that spirit or contribute to it in the least degree. We should stand with a front like flint against every spirit or species of contempt or disrespect for the constitution of our country and the constitutional laws of our land.'"10

And finally, he summarized:

I have just one little short sermon: Get out of debt; keep out of debt; never mortgage your homes nor your farms.

Put down intemperance, and be a wise and sober people. Do not make war on, but love your neighbors. Keep the word of wisdom. Be wise and moderate in your amusements, and let your amusements be innocent and your enjoyment pure. Card-playing is an evil; pool-playing is an evil; gambling is an evil. Avoid every evil, and the waste of your time. Honor the Sabbath day and divine authority. Keep yourself pure and unspotted from the world... Be not scoffers, but show kindness and sympathy to all, and especially to the unfortunate.11

With every fiber of his being, Joseph F. believed in these and every other doctrine of the Lord's restored Church. "'There is nothing under the heavens,'" he declared, "'of so much importance to me or to the children of men as the great plan of life and salvation.'"12 In fact, he felt so strongly about these doctrines of Christ—and about the eternal consequences of obeying or not obeying the principles of the Gospel, that he declared the following in the October, 1909, general conference:

I may be pardoned, since it is pretty well known everywhere, I believe, that I speak my mind if I speak at all, if I say to you, Mormon, Jew, and Gentile, believer and unbeliever, present in this congregation, I would rather take one of my children to the grave than I would see him turn away from this Gospel. I would rather take my children to the cemetery, and see them buried in innocence, than I would see them corrupted by the ways of the world. I would rather go myself to the grave than to be associated with a wife outside of the bonds of the new and everlasting covenant. Now, I hold it just so sacred... There is nothing I can think of, in a religious way, that would grieve me more intensely than to see one of my boys marry an unbelieving girl, or one of my girls marry an unbelieving man. While I live, and they will listen to my voice, you can depend upon it, none of them will ever do it.13

Despite such stern-sounding preachments, President Joseph F. was much beloved—a man of the people. During a tour of the southern Utah settlements in 1916, it was observed by one who accompanied him: "'He is one of the people, not apart from them; and, like the apostles of old, he mingles with them on terms of equality and fellowship. The humblest member may stand up like a man and greet him as his brother.'"14

Though by nature affable, kind, sympathetic, even jovial and happy, with a marvelous sense of humor, taken all-in-all, Joseph F. lived a life that tended to be somber, reflective, and rather lonely. This was in part because of the tragic events of his youth. In all sincerity, he could say:

> *Out of myself, dear Lord,*
> *O lift me up!*
> *No more I trust myself in life's dim maze;*
> *Sufficient to myself is all its devious ways.*
> *I trust no more, but humbly at Thy throne*
> *Pray, "Lead me, for I cannot go alone."*

> *Out of my weary self*
> *O lift me up!*
> *I faint, the road winds upward all the way;*
> *Each night but ends another weary day.*
> *Give me Thy strength, and may I be so blest*
> *As on "the heights" to find the longed for rest.*

Out of my lonely self,
O lift me up!
Though other hearts with love are running o're;
Though dear ones fill my lonely home no more;
Though every day I miss the fond caress;
Help me to join in others' happiness.

Out of my doubting self,
O lift me up!
Help me to feel that Thou art always near;
E'en though 'tis night and all around seems drear,
Help me to know that, though I cannot see,
It is my Father's hand that leadeth me![15]

Early in January of 1918, President Joseph F.'s son Hyrum, a member of the Council of the Twelve, developed appendicitis. Putting it off as of little consequence, when surgery finally did take place the appendix had ruptured, and within days Elder Smith had died of peritonitis. "President Anthon H. Lund provides a poignant word-picture of President Joseph F.'s final farewell to his beloved son: 'Prest. Smith broke down and groaned when he came in to take the last look of his son, witnessed a very sad scene.'"[16]

Hyrum's death was a severe trial to the aged President, who from that time began to decline in vigor and in health. Nevertheless, in April conference he told the assembled Saints: " 'I may have physical ailments, ...but it appears to me that my spiritual status not only remains steadfast as in times past, but is developing, growing, becoming more thoroughly established in the faith of the gospel, in the love of truth, and in a desire to devote all the energy, time, wisdom and ability the Lord may give me to build up Zion in these latter days'."[17] He then issued an official document titled "An Authoritative Declaration," which reads:

Joseph F. Smith with his
greatest treasure – his family.

13 November 1904

Church Archives, The Church of Jesus Christ of Latter-day Saints

The Church of Jesus Christ of Latter-day Saints is no partisan Church. It is not a sect. It is THE CHURCH OF JESUS CHRIST OF LATTER-DAY SAINTS. It is the only one today existing in the world that can and does legitimately bear the name of Jesus Christ and His divine authority. I make this declaration in all simplicity and honesty before you and before all the world, bitter as the truth may seem to those who are opposed and who have no reason for that opposition. It is nevertheless true and will remain true until He who has a right to rule among the nations of the earth and among the individual children of God throughout the world shall come and take the reins of government and receive the bride that shall be prepared for the coming of the Bridegroom.

Many of our great writers have recently been querying and wondering where the divine authority exists today to command in the name of the Father and of the Son and of the Holy Ghost, so that it will be in effect and acceptable at the throne of the Eternal Father. I will announce here and now, presumptuous as it may seem to be to those who know not the truth, that the divine authority of Almighty God, to speak in the name of the Father and of the Son, is here in the midst of these everlasting hills, in the midst of this intermountain region, and it will abide and will continue, for God is its source, and God is the power by which it has been maintained against all opposition in the world up to the present, and by which it will continue to progress and grow and increase on the earth until it shall cover the earth from sea to sea. This is my testimony to you, my brethren and sisters, and I have a fullness of joy and of satisfaction in being able to declare this without regard to, or fear of, all the adversaries of the truth.18

Through the summer and fall President Joseph F. continued at his labors and still spent as much time as possible with his family and fellow Saints. Nevertheless, his body was racked by a series of illnesses which he could not seem to overcome. As he weakened in physical strength, however, the President grew stronger and stronger in the Spirit. On October 4TH, 1918, to the Saints in General Conference, he stated: "As most of you, I suppose, are aware, I have been undergoing a siege of very serious illness for the last five months...

" 'I will not, I dare not, attempt to enter upon many things that are resting upon my mind this morning, and I shall postpone until some future time, the Lord being willing, my attempt to tell you of some of the things that are in my mind, and that dwell in my heart. I have not lived alone these last five months. I have dwelt in the spirit of prayer, of supplication, of faith and of determination; and I have had my communication with the Spirit of the Lord continuously...' "19

What the Saints did not learn, at least until two months later, was that President Joseph F., the boy who had struggled so to overcome his temper and to endure silently the jeers of the world; the young man who had suffered through a bitter divorce but who had reared a most wonderfully loving family; the orphaned child who had so missed his parents but had willingly spent years of lonely service away from his family; the heartbroken father who had buried thirteen beloved children and one precious wife but yet bore continuing witness to the goodness and mercy of God; this man had finally "received the reward of his endurance, faith, and meekness. The veil [had grown] so thin that he [had seen] the Savior, the spirit world, and the things of God."20 "He saw his father Hyrum, the Prophet Joseph, and others, and learned 'that the faithful elders of this dispensation, when they depart from mortal life, continue their labors in the preaching of the gospel.'"21

Apparently a series of visions and manifestations which he had shared with his son Joseph Fielding had culminated only the day before Conference began in a remarkable vision which is now known as the "Vision of the Redemption of the Dead." Presented to his counselors, the Twelve, and the Church patriarch on October 31, 1918, and unanimously accepted, this vision of President Joseph F.'s was published in the December 1918 Improvement Era and was accepted by the Church as canonized scripture in 1976. It is now contained in Doctrine and Covenants, Section 138. In part it reads:

> On the third of October, in the year nineteen hundred and eighteen, I sat in my room pondering over the scriptures; And reflecting upon the great atoning sacrifice that was made by the Son of God, for the redemption of the world; And the great and wonderful love made manifest by the Father and the Son in the coming of the Redeemer into the world; That through his atonement, and by obedience to the principles of the gospel, mankind might be saved.
>
> While I was thus engaged, my mind reverted to the writings of the apostle Peter...
>
> As I pondered over these things which are written, the eyes of my understanding were opened, and the Spirit of the Lord rested upon me, and I saw the hosts of the dead, both small and great. And there were gathered together in one place an innumerable company of the spirits of the just, who had been faithful in the testimony of Jesus while they lived in mortality; And who had offered sacrifice in the similitude of the great sacrifice of the Son of God, and had suffered tribulation in their Redeemer's name. All these had departed the mortal life, firm in the hope of a glorious resurrection, through the grace of God the Father

and his Only Begotten Son, Jesus Christ. I beheld that they were filled with joy and gladness, and were rejoicing together because the day of their deliverance was at hand. They were assembled awaiting the advent of the Son of God into the spirit world, to declare their redemption from the bands of death. Their sleeping dust was to be restored unto its perfect frame, bone to his bone, and the sinews and the flesh upon them, the spirit and the body to be united never again to be divided, that they might receive a fullness of joy.

While this vast multitude waited and conversed...the Son of God appeared... But unto the wicked he did not go, and among the ungodly and the unrepentant who had defiled themselves while in the flesh, his voice was not raised; Neither did the rebellious who rejected the testimonies and the warnings of the ancient prophets behold his presence, nor look upon his face. Where these were, darkness reigned, but among the righteous there was peace; And the saints rejoiced in their redemption, and bowed the knee and acknowledged the Son of God as their Redeemer and Deliverer from death and the chains of hell. Their countenances shone, and the radiance from the presence of the Lord rested upon them, and they sang praises unto his holy name...

And I wondered at the words of Peter—wherein he said that the Son of God preached unto the spirits in prison, who sometime were disobedient, when once the long-suffering of God waited in the days of Noah—and how it was possible for him to preach to those spirits and perform the necessary labor among them in so short a time.

And as I wondered, my eyes were opened, and my

understanding quickened, and I perceived that the Lord went not in person among the wicked and the disobedient who had rejected the truth, to teach them; But behold, from among the righteous, he organized his forces and appointed messengers, clothed with power and authority, and commissioned them to go forth and carry the light of the gospel to them that were in darkness, even to all the spirits of men; and thus was the gospel preached to the dead...

And so it was made known among the dead, both small and great, the unrighteous as well as the faithful, that redemption had been wrought through the sacrifice of the Son of God upon the cross. Thus was it made known that our Redeemer spent his time during his sojourn in the world of spirits, instructing and preparing the faithful spirits of the prophets who had testified of him in the flesh; That they might carry the message of redemption unto all the dead, unto whom he could not go personally, because of their rebellion and transgression, that they through the ministration of his servants might also hear his words...

I beheld that the faithful elders of this dispensation, when they depart from mortal life, continue their labors in the preaching of the gospel of repentance and redemption, through the sacrifice of the Only Begotten Son of God, among those who are in darkness and under the bondage of sin in the great world of the spirits of the dead. The dead who repent will be redeemed, through obedience to the ordinances of the house of God. And after they have paid the penalty of their transgressions, and are washed clean, shall receive a reward according to their works, for they are heirs of salvation.

Thus was the vision of the redemption of the dead revealed to me, and I bear record, and I know that this record is true, through the blessing of our Lord and Savior, Jesus Christ, even so. Amen.

On the anniversary of the day he was sustained as President of the Church, November 10, 1918, the children, grandchildren, and wives of Joseph F. gathered to pay him honor. To them he declared, "'If there is anything on earth I have tried to do as much as anything else, it is to keep my word, my promises, my integrity, to do what it was my duty to do.'"22

Within a few days of this grand family reunion, to which all had come in the spirit of fasting and prayer, President Joseph F. grew seriously ill with what was then called pleurisy, "which continued to grow in intensity, finally developing into pleuro-pneumonia..."23 His office in the Beehive House next door to the Church Office Building became his sickroom, and there his son David, as well as other members of his family, watched over him. And it was there, on November 18, that he met with and blessed Heber J. Grant.

Following the blessing given him by the dying Prophet, Elder Grant recorded in a letter to the family of President Smith: "Sister Bowman entered and kissed and wept over her father, and I walked into the little front office and wept, feeling that the last words I would ever hear from his beloved lips had been spoken when he said to me, 'The Lord bless you, my boy, the Lord bless you, you have a great responsibility. Always remember this is the Lord's work and not man's. The Lord is greater than any man. He knows whom He wants to lead His Church and never makes any mistakes. The Lord bless you.'

"I returned to my office, but I did not even have the heart to mail some letters which I had written earlier in the day. I went home and after eating supper I again visited the President, whom

Heber J. Grant

CA. *about 1908*

Church Archives, The Church of Jesus Christ of Latter-day Saints

I found in great pain, and he asked President Lund who was there to bless him and supplicate the Lord to release him, and call him home. We placed our hands upon his head and President Lund told the Lord how much we loved our President and of our gratitude for the joy and happiness we had had in laboring with him, but asked that he be called home if his life could not be spared to us.

"The next morning I awoke at one o'clock and was not able to get to sleep until after six-thirty, as my mind was with the President. I got the November *Era* and reread the President's talk at the October conference, and after doing so I wrote in my *Era* at the close of his talk:

"'Nov. 19/18. Re-read twice and wept as I think of how near death's door the President is.

"'It is 3:45 and I have been awake since one a.m.—Heber J. Grant.

"The President lived but one hour and five minutes after I had written that he was near death's door."24

It was 4:50 Tuesday morning, November 19, 1918, six days after his eightieth birthday. President Smith was buried on the cold, rainy afternoon of November 22ND. "No public funeral could be held as the city and state were under quarantine because of an epidemic of influenza which was sweeping over all the earth... As the solemn cortege quietly passed from the Bee Hive House to the City Cemetery, thousands of people thronged the streets with bowed heads, many of these had in the past expressed bitterness and enmity towards President Smith, but now they stood and mourned. As the remains passed the Cathedral of the Madeleine, the bells in the tower tolled solemnly and the Catholic priests paid silent respect to the distinguished dead."25

A short but lovely graveside service was held, and the Salt Lake City newspapers, including those controlled or written by his former enemies, eulogized Joseph F.'s name and memory with praise, honor,

Joseph F. Smith   *13 November 1913*

and glory.

Because the influenza epidemic, which had slain more than 21 million people worldwide, still raged the following April, no General Conference was held. But in June 1919, conditions were such that the eighty-ninth annual Conference could be held on Temple Square. Conducted by President Heber J. Grant, the speakers were instructed to "'devote the time and their remarks to the memory of President Joseph F. Smith.'"[26]

A host of General Authorities then paid marvelous tributes — among them the following by President Heber J. Grant:

> "I bear witness to you that from my early childhood days, when I could not thoroughly understand and comprehend the teachings of the gospel, that I have had my very being thrilled, and tears have rolled down my cheeks, under the inspiration of the living God, as I have listened to Joseph F. Smith when preaching the gospel. I believe that Joseph F. Smith and his son Hyrum M. Smith more than any other men to whom I have listened, who were born in the Church of Christ in our day, were the greatest preachers of righteousness. I know that whenever I heard that Joseph F. Smith was going to speak in one of the wards, that time and time again as a young man I have left my own ward and gone to listen to him, because he always filled my being and lifted me up as I listened to him proclaim the gospel of Jesus Christ. I bear witness that he was one of the greatest prophets of God that has ever lived; that God was with him from the day that he went forth as a little boy of fifteen years of age, to proclaim the gospel of Jesus Christ in the Hawaiian Islands, until the day when, after giving sixty-five years of his life to the work of God, he closed his earthly career.

"May God bless each and all of us who have a knowledge of the divinity of the work in which we are engaged, and may we be as faithful to the end as our prophet was, our beloved leader who has left us, Joseph F. Smith, is my prayer, and I ask it in the name of Jesus Christ. Amen."27

END NOTES

CHAPTER 1

1   Joseph Fielding Smith, *The Life of Joseph F. Smith*
     (Salt Lake City: Deseret News Press, 1938), p. 445.

2   Leonard J. Arrington, ed., and Scott Kenney, essayist,
     The Presidents of the Church—Biographical Essays—
     Joseph F. Smith (Salt Lake City: Deseret Book, 1986), p. 184.

3   Ibid., pp. 185–86.

4   *Teachings of Presidents of the Church—Joseph F. Smith* (Salt Lake City:
     The Church of Jesus Christ of Latter-day Saints, 1998), p. 95.

5   Joseph Fielding Smith, *The Life of Joseph F. Smith*, pp. 445–47.

6   Ibid., p. 176–77.

CHAPTER 2

1   Joseph Fielding Smith, *The Life of Joseph F. Smith*
     (Salt Lake City: Deseret News Press, 1938), p. 38.

2   Ibid., p. 31.

3   LeRoy S. Wirthlin, "Nathan Smith (1762–1828) Surgical
     Consultant to Joseph Smith," *BYU Studies 17* (Spring 1977):
     p. 327. In all the early documents this disease was referred to
     as typhus, though it has been correctly identified as typhoid fever.
     It is not likely that even Nathan Smith understood the difference.

4   Lucy Mack Smith, *History of Joseph Smith, by His Mother*
     (Salt Lake City: Bookcraft, 1958), p. 55.

5   Ibid., p. 55.

6   Pearson Corbett, *Hyrum Smith, Patriarch*, p. 10.
7   Ibid., p. 18.
8   Ibid., p. 19.
9   Ibid., p. 20.
10   Ibid., pp. 24–25.
11   Ibid., p. 25.
12   Ibid., p. 26.
13   Lucy Mack Smith, *History of Joseph Smith...*, pp. 75, 77.
14   Ibid., p. 87.
15   Ibid., p. 89.
16   Pearson Corbett, *Hyrum Smith...*, 39. In a footnote, Corbett states: "This chest, the first such repository for the gold plates and the Urim and Thummim, is in the possession of Hyrum's descendants. Its inside measurements are 16¼″ by 14½″. It has a sloping lid, attached by metal hinge to a four-inch wide strip across the back of the top side. A keyhole is located in the outside center of the lid through the wood to the metal lock. On the right of the lock craved (*sic*) in the inch board is the word 'Alvin.' Joints are dove tail construction, and the floor of the chest is one piece of inch lumber."
17   Doctrine and Covenants 11:23–26, 28–30.
18   Doctrine and Covenants 11:1–22.

CHAPTER 3
1   Don C. Corbett, *Mary Fielding Smith, Daughter of Britain* (Salt Lake City: Deseret Book, 1974), p. 11.
2   Ibid., p. 14.
3   Susa Y. Gates, "Mothers in Israel," *Relief Society Magazine* III (March 1916): p. 123.
4   Parley P. Pratt, *Autobiography of Parley P. Pratt* (Salt Lake City: Deseret Book, 1938), p. 110.
5   Ibid., p. 128.
6   Ibid., p. 128.
7   Don Corbett, *Mary Fielding Smith...*, p. 20.
8   Gates, "Mothers in Israel," p. 123. See also Don Corbett, *Mary Fielding Smith*, pp. 19–20.
9   Edward W. Tullidge, *The Women of Mormondom* (New York: Tullidge & Crandall, 1877), p. 250.

10 Orson F. Whitney, *Life of Heber C. Kimball* (Salt Lake City: The Kimball Family and The Juvenile Instructor Office, 1888), p. 116.

11 Joseph Smith, *History of the Church of Jesus Christ of Latter-day Saints* (Salt Lake City: Deseret Book, 1948), 2:492.

12 Tullidge, *Women of Mormondom*, p. 252.

13 Don Corbett, *Mary Fielding Smith...*, p. 34.

14 Ibid., pp. 36–39.

Chapter 4

1 Joseph Fielding Smith, *The Life of Joseph F. Smith* (Salt Lake City: Deseret News Press, 1938), p. 117.

2 Joseph Fielding Smith, *Life of Joseph F....*, p. 123.

3 Pearson H. Corbett, *Hyrum Smith, Patriarch* (Salt Lake City: Deseret Book, 1963), pp. 171–72.

4 Brigham H. Roberts, "A Comprehensive History of the Church" (Provo, Utah: Brigham Young University Press, 1965) 1:421. It was there, according to revelation received by Joseph Smith, where Adam had lived following his expulsion from the Garden and where Adam " 'shall come to visit his people or the Ancient of Days shall sit, as spoken of by Daniel the prophet.' "

5 Pearson Corbett, *Hyrum Smith...*, 59.

6 Joseph Smith, *History of the Church...*, 2:487–88.

7 Roberts, "A Comprehensive History of the Church," 1:438–39.

8 Pearson Corbett, *Hyrum Smith...*, p. 176–77.

9 Ibid., p. 180.

10 Don C. Corbett, *Mary Fielding Smith, Daughter of Britain* (Salt Lake City: Deseret Book, 1974), p. 73.

11 Ibid., pp. 75–76.

12 Parley P. Pratt, *Autobiography of Parley P. Pratt* (Salt Lake City: Deseret Book, 1938), p. 162.

13 Joseph Smith, *History of the Church...*, 3:190.

14 Ibid., 3:190–91.

15 Don Corbett, *Mary Fielding Smith...*, 77, 78.

16 Ibid., p. 77–78.

17 Ibid., pp. 77, 78.

18 Pratt, *Autobiography*, p. 179.

19 Joseph Smith, *History of the Church...*, 3:422.

CHAPTER 5

1 Joseph Fielding Smith, *The Life of Joseph F. Smith* (Salt Lake City: Deseret News Press, 1938), 123.

2 Joseph Fielding Smith, *Life of Joseph F....*, pp. 123–24, 33 Richard Neitzel Holzapfel and R. Q. Shupe, *Joseph F. Smith, Portrait of a Prophet* (Salt Lake City: Deseret Book, 2000), p. 352.

4 Don C. Corbett, *Mary Fielding Smith, Daughter of Britain* (Salt Lake City: Deseret Book, 1974), p. 80.

5 Joseph Smith, *History of The Church of Jesus Christ of Latter-day Saints* (Salt Lake City: Deseret Book, 1974), 3:244.

6 Don Corbett, *Mary Fielding Smith...*, p. 84.

7 Ibid., p. 85.

8 *Teachings of Presidents of the Church—Joseph F. Smith* (Salt Lake City: The Church of Jesus Christ of Latter-day Saints, 1998), 147.

9 Pearson H. Corbett, *Hyrum Smith, Patriarch* (Salt Lake City: Deseret Book, 1963), p. 203.

10 Pearson Corbett, *Hyrum Smith...*, p. 213.

11 Joseph Smith, *History of The Church...*, 3:285–86.

12 Ibid., 3:289–305.

13 Ibid., 3:321.

14 Lucy Mack Smith, *History of Joseph Smith, by His Mother* (Salt Lake City: Bookcraft, 1958), p. 301.

15 Ibid., pp. 301–02.

16 Pearson Corbett, *Hyrum Smith...*, pp. 215–16.

CHAPTER 6

1 Pearson H. Corbett, *Hyrum Smith, Patriarch* (Salt Lake City: Deseret Book, 1963), p. 223.

2 Joseph Smith, *History of The Church of Jesus Christ of Latter-day Saints*, 4:268. See also Brigham H. Roberts, "A Comprehensive History of the Church" (Provo, Utah: Brigham Young University Press, 1965), 2:11.

3 Don C. Corbett, *Mary Fielding Smith, Daughter of Britain* (Salt Lake City: Deseret Book, 1974), pp. 98–100.

4 Hyrum Smith, "To the Saints Scattered Abroad," *Times and Seasons* 1, no. 2 (December 1839): 17–23.

5 Don Corbett, *Mary Fielding Smith...*, 125–26.

6   Ibid., p. 139.

7   Pearson Corbett, *Hyrum Smith...*, p. 274.

8   Preston Nibley, *Joseph Smith the Prophet*
     (Salt Lake City: Deseret News Press, 1944), 488–89.

9   Joseph Smith, *History of The Church...*, 6:520.

10   Ibid., 6:545–46.

11   Pearson Corbett, *Hyrum Smith...*, p. 385; see footnote.

12   Ibid., p. 390.

13   Ibid., p. 422.

14   Ibid., p. 426.

15   Don Corbett, *Mary Fielding Smith...*, pp. 171–72.
     See also footnote 3 on p. 172.

16   Lucy Mack Smith, *History of Joseph Smith, by His Mother*
     (Salt Lake City: Bookcraft, 1958), pp. 324–25.

Chapter 7

1   Don C. Corbett, *Mary Fielding Smith, Daughter of Britain*
     (Salt Lake City: Deseret Book, 1974), p. 178.

2   Don Corbett, *Mary Fielding Smith...*, p. 189.

3   Ibid., p. 189–90.

4   Leonard J. Arrington, ed., and Scott Kenney, essayist,
     "The Presidents of the Church—Biographical Essays—
     Joseph F. Smith" (Salt Lake City: Deseret Book, 1986), p. 181.

5   Don Corbett, *Mary Fielding Smith...*, p. 186.

6   Brigham H. Roberts, "A Comprehensive History of the Church"
     (Provo, Utah: Brigham Young University Press, 1965), 2:538–39.

7   Ibid., 2:538–39.

8   Don Corbett, *Mary Fielding Smith...*, p. 188. See also footnote 4.

9   Ibid., p. 195, footnote 18.

10   Joseph Fielding Smith, Journal, Book 5 (Salt Lake City, LDS
     Historian's Office, 1839–1859. Reproduced in mimeographed
     form, June 1963), p. 90, 91.

11   Ibid., pp. 5:100–01.

12   Pearson H. Corbett, *Hyrum Smith, Patriarch*
     (Salt Lake City: Deseret Book, 1963), pp. 442–43.

13   Pearson Corbett, *Hyrum Smith...*, p. 443, footnote 3.

14   Don Corbett, *Mary Fielding Smith...*, p. 198.

15 Ibid., p. 197. See also Journal History, October 7, 1846.
16 Ibid., pp. 196–97.
17 Fielding Smith, Journal, 5:103.

Chapter 8
1 Joseph Fielding Smith, *The Life of Joseph F. Smith*
(Salt Lake City: Deseret News Press, 1938), pp. 133–34.
2 Don C. Corbett, *Mary Fielding Smith, Daughter of Britain*
(Salt Lake City: Deseret Book, 1974), p. 200.
3 *Teachings of Presidents of the Church—Joseph F. Smith* (Salt Lake City:
The Church of Jesus Christ of Latter-day Saints, 1998), p. 31.
4 Joseph Fielding Smith, *Life of Joseph F....*, p. 143.
5 Don Corbett, *Mary Fielding Smith...*, p. 201.
6 Smith Fielding, Journal, 5:108.
7 Smith Fielding, Journal, 5:112.
8 Don Corbett, *Mary Fielding Smith...*, pp. 205–06.
9 *Teachings of Presidents...*, pp. 31–32.
10 Leonard J. Arrington, ed., and Scott Kenney, essayist, "The
Presidents of the Church—Biographical Essays—Joseph F. Smith"
(Salt Lake City: Deseret Book, 1986), 182.
11 Joseph Fielding Smith, *Life of Joseph F....*, pp. 134–37.

Chapter 9
1 *Teachings of Presidents of the Church—Joseph F. Smith* (Salt Lake City:
The Church of Jesus Christ of Latter-day Saints, 1998), p. 31.
2 Don Corbett, *Mary Fielding Smith...*, p. 231.
See also, Journal History, June 6, 1848.
3 Joseph Fielding Smith, *The Life of Joseph F. Smith*
(Salt Lake City: Deseret News Press, 1938), p. 149.
4 Smith Fielding, Journal, 5: 233.
5 Don Corbett, *Mary Fielding Smith...*, p. 233.
6 Ibid., p. 234.
7 Ibid., p. 149.
8 Ibid., p. 149–50.
9 Ibid., p. 150.
10 Ibid., p. 150.
11 Ibid., p. 150.

12 Ibid., p. 151.

13 Joseph Fielding Smith, *Life of Joseph F....*, pp. 155–56.

14 Ibid., p. 151–52.

15 Don Corbett, *Mary Fielding Smith...*, pp. 238–39.

16 Ibid., p. 239.

17 Joseph Fielding Smith, *Life of Joseph F....*, p. 153.

18 Ibid., p. 153.

19 Ibid., p. 153.

20 Ibid., p. 154.

21 Ibid., p. 154–55.

Chapter 10

1 Leonard J. Arrington, ed., and Scott Kenney, essayist, "The Presidents of the Church—Biographical Essays—Joseph F. Smith" (Salt Lake City: Deseret Book, 1986), p. 181.

2 Joseph Fielding Smith, *The Life of Joseph F. Smith* (Salt Lake City: Deseret News Press, 1938), p. 158.

3 Ibid., p. 157.

4 Don C. Corbett, *Mary Fielding Smith, Daughter of Britain* (Salt Lake City: Deseret Book, 1974), p. 251.

5 Joseph Fielding Smith, Journal, Book 5 (Salt Lake City, LDS Historian's Office, 1839–1859. Reproduced in mimeographed form, June 1963), p. 147.

6 Joseph Fielding Smith, Journal, 5:148.

7 Ibid., 5:148.

8 Joseph Fielding Smith, *Life of Joseph F....*, p. 159.

9 "Hoof" was a pioneer expression meaning hoofed animal.

10 Joseph Fielding Smith, *Life of Joseph F....*, p. 164.

11 Ibid., p. 164.

12 Don Corbett, *Mary Fielding Smith...*, pp. 255–56.

13 Joseph Fielding Smith, *Life of Joseph F....*, pp. 158–59.

14 Ibid., p. 159.

15 Ibid., p. 159–60.

16 Don Corbett, *Mary Fielding Smith...*, pp. 258–59.

17 Ibid., p. 259.

18 *Teachings of Presidents...*, p. xv.

19 Don Corbett, *Mary Fielding Smith*, p. 261.

20 *Teachings of Presidents...*, p. 59.
21 Don Corbett, *Mary Fielding Smith*, p. 262.
22 Ibid., p. 263.
23 Ibid., p. 265.
24 Ibid., p. 265.
25 Joseph Fielding Smith, *Life of Joseph F....*, p. 161.
26 *Teachings of Presidents...*, p. xv.
27 Joseph Fielding Smith, *Life of Joseph F....*, p. 163.
28 Ibid., p. 162–63.
29 *Teachings of Presidents...*, pp. 32–33.

CHAPTER 11
1 Richard Neitzel Holzapfel and R. Q. Shupe, *Joseph F. Smith, Portrait of a Prophet* (Salt Lake City: Deseret Book, 2000), p. 341.
2 Joseph Fielding Smith, *The Life of Joseph F. Smith* (Salt Lake City: Deseret News Press, 1938), p. 166.
3 Joseph Fielding Smith, *Life of Joseph F....*, pp. 166–67.
4 Ibid., p. 169.
5 Leonard J. Arrington, ed., and Scott Kenney, essayist, "The Presidents of the Church—Biographical Essays—Joseph F. Smith" (Salt Lake City: Deseret Book, 1986), p. 184.
6 Joseph Fielding Smith, *Life of Joseph F....*, p. 173.
7 Ibid., p. 172.
8 Ibid., p. 173.
9 Ibid., p. 179.
10 Ibid., p. 179.
11 *Teachings of Presidents of the Church—Joseph F. Smith* (Salt Lake City: The Church of Jesus Christ of Latter-day Saints, 1998), pp. 67–68.
12 Joseph Fielding Smith, *Life of Joseph F....*, p. 179.
13 Ibid., p. 179.
14 Ibid., p. 180.
15 Ibid., p. 180–81.
16 Ibid., p. 182.
17 Arrington and Kenney, "...Presidents of the Church...," p. 185.
18 Joseph Fielding Smith, *Life of Joseph F....*, pp. 183–84.
19 Ibid., p. 184.
20 Ibid., p. 184.

21 Ibid., p. 190–92.

22 Arrington and Kenney, "...Presidents of the Church...," p. 186.

23 Emerson Roy West, *Latter-day Prophets, Their Lives, Teachings, and Testimonies, with Profiles of Their Wives* (American Fork, Utah: Covenant Communications, Inc., 1997), p. 231.

24 Ibid., p. 231.

25 Joseph Fielding Smith, *Life of Joseph F....*, p. 186.

26 Holzapfel and Shupe, *Portrait...*, p. 21.

Chapter 12

1 Joseph Fielding Smith, *The Life of Joseph F. Smith* (Salt Lake City: Deseret News Press, 1938), p. 195.

2 Leonard J. Arrington, ed., and Scott Kenney, essayist, "The Presidents of the Church—Biographical Essays—Joseph F. Smith" (Salt Lake City: Deseret Book, 1986), p. 187.

3 Joseph Fielding Smith, *Life of Joseph F....*, p. 197.

4 Ibid., p. 197.

5 Ibid., p. 197–98.

6 Ibid., p. 198.

7 Ibid., p. 198.

Chapter 13

1 It should be noted that the author has found no specific documentation that Levira's childlessness led to her nervous condition. Therefore, this dialogue is based entirely on his assumptions, and is his own creation.

2 Joseph Fielding Smith, *The Life of Joseph F. Smith* (Salt Lake City: Deseret News Press, 1938), p. 199.

3 Leonard J. Arrington, ed., and Scott Kenney, essayist, "The Presidents of the Church—Biographical Essays—Joseph F. Smith" (Salt Lake City: Deseret Book, 1986), p. 187.

4 Joseph Fielding Smith, *Life of Joseph F....*, p. 199.

5 Ibid., p. 199.

6 Ibid., pp. 199–200.

7 Ibid., p. 200.

8 Ibid., p. 200.

9 Ibid., p. 200.

10   Ibid., p. 201.

11   Ibid., p. 201.

12   Andrew F. Ehat and Lyndon W. Cook, eds. and comps.,
     The Words of Joseph Smith (Provo, Utah: Brigham Young
     University Religious Studies Center, 1980), pp. 244–47, 256.

13   Arrington and Kenney, "...Presidents of the Church...," p. 188.

14   Ibid., p. 188.

15   Ibid., p. 188.

16   Joseph Fielding Smith, *Life of Joseph F....*, p. 202.

17   Ibid., p. 202.

18   Ibid., p. 203.

19   Arrington and Kenney, "...Presidents of the Church...," p. 188.

20   Ibid., p. 188.

21   Joseph Fielding Smith, *Life of Joseph F....*, p. 203.

22   James B. Allen and Glen M. Leonard, *The Story of the Latter-day Saints*
     (Salt Lake City: Deseret Book, 1976), pp. 312–13.

23   Doctrine and Covanents 87.

24   Joseph Fielding Smith, *Life of Joseph F....*, p. 204.

25   Ibid., p. 204.

26   Arrington and Kenney, "...Presidents of the Church...," p. 188.

Chapter 14

1   Joseph Fielding Smith, *The Life of Joseph F. Smith*
     (Salt Lake City: Deseret News Press, 1938), 213–14.

2   Joseph Fielding Smith, *Life of Joseph F....*, 214.

3   Ibid., p. 216.

4   Ibid., p. 216.

5   Leonard J. Arrington, ed., and Scott Kenney, essayist, "The
     Presidents of the Church—Biographical Essays—Joseph F. Smith"
     (Salt Lake City: Deseret Book, 1986), p. 189.

6   Joseph Fielding Smith, *Life of Joseph F....*, p. 218.

7   Ibid., p. 218.

8   Ibid., p. 220.

9   Ibid., p. 220.

10   Ibid., p. 221.

11   Ibid., p. 221.

12   Ibid., p. 222.

13 Ibid., p. 222.

14 Ibid., p. 223.

15 Arrington and Kenney, "...Presidents of the Church...," p. 189.

16 Ibid., p. 189.

CHAPTER 15

1 Joseph Fielding Smith, *The Life of Joseph F. Smith* (Salt Lake City: Deseret News Press, 1938), pp. 226–27.

2 Leonard J. Arrington, ed., and Scott Kenney, essayist, "The Presidents of the Church—Biographical Essays—Joseph F. Smith" (Salt Lake City: Deseret Book, 1986), p. 190.

3 Arrington and Kenney, "...Presidents of the Church...," p. 190.

4 Joseph Fielding Smith, *Life of Joseph F....*, p. 231.

5 Arrington and Kenney, "...Presidents of the Church...," p. 190.

6 Joseph Fielding Smith, *Life of Joseph F....*, p. 227.

7 Ibid., p. 226.

8 Ibid., p. 226.

9 Arrington and Kenney, "...Presidents of the Church...," p. 191.

10 Joseph Fielding Smith, *Life of Joseph F....*, p. 231.

11 Arrington and Kenney, "...Presidents of the Church...," p. 191.

12 *Teachings of Presidents of the Church—Joseph F. Smith* (Salt Lake City: The Church of Jesus Christ of Latter-day Saints, 1998), p. 295.

13 Ibid., pp. 295–296.

14 Emerson Roy West, *Latter-day Prophets, Their Lives, Teachings, and Testimonies, with Profiles of Their Wives* (American Fork, Utah: Covenant Communications, Inc., 1997), pp. 62–63. See also Joseph Fielding Smith, *Life of Joseph F....*, p. 4.

15 Joseph Fielding Smith, *Life of Joseph F....*, p. 228.

16 Ibid., p. 228–29.

17 Arrington and Kenney, "...Presidents of the Church...," p. 192.

18 Joseph Fielding Smith, *Life of Joseph F....*, p. 230.

19 *Teachings of Presidents...*, p. 163.

20 Ibid., p. 302.

21 Joseph Fielding Smith, *Life of Joseph F....*, p. 230.

22 Arrington and Kenney, "...Presidents of the Church...," p. 196.

23 Ibid., p. 196.

24 *Teachings of Presidents...*, p. 128.

25   Ibid., p. 129.

CHAPTER 16

1   *Teachings of Presidents of the Church—Joseph F. Smith* (Salt Lake City: The Church of Jesus Christ of Latter-day Saints, 1998), p. 210.

2   Joseph Fielding Smith, *The Life of Joseph F. Smith* (Salt Lake City: Deseret News Press, 1938), pp. 231–32.

3   Ibid., p. 232.

4   Emerson Roy West, *Latter-day Prophets, Their Lives, Teachings, and Testimonies, with Profiles of Their Wives* (American Fork, Utah: Covenant Communications, Inc., 1997), p. 229.

5   West, "Latter-day Prophets," p. 229. In the second paragraph, the author is quoting from Francis M. Gibbons, *Dynamic Disciples, Prophets of God—Joseph F. Smith* (Salt Lake City: Deseret Book, 1996), p. 236.

6   Leonard J. Arrington, ed., and Scott Kenney, essayist, "The Presidents of the Church—Biographical Essays—Joseph F. Smith" (Salt Lake City: Deseret Book, 1986), p. 193.

7   Gibbons, *Dynamic Disciples...*, p. 138.

8   West, *Latter-day Prophets...*, p. 232.

9   Joseph Fielding Smith, *Life of Joseph F....*, p. 232.

10   *Teachings of Presidents...*, p. 147.

11   Gibbons, *Dynamic Disciples...*, p. 139.

12   Joseph Fielding Smith, *Life of Joseph F....*, pp. 457–58. As a postcript to her husband's letter, written in 1929, long after Joseph F.'s death, Julina added, "The little girl he speaks of, 'Dodo,' is my firstborn. Ella was Sarah's baby, and it only lived a few days... [Joseph]...never got over losing his first born. She was an extra bright child and clung to her papa. She always ran to meet him and would ask so many questions that sometimes he would almost tire of answering. She came to us when he needed comfort, and she filled the bill, although when she died we had another baby girl, Mamie, which he used to take in his arms, walk the floor and cry. I have had eleven children; he has loved them all with as great a love as a human could, but he never got where he could talk of his 'Dodo' without tears in his eyes."

13   West, *Latter-day Prophets...*, p. 232.

14 Joseph Fielding Smith, *Life of Joseph F.…*, p. 233.
15 Arrington and Kenney,"…Presidents of the Church…," p. 193.
16 Ibid., p. 193.
17 Joseph Fielding Smith, *Life of Joseph F.…*, pp. 234–35.
18 Ibid., p. 235.
19 Arrington and Kenney, "…Presidents of the Church…," p. 194.
20 Ibid., p. 194.
21 Andrew Jensen, "Whitmer, David," Latter-day Saint Biographical Encyclopedia—"A Compilation of Biographical Sketches of Prominent Men and Women in The Church of Jesus Christ of Latter-day Saints" (Salt Lake City: n.p., 1901–1936), 1:263ff. The majority of this interview comes word-for-word from the Jensen account. Additional material has also been supplemented from Joseph Fielding Smith's biography and an account of the translation process published by David Whitmer, which is also found in the Jensen article.
22 Ibid., 1:263ff. See also *Millennial Star,* 53:421, etc.
23 Ibid., 1:263ff. See also: *Millennial Star*, Vol. 53, p. 421, etc.
24 Ibid., 1:263ff. See also: *Millennial Star*, Vol. 53, p. 421, etc.
25 Joseph Fielding Smith, *Life of Joseph F.…*, p. 246. In a footnote on this page Smith writes: "It seems apparent from this conversation that neither Orson Pratt nor Joseph F. Smith knew exactly where the original manuscript of the Book of Mormon was. This knowledge, however, was shortly made known to them. For they discovered in one of the manuscript records kept by the Prophet Joseph Smith, and written in Nauvoo, that he deliberately and knowingly placed the original manuscript of the Book of Mormon in the cornerstone of the Nauvoo House when it was being built…"
26 Joseph Fielding Smith, *Life of Joseph F.…*, 241–46. See also Brigham H. Roberts, A Comprehensive History of the Church (Provo, Utah: Brigham Young University Press, 1965) 1:123–46. See also Jensen, "Whitmer, David," 1:263ff. See also *Millennial Star* 45:538; 48:35, 341, 420, 436, etc.; and "Historical Record," Vol. 7, p. 622.
27 Joseph Fielding Smith, *Life of Joseph F.…*, p. 249.

CHAPTER 17

1   Francis M. Gibbons, *Dynamic Disciples, Prophets of God—Joseph F. Smith* (Salt Lake City: Deseret Book, 1996), pp. 140–41.

2   Joseph Fielding Smith, *The Life of Joseph F. Smith* (Salt Lake City: Deseret News Press, 1938), p. 253.

3   Ibid., p. 253.

4   Richard Neitzel Holzapfel and R. Q. Shupe, *Joseph F. Smith, Portrait of a Prophet* (Salt Lake City: Deseret Book, 2000), p. 64.

5   Emerson Roy West, *Latter-day Prophets, Their Lives, Teachings, and Testimonies, with Profiles of Their Wives* (American Fork, Utah: Covenant Communications, Inc., 1997), p. 232.

6   Gustive O. Larson, *Outline History of Territorial Utah* (Provo, Utah: Brigham Young University Press, 1958), p. 265.

7   Gustive O. Larson, *The "Americanization" of Utah for Statehood* (San Marino, California: The Huntington Library, 1971), pp. 92–94. It is interesting to note that among those advocating Federal intervention to crush Mormon political power in Utah and abolish polygamy were the leaders of the Reorganized Church of Jesus Christ of Latter-day Saints, with headquarters in Iowa, who claimed that polygamy was Brigham Young's innovation following the death of Joseph Smith. Their idea was to establish Joseph Smith III in as governor to Utah and let his Church's missionary efforts encourage an antipolygamy revolt among the Saints.

8   Ibid., p. 94.

9   Ibid., p. 95.

10   Ibid., p. 96–97.

11   Joseph Fielding Smith, *Life of Joseph F....*, pp. 253–54.

12   Ibid., p. 255.

13   Larson, *Outline History...*, p. 272.

14   Joseph Fielding Smith, *Life of Joseph F....*, p. 255.

15   Larson, *Outline History...*, pp. 272–73. This principle was finally overruled by the U.S. Supreme Court in 1877.

16   Joseph Fielding Smith, *Life of Joseph F....*, p. 258.

17   Ibid., p. 258.

18   Holzapfel and Shupe, *...Portrait of a Prophet*, pp. 69–70.

19   Joseph Fielding Smith, *Life of Joseph F....*, pp. 260–61.

20   Ibid., pp. 261–62.

21 Ibid., p. 262.

22 Ibid., p. 262.

23 Joseph Fielding Smith, *Life of Joseph F....*, p. 263. Smith continues: "From this time forth President Smith kept up a correspondence with her, frequently sent her money in her old age when she was in need, and thus broke down much of her prejudice, but never was he able to remove it all, so deep rooted had it become due to false impressions in her childhood and youth."

24 Kenneth W. Godfrey, Audrey M. Godfrey, and Jill Mulvay Derr, *Women's Voices, An Untold History of the Latter-day Saints, 1830–1900* (Salt Lake City: Deseret Book, 1982), pp. 343–57.

25 Ibid., pp. 355–56.

26 Joseph Fielding Smith, *Life of Joseph F....*, p. 461.

27 Ibid., pp. 265–66.

28 Ibid., pp. 268–69.

29 Ibid., p. 281.

30 Ibid., pp. 284, 285.

31 *Teachings of Presidents of the Church—Joseph F. Smith* (Salt Lake City: The Church of Jesus Christ of Latter-day Saints, 1998), p. 173.

32 Leonard J. Arrington, ed., and Scott Kenney, essayist, "The Presidents of the Church—Biographical Essays—Joseph F. Smith" (Salt Lake City: Deseret Book, 1986), pp. 196–97.

33 Emerson Roy West, *Latter-day Prophets, Their Lives, Teachings, and Testimonies, with Profiles of Their Wives* (American Fork, Utah: Covenant Communications, Inc., 1997), pp. 232–33.

Chapter 18

1 Leonard J. Arrington, ed., and Scott Kenney, essayist, "The Presidents of the Church—Biographical Essays—Joseph F. Smith" (Salt Lake City: Deseret Book, 1986), p. 197.

2 Joseph Fielding Smith, *The Life of Joseph F. Smith* (Salt Lake City: Deseret News Press, 1938), pp. 288–89.

3 Ibid., p. pp. 289–90.

4 Ibid., p. 290.

5 Ibid., pp. 290–91.

6 Francis M. Gibbons, *Dynamic Disciples, Prophets of God—Joseph F. Smith* (Salt Lake City: Deseret Book, 1996), p. 143.

7   Joseph Fielding Smith, *Life of Joseph F....*, p. 295.

8   Ibid., pp. 295–96.

9   Leonard J. Arrington, ed., and Scott Kenney, essayist, "The Presidents of the Church—Biographical Essays—Joseph F. Smith" (Salt Lake City: Deseret Book, 1986), p. 198.

10 Arrington and Kenney, "...Presidents of the Church...," p. 198.

11 Gibbons, *Dynamic Disciples*, pp. 143–44.

12 Joseph Fielding Smith, *Life of Joseph F....*, pp. 297–98.

13 Gustive O. Larson, *The "Americanization" of Utah for Statehood* (San Marino, California: The Huntington Library, 1971), pp. 261–62. It should be noted that Frank Cannon, son of George Q. Cannon, penned these lines about his father and Joseph F. Smith some years after the fact, seeing them published in 1911. By that time he had become estranged from the Church and was also one of Joseph F. Smith's most bitter enemies, having failed to retain Church support for reelection to the U.S. Senate.

14 Arrington and Kenney, "...Presidents of the Church...," pp. 198–99.

15 Ibid., p. 199.

16 Richard Neitzel Holzapfel and R. Q. Shupe, *Joseph F. Smith, Portrait of a Prophet* (Salt Lake City: Deseret Book, 2000), p. 331.

17 *Teachings of Presidents of the Church—Joseph F. Smith* (Salt Lake City: The Church of Jesus Christ of Latter-day Saints, 1998), p. 305.

18 Arrington and Kenney, "...Presidents of the Church...," p. 199.

19 Klaus J. Hansen, *Quest For Empire, the Political Kingdom of God and the Council of Fifty in Mormon History* (Lincoln: University of Nebraska Press, 1974), p. 170.

20 Joseph Fielding Smith, *Life of Joseph F....*, p. 463.

21 Ibid., p. 302.

22 Ibid., p. 303.

23 Ibid., p. 304.

24 Ibid., pp. 308–09.

25 Ibid., p. 451.

26 *Teachings of Presidents...*, p. 295.

27 Emerson Roy West, *Latter-day Prophets, Their Lives, Teachings, and Testimonies, with Profiles of Their Wives* (American Fork, Utah: Covenant Communications, Inc., 1997), p. 233.

28 Ibid., pp. 233–34.

29 *Deseret News 1999–2000 Church Almanac*
(Salt Lake City: Deseret News, 1998), p. 47.

CHAPTER 19

1 Joseph Fielding Smith, *The Life of Joseph F. Smith*
(Salt Lake City: Deseret News Press, 1938), pp. 314–15.

2 Ibid., p. 315.

3 Emerson Roy West, *Latter-day Prophets, Their Lives, Teachings,
and Testimonies, with Profiles of Their Wives* (American Fork, Utah:
Covenant Communications, Inc., 1997), p. 62.

4 Richard Neitzel Holzapfel and R. Q. Shupe, *Joseph F. Smith,
Portrait of a Prophet* (Salt Lake City: Deseret Book, 2000), pp. 123,
125. Holzapfel and Shupe are quoting from Edward H. Anderson,
"Joseph Fielding Smith: Sixth President of the Church of Jesus
Christ of Latter-day Saints," *Improvement Era* 5 (December 1901):138.

5 Leonard J. Arrington, ed., and Scott Kenney, essayist, "The
Presidents of the Church—Biographical Essays—Joseph F. Smith"
(Salt Lake City: Deseret Book, 1986), pp. 201–02.

6 *Teachings of Presidents of the Church—Joseph F. Smith* (Salt Lake City:
The Church of Jesus Christ of Latter-day Saints,1998), p. 221.

7 Ibid., p. 202.

8 Ibid., p. xii.

9 Ibid., p. 11.

10 Ibid., p. xii.

11 Ibid., p. 39.

12 Ibid., pp. 11–12.

13 Ibid., p. 201.

14 Ibid., pp. 201–02.

15 Holzapfel and Shupe, *...Portrait of a Prophet*, p. 153.

16 Joseph Fielding Smith, *Life of Joseph F....*, p. 372.

17 Ibid., p. 328.

18 Ibid., p. 328.

19 Ibid., pp. 331–32.

20 Holzapfel and Shupe, *...Portrait of a Prophet*, p. 320.

21 Arrington and Kenney, "...Presidents of the Church...," p. 202.

22 Joseph Fielding Smith, *Life of Joseph F....*, p. 334.

23 Ibid., p. 354.

24 Arrington and Kenney, "...Presidents of the Church...," p. 203.

25 Ibid., p. 203.

26 West, *Latter-day Prophets*, p. 233.
    See also *Teachings of Presidents...*, p. 257.

27 Truman G. Madsen, *Lectures on Tape, The Presidents of the Church,
    Insights into the Life and Teachings of Each Church President*—Joseph F.
    Smith (Salt Lake City, Bookcraft, 1999), Side B.

28 *Teachings of Presidents...*, p. 260.

29 Ibid., p. 260.

30 Joseph Fielding Smith, *Life of Joseph F....*, p. 374.

31 Ibid., p. 374.

32 Holzapfel and Shupe, *...Portrait of a Prophet*, pp. 158–59.

33 Joseph Fielding Smith, *Life of Joseph F....*, pp. 428–29.

34 Ibid., p. 428–29.

35 Madsen, *Lectures on Tape...*, Side B.

36 Holzapfel and Shupe, *...Portrait of a Prophet*, p. 349.

37 West, *Latter-day Prophets...*, p. 63.

38 West, *Latter-day Prophets...*, pp. 63–64.

39 Joseph Fielding Smith, *Life of Joseph F....*, p. 419.

40 Ibid., p. 478.

41 Holzapfel and Shupe, *...Portrait of a Prophet*, pp. 224–25.

42 Joseph Fielding Smith, *Life of Joseph F....*, p. 478.

CHAPTER 20

1   *Teachings of Presidents of the Church—Joseph F. Smith* (Salt Lake City:
    The Church of Jesus Christ of Latter-day Saints, 1998), p. 147.

2   Joseph Fielding Smith, *The Life of Joseph F. Smith*
    (Salt Lake City: Deseret News Press, 1938), p. 433.

3   Ibid., p. 403.

4   Ibid., pp. 405–06.

5   Joseph F. Smith, *Gospel Doctrine, Sermons and Writings of Joseph F.
    Smith* (Salt Lake City: Deseret Book Company, 1939, 1986),
    pp. 312–13.

6   Joseph F. Smith, *Gospel Doctrine...*, p. 309.

7   Ibid., 309–10.

8   Emerson Roy West, *Latter-day Prophets, Their Lives, Teachings, and Testimonies, with Profiles of Their Wives* (American Fork, Utah: Covenant Communications, Inc.1997), p. 66.

9   West, *Latter-day Prophets...*, p. 67.

10 *Teachings of Presidents...*, p. 122.

11 Joseph Fielding Smith, *Life of Joseph F....*, p. 406.

12 *Teachings of Presidents...*, p. 147.

13 Joseph Fielding Smith, *Life of Joseph F....*, pp. 404–05.

14 Richard Neitzel Holzapfel and R. Q. Shupe, *Joseph F. Smith, Portrait of a Prophet* (Salt Lake City: Deseret Book, 2000), p. 215.

15 Joseph Fielding Smith, *Life of Joseph F....*, pp. 464–65.

16 Holzapfel and Shupe, *...Portrait of a Prophet*, p. 220.

17 Leonard J. Arrington, ed., and Scott Kenney, essayist, "The Presidents of the Church—Biographical Essays—Joseph F. Smith" (Salt Lake City: Deseret Book, 1986), p. 207.

18 Holzapfel and Shupe, *...Portrait of a Prophet*, pp. 220–22.

19 Joseph Fielding Smith, *Life of Joseph F....*, p. 466.

20 West, *Latter-day Prophets...*, p. 235.

21 Arrington and Kenney, "...Presidents of the Church...," p. 208.

22 *Teachings of Presidents...*, p. 416.

23 Joseph Fielding Smith, *Life of Joseph F....*, p. 479.

24 Holzapfel and Shupe, *...Portrait of a Prophet*, pp. 271–72.

25 Joseph Fielding Smith, *Life of Joseph F....*, p. 479.

26 Holzapfel and Shupe, *...Portrait of a Prophet*, p. 267.

27 Ibid., p. 263–64. See also Conference Report, June 1919, pp. 13–14.

22

BIBLIOGRAPHY

Allen, James B., and Glen M. Leonard. *The Story of the Latter-day Saints*
(Salt Lake City: Deseret Book Company, 1976).

Arrington, Leonard J., Editor, and Scott Kenney, Essayist, "The
Presidents of the Church Biographical Essays Joseph F. Smith"
(Salt Lake City: Deseret Book, 1986).

Bailey, Paul, Holy Smoke, *A Dissertation on the Utah War*
(Los Angeles: Westernlore Books, 1978).

Cannon, George Q., *Life of Joseph Smith The Prophet*
(Salt Lake City: Deseret Book Company, 1986).

Corbett, Don C., *Mary Fielding Smith, Daughter of Britain*
(Salt Lake City: Deseret Book Company, 1974).

Corbett, Pearson H., *Hyrum Smith, Patriarch*
(Salt Lake City: Deseret Book Company, 1963).

Deseret News 1999-2000 Church Almanac
(Salt Lake City: Deseret News, 1998).

Fielding, Joseph, Journal, 5 Books, (Salt Lake City:, L.D.S. Historian's
Office, 1839–1859). Reproduced in mimeographed form, June 1963.

Flanders, Robert Bruce, Nauvoo, *Kingdom on the Mississippi,* Urbana and
Chicago (University of Illinois Press, 1965).

Foote, Warren, *Warren Foote Autobiography* typescript, BYU-S, (Undated).

Furniss, Norman F., *The Mormon Conflict, 1850-1859*
(New Haven, Yale University Press, 1960).

Gates, Susa Y., "Mothers in Israel" (*Relief Society Magazine*, III,
Salt Lake City, March, 1916).

Gibbons, Francis M., *Dynamic Disciples, Prophets of God*
(Salt Lake City: Deseret Book Company, 1996).

Godfrey, Kenneth W., Godfrey, Audrey M., and Derr, Jill Mulvay,
Women's Voices, An Untold History of the Latter-day Saints, 1830–1900
(Salt Lake City: Deseret Book Company, 1982).

Hammond, Otis G., Editor, *The Utah Expedition, 1857–1858* (Letters of
Capt. Jesse A. Gove, 10TH Inf., U.S.A., of Concord, N.H., to Mrs.
Gove, and special correspondence of the New York Herald, Concord,
New Hampshire Historical Society, 1928).

Hansen, Klaus J., *Quest For Empire, The Political Kingdom of God and The
Council of Fifty in Mormon History* (Lincoln, University of Nebraska
Press, 1974).

Holzapfel, Richard Neitzel, and R.Q. Shupe, *Joseph F. Smith, Portrait
of a Prophet* (Salt Lake City: Deseret Book Company, 2000).

Jakeman, James T., *Daughters of Utah Pioneers and Their Mothers,
Biographical Sketches* (Salt Lake City, 1915).

Jensen, Andrew, *Church Chronology*
(Salt Lake City; Deseret News, 1899).

Jensen, Andrew, *Latter-day Saint Biographical Encyclopedia – A Compilation
of Biographical Sketches of Prominent Men and Women in the Church of Jesus
Christ of Latter-Day Saints*, 4 Volumes (Salt Lake City, 1901–1936).

Johnson, Clark V., Editor, *Mormon Redress Petitions – Documents of the
1833–1838 Missouri Conflict* (Provo, Utah: Brigham Young University
Religious Studies Center, 1992).

Larson, Gustive O., *The "Americanization" of Utah For Statehood*
(San Marino, California: The Huntington Library, 1971).

Larson, Gustive O., *Outline History of Utah and the Mormons* (also titled, *Outline History of Territorial Utah*), (Salt Lake City: Deseret Book Company, 1958, 1965).

Madsen, Truman G., *Joseph Smith The Prophet* (Salt Lake City: Bookcraft, Inc., 1989).

Madsen, Truman G., *The Presidents of the Church, Insights Into The Life And Teachings Of Each Church President – Joseph F. Smith* (Lectures on Tape, Salt Lake City, Bookcraft, 1999).

Newell, Linda King, and Valeen Tippetts Avery, *Mormon Enigma: Emma Hale Smith, Prophet's Wife, Elect Lady, Polygamy's Foe* (New York: Doubleday and Company, 1984).

Nibley, Preston, *Joseph Smith The Prophet* (Salt Lake City: Deseret News Press, 1944).

Pratt, Parley P., *Autobiography of Parley P. Pratt*, (Salt Lake City: Deseret Book Company, 1938).

Roberts, Brigham H., *A Comprehensive History of the Church of Jesus Christ of Latter-day Saints*, 6 Volumes (Provo, Utah: Brigham Young University Press, 1965).

Roberts, Brigham H., *The Rise And Fall Of Nauvoo* (Salt Lake City: The Deseret News Publishers, 1900).

Smith, Hyrum, *Times And Seasons*, "To The Saints Scattered Abroad," Vol. 1, No. 2 [Commerce, Illinois, December 1839], pp. 17–23.

Smith, Joseph, *History of the Church*, Period 1, Six Volumes (Salt Lake City: Deseret Book Company, 1974).

S[mith], J[oseph] F., "A Noble Woman's Experiences" (Salt Lake City: *The Heroines of Mormondom, Noble Womens' Lives Series*, Book 2, 1884).

Smith, Joseph F., *Gospel Doctrine, Sermons and Writings Of Joseph F. Smith* (Salt Lake City: Deseret Book Company, 1939, 1986).

Smith, Joseph Fielding, *The Life of Joseph F. Smith* (Salt Lake City: Deseret News Press, 1938).

Smith, Lucy Mack, *History of Joseph Smith, by his Mother* (Salt Lake City: Bookcraft, 1958).

Teachings of Presidents of the Church – Joseph F. Smith
(Salt Lake City: The Church of Jesus Christ of Latter-day Saints, 1998).

The Latter-Day Saints' Millennial Star
Liverpool, England, A. Carrington.

Tullidge, Edward W., *The Women of Mormondom*
(New York, Tullidge & Crandall, 1877).

West, Emerson Roy, *Latter-day Prophets, Their Lives, Teachings, and Testimonies, with Profiles of Their Wives* (American Fork, Utah: Covenant Communications, Inc., 1997).

Whitney, Orson F., *Life of Heber C. Kimball*
(Salt Lake City: The Kimball Family and
The Juvenile Instructor Office, 1888).

Whitney, Orson F., *Popular History of Utah* (Salt Lake City, 1916).

Widtsoe, John A., *Joseph Smith, Seeker after Truth, Prophet of God*
(Salt Lake City: Deseret News Press, 1951).

Wirthlin, LeRoy S., "Joseph Smith's Boyhood Operation: An 1813 Surgical Success" BYU Studies, 21, (Provo, Utah, [Spring 1981]).

Wirthlin, LeRoy S., "Nathan Smith (1762–1828) Surgical Consultant to Joseph Smith" BYU Studies, 17, (Provo, Utah, [Spring 1977]).

Topical Index

Buchanan, James; U.S. President,
  sends army to Utah, 172, 191, 193;
  sends proclamation to the Saints, 195
Bull, Mrs. Norman, 66
Burdick, Alden and Thomas, 121
Burton, Rachel Fielding
  cousin of JFS takes in orphan boy, 215

C

Cahoon, Reynolds, 42
Cain, Margaret N., (photo) 326
Cain, John T., 315, (photo) 326
Caldwell County, Missouri
  Saints seek refuge in, 41
California; JFS meets Governor of, 298
Calvinists and nonconformists, 30
Canada, 329
Cannon, Frank J., 321, 328;
  anti-Mormon editor of SL Tribune, 351;
  "Furious Judas," 350-351;
  son of George Q., 350;
Cannon, George Q.
  called in 1860 as Apostle, 216; called in
  1880 to First Presidency, 288; death of, 331;
  first counselor to Pres. Woodruff, 309, 316;
  gives JFS overcoat, 171; lifelong friend-
  ship to JFS, 216; photo, First Presidency,
  289, 318; presides over British Isles, 216;
  San Francisco meeting, 309
Carroll County, Missouri
  Saints driven from, 47
Carthage Jail
  illustration, 88; JFS visits, 355–356;
  Smith brothers martyred in, 73, 87
Children's Friend, The
  Primary publication, 359
Church line of authority
  challenged by William Smith, 96;
  succession following martyrdom, 98
Church of Christ, apostates of LDS Church
  create, 38; dissenter members of, 38
Church of the English Crown, 30
Civil War; prophesied by JS, 218;
  riots witnessed by JFS, 218
Clark, General, role of, in militia/mob, 52
Clawson, Rudger, 340
Cluff, William W.
  account of near drowning in Hawaii, 225;

counselor to JFS in Hawaii mission, 234;
  Elder, Hawaii mission, 220–221; photo, 235
Commerce, Illinois; Mississippi river town,
  73; name changed to Nauvoo, 74;
  transformation to Nauvoo, 79
Coolbrith, Agnes
  wife of Don Carlos Smith, 81;
  JFS visits aunt in San Francisco, 236
Coolbrith, Ina, (see Josephine Donna Smith)
  apostasy of, 300; cousin of JFS, letter to,
  186–187; daughter of Don Carlos, 300;
  JFS visits in San Francisco, 236, 300;
  pen name of Josephine Donna Smith, 186;
  Poet Laureate of California, 300
Corrill, John
  quote, meaning of Adam-ondi-Ahman, 44
Cowdery, Oliver
  Book of Mormon translation handwrit-
  ten by, 282; manuscript of, 258–283;
  gives manuscript to David Whitmer, 261
Cowley, Matthias F., 340, 354
Crooked River; mob slays Saints at, 60
Crisman, George
  employer of JFS, 168–169, 171
Cummings, Governor, 191
Cumorah
  D. Whitmer account of going to, 278

D

Davis, Albert W., brother-in-law of JFS, 284
Daviess County, Missouri
  Mobs prevent Saints from voting, 47;
  Saints seek refuge in, 41; Saints driven
  from, 47
Debt; JFS counsel about, 370
Declaration of Independence;
  Mormon speech by Sidney Rigdon, 46
Deming, General, of mob/militia, 89
Deseret News; announces new First
  Presidency, 339–340; prints report on
  Spaulding Manuscript, 304; reports death
  of MFS, 163
Dewitt, Missouri; mob action in, 47
Doctrine and Covenants; sections
  originate as letters from Liberty Jail, 67
Doniphan, Militia Brigadier-General, 47;
  role of, in extermination order, 50–51;
  letter reply from, 51

Independence, Missouri, temple site, 259
Jail at Carthage, attacked, 87;
   JFS emotional visit to, 356
Jail at Richmond, Missouri, 261
Jennings, William O.
   Colonel, mob/militia at Haun's Mill, 49
Johnson, Lyman; Apostle, 46;
   excommunication, 46
Johnson, Sixtus E., 171, 183
Johnston, Albert Sidney; Army General, 193;
   Johnston's Army, 173

K

Kearns, Thomas; anti-Mormon American
   Party, organizer, 350; Senator, 350;
   Salt Lake Tribune owner, 350
Keokuk, Indian chief, 84;
   vision of prophet Joseph, 84
Keokuk, Iowa, reinforcements found in, 107
Kimball, [Smith] Alice Ann
   children prior to JFS marriage, 253;
   children with JFS, 253; daughter of Heber
   C., 253; photo, 254; plural marriage to
   JFS, 253
Kimball, Heber C.; baptisms in England, 41;
   baptizes JFS, 161; daughter marries JFS,
   253; gift of prophecy, 34; first sermon in
   foreign land, given by, 37; mission to
   England, 36–37; mission donation given
   by MFS, 37; photo, 160; plural marriages
   of, 101; prophetic prayer to P.P. Pratt, 34;
   seals JFS to plural wife, Julina, 239; seized
   by evil spirit, 41; step father of JFS, 126
Kipling, Rudyard, 310
King, William, 171
Kirtland; exodus from, 44; mob spirit
   permeates, 41; spirit of apostasy in, 41, 44
Kirtland Temple; awe inspiring sight of, 36;
   builders of, 42; sacrifices for, 42
Kula, Maui, Hawaii
   JFS mission experiences in, 178, 180
Laie, Hawaii
   JFS exiled on plantation in, 286
Lahaina Harbor, Maui
   JFS senses danger in, 220–228;
   violent storm in, story, 221–228
Lambs to the slaughter, 86
Lambson, [Smith] Edna

photo, 245; death of child, Robert, 287,
   300; ten children with JFS, 253; third
   plural wife of JFS, 253; youngest sister of
   Julina, 253
Lambson, [Smith] Julina Bigler
   children with JFS, 253, 285; exiled with
   JFS, 285; gives birth to first child of JFS,
   248; death of first child, Mercy Josephine,
   256; JFS courts, 239; niece to George and
   Bathsheba, 238, 244; photo, 245; plural
   wife of JFS, 239, 253, 285; professes love
   for JFS, 244
Lanai, Hawaii
   apostate W. Gibson "kingdom" in, 228;
   JFS first mission labors in, 184
Letters from Liberty Jail become
   Doctrine &Covenants sections, 67
Liberty, land of, town of, jail of, irony of, 61
Liberty Jail, 54–69;
   conditions in, 56, 61; entrance guard,
   story of, 55; escape from, rumor of, 64;
   escape attempts from, 67; Hyrum greets
   infant, JFS, 56; imprisonment in, 53;
   letters from, become D&C sections, 67;
   perilous journey to, 63; photo, 62; request
   to see prisoners in, story, 55;
   reunion of Hyrum and Mary in, 56;
   reunion illustration, 57
Liberty Park in SLC, 253
Lincoln, Abraham
   and Antibigamy Law, 287, 291; attitude
   toward Mormons, 217; Civil War conflict,
   218; JFS and Saints respect, 218
Line of authority
   challenged by William Smith, 96
Little Mountain
   last stop before Salt Lake valley, 143
Lott, Cornelius P.; animosity between
   Smith party and, 137, 141; captain, pioneer
   company, 128; contest between MFS and,
   138–139; thorn in the side of MFS, 129–135
Lucas, Samuel D.
   militia General attacks Far West, 49
   orders death of J S and prisoners, 50–51
Lund, Anthon H.; counselor to JFS, 339;
   photo of First Presidency, 337
Lyman, Amasa M., 50, 203, 249
Lyman, Francis M., photo, 272

Smith, Joseph F. (JFS)
Early life
adventure found in crossing plains, 116;
affected by meeting with Uncle Joseph
and Indians, 84; as infant baby, story, mob
swarms house, 60; as lad on lap of Uncle
JS, 87; birth of, 53, 64; divinely appointed
dream, 8; experience with Indians at nine
years of age, 121; finds lost oxen, 109–114;
firstborn of Mary Fielding, 53; gazes at
father's martyred body, 90; growth as
infant, 74; impressionable boy, 84, 114;
last meeting with father, 73; maturity as a
youth, 82, 152, 156; mother's lasting
impression on, 119, 165–167; prayer to
find oxen, 109–114; remembers leaving
Nauvoo, 116; responsibilities as a boy, 116,
127, 152, 156; sees father, Hyrum, for the
first time, 56–58; seventh child of Hyrum
Smith, 53; similarities to father, 82; trauma
as infant, affects life of, 64, 73; trek across
Iowa, adventure for JFS, 116
As a youth
anger, temper of, 2, 149–150, 159, 167;
baptism at 14 in Salt Lake, 161; confrontation with teacher, 150; fractures hand, 159;
friends, role models of, grown-up duties
of, 116, 140, 154–155, 156; home in Mill
Creek, 147, 155–156; learns efficacy of
prayer, 114; participation in Mormon
militia, 190–203; photo as a youth, 3;
schooling of, 146–150, 247; typical boyhood experiences, 158–159; weakness of
temper, 150, 167, 247; whips the schoolmaster, 149–150, 167, 247, 251
Adult life and family
alias names used by JFS, 286, 299, 315;
appears before the U.S. Senate, 348–349;
birth of first child, 248; character
described, 342; children of, 248, 360;
courts Levira, 199; death of JFS, 380–382;
death of Robert, child of JFS and Edna,
287, 300; death of Ruth, child of JFS, 325;
death of son, Hyrum, 373; death of 12
children of JFS, 256; divorce from Levira,
247; employment in NYC, 218; employment, Historian's Office, 263; exile of,
285–286, 295–301, 308; family photo, 374;

farming and losing the homestead, 263–64;
fifth wife, Mary Taylor Schwartz, 253;
"fighting apostle," label of, 288; fourth
wife, Alice Ann Kimball, 253; friendship
with Charles W. Nibley, 249, 265; frugal,
methodical, and organized, 265; grandchildren of, 360; grief at death of 12 of his
children, 256; health fails, illness of, 376;
hymn verses written by JFS, 301; Julina
Lambson, second plural wife, 253; labors
performed in SLC, 199; love for his children, 248, 249, 256, 307, 325, 327, 329, 360;
man of the people, 372; marriage to
Levira, 199–200; meets Levira in San
Francisco, 236; opposition to bond
commission, 328; persecution, personal
attacks on, 351; photos, 3, 70, 188, 243,
245, 332, 358, 383; physical description, 342;
political agent of the Church, 315;
powerful church speaker, 264, 288;
plural marriage to Julina Lambson, 239,
244; plural marriage to Sarah Ellen
Richards, 251; plural wives of JFS, 284;
prayers with the family, 330; preparation
for greatness, 288, 290; revelation given
to JFS on eternal nature of families, 257;
sealed in Endowment House, 239; secures
Church historical sights, 345–347; separation from Levira, 247; spirituality of, 265,
356; teeth pulled, 296; temper lamented,
2, 247, 336; testimony 34, 344; third plural
wife, Edna Lambson, 253; tireless missionary work, 218; train trip across country,
irony of, 259; train travels, 298–299, 356;
tribute by Heber J. Grant, 384–385;
two-fold mission of, 343; visits Aunt in
San Francisco, 236; visits Hawaii again
1899, 329
Church Callings and Accomplishments
Apostleship kept confidential, 242, 246;
called to European Mission, 263; called to
Sandwich Isles Mission at 15, 7; called to
third European Mission, 270; called to
Stake High Council, 200; Cardston,
Alberta ,Temple dedicated, 357; *Children's
Friend*, [*The*], published, 359; Church
historical sites acquired, 359; Church
Office Building built, 357; Church

Smith, William
  Apostle, excommunication of, 95; apostasy,
  rebellion of, 94–95, 102; challenges line of
  authority, 96; last remaining Smith family
  brother, 93; mission service, 94; physically
  attacks brother, JS, 94; teaches false
  doctrine, 94; verbally attacks MFS, 94,
  96–97; wayward nature of, 93–94
Smoot, Abraham O.
  Bishop, Mayor, of Provo, 251;
  BY calls to Provo, 251
Smoot, Reed, 340;
  Apostle elected to U.S. Senate, 348
Snow, Lorenzo
  Apostle visits Hawaii, 221; bonds issued
  by, 328; calls for sustaining vote of
  Manifesto, 322; death of, 331; foretells JFS
  will be a prophet, 228; focus on law of
  tithing, 328; near drowning in Hawaiian
  waters, 221; meets with apostate leader,
  230; photo, 229; reacts to JFS storm
  warning, 224; responds to anti-Mormonism,
  347; sustained President of Church, 327
Spaulding, Solomon (Spaulding Story)
  false version of Book of Mormon, 302;
  JFS copies manuscript of, 304;
  manuscript title page, 303
Speight
  alias name used by JFS, 300
Spirit of Apostasy
  spreads in Missouri, 45–46
Spirit of Gathering
  Fielding family responds to, 35
St. George Temple; conference held in, 270;
  dedication of, 270
St. Joseph, Missouri
  journey from Winter Quarters, 110;
  mortality rate of the Saints in, 120;
  provisions purchased in, 110, 120
Stanford, Leland; California Governor, 298
Steward, John J., 296
Stout, Hosea; Brigadier-General, 89
Sugar Creek, Iowa, temporary camp, 101

T

Talmage, Reverend DeWitt, 290
Taylor, John
  called as Judge in Provo, 251; conference

statement on polygamy, 292; death of, 308;
in hiding, 307; Methodist minister in
Canada, 33; niece of, marries JFS, 253;
photo, 289; sends JFS to Hawaii exile,
299; wife, Leonora, 34; wounded at
Carthage, 89
Taylor, John W., 340, 354
Taylor, Thomas
  Elder writes in the *Millennial Star*, 217
Teacher in school,
  at age 15, JFS has confrontation with, 6,
  146–150
Teasdale, George, 336
Temple
  awe inspiring sight of Kirtland, 36;
  builders of Kirtland, 42;
  Far West cornerstones laid, 46;
  revelation to build Nauvoo, 79;
  Salt Lake capstone, dedication, 323;
  St. George dedication, 270
Territory of Utah
  anti-Mormon legislation, 217;
  Morrill Anti-Bigamy Act, 217
Tithes, tithing
  waived for MFS and Mercy Rachel, 118;
  diligence of MFS family in paying,
  156–157; office visited by MFS family 157;
  sufficient to pay Church debt, 354–355
Thompson, [Taylor] Mary Jane
  baby daughter of Mercy Rachel, 65;
  photo, 70
Thompson, Mercy Rachel Fielding
  (see Fielding, Mercy Rachel)
Thompson, Robert B.
  marriage to Mercy Rachel Fielding, 36;
  partner with Don Carlos in printing
  business, 81; pneumonia causes death of,
  81; serves mission to Canada with wife, 36
Thompson, William
  apostasy of, 158; tithing office clerk, 157
typhoid fever epidemic, 18–19

U–W

United Order, 270, 287
Utah; politics in 324–325, 347;
  state constitution and polygamy, 293;
  statehood, 322, 325, 347;
  territory known as Deseret, 293